# THE GLOBAL HISTORY SERIES

Leften Stavrianos, *Northwestern University*
General Editor

This series aims to present history in global perspective, going beyond national or regional limitations, and dealing with overriding trends and forces. The various collections of original materials span the globe, range from prehistoric times to the present, and include anthropology, economics, political science, and religion, as well as history.

S. N. Eisenstadt, the editor of this volume, is Professor of Sociology and Chairman of the Department at The Hebrew University, Jerusalem. In 1964 he was presented the McIver Award for his book, *The Political Systems of Empires,* by the American Sociological Association. Among his other books are *Essays on Comparative Institutions* and *Modernization: Protest and Change,* and he is a frequent contributor to numerous professional journals.

## Also in the Global History Series

Africa in the Days of Exploration, *edited by Roland Oliver and Caroline Oliver,* S-123

The Americas on the Eve of Discovery, *edited by Harold E. Driver,* S-93

Asia on the Eve of Europe's Expansion, *edited by Donald F. Lach and Carol Flaumenhaft,* S-125

Christianity in the Non-Western World, *edited by Charles W. Forman,* S-150

Man Before History, *edited by Creighton Gabel,* S-92

The Muslim World on the Eve of Europe's Expansion, *edited by John J. Saunders,* S-144

The Political Awakening of Africa, *edited by Rupert Emerson and Martin Kilson,* S-124

Russia's Eastward Expansion, *edited by George Alexander Lensen,* S-94

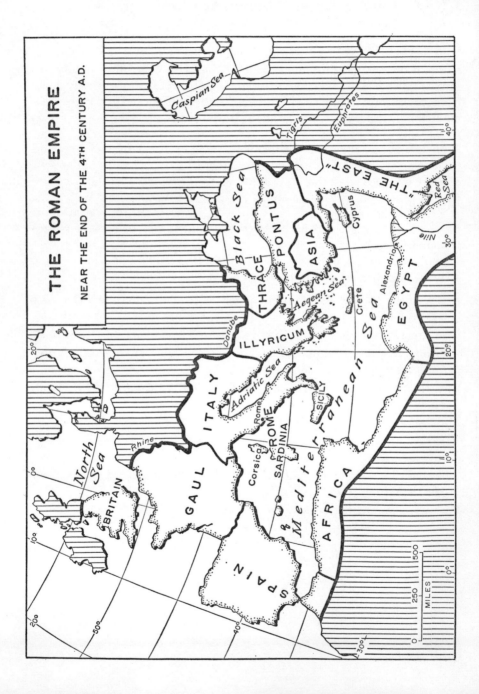

## THE ROMAN EMPIRE

### NEAR THE END OF THE 4TH CENTURY A.D.

Caspian Sea

Black Sea

Tigris

Euphrates

"THE EAST"

Red Sea

PONTUS

THRACE

ASIA

Cyprus

Nile

Aegean Sea

Crete

Alexandria

EGYPT

ILLYRICUM

Danube

ITALY

Adriatic Sea

Rome

ROME

SARDINIA

SICILY

Mediterranean Sea

Corsica

North Sea

Rhine

BRITAIN

GAUL

SPAIN

AFRICA

MILES

0    250    500

# THE DECLINE OF EMPIRES

EDITED BY S. N. EISENSTADT

 Prentice-Hall, Inc. / *Englewood Cliffs, N.J.*

# PREFACE

The major purpose of this book is to illustrate the pattern that prevails in the destinies of the great empires of history. The common theme that reveals itself in a study of these empires does not obscure—but, rather, complements—the great differences in geographical setting, cultural background, and specific historical circumstances that characterize each. It is not possible, of course, within this book to discuss all the great empires of the past, but the ones chosen are representative of the whole and serve as examples of our basic thesis.

I would like to extend my thanks to Professor L. Stavrianos, the editor of this series, for his helpful criticism of the manuscript, and to Mrs. R. Shaco, for her help in its preparation.

S.N.E.

# CONTENTS

## Maps

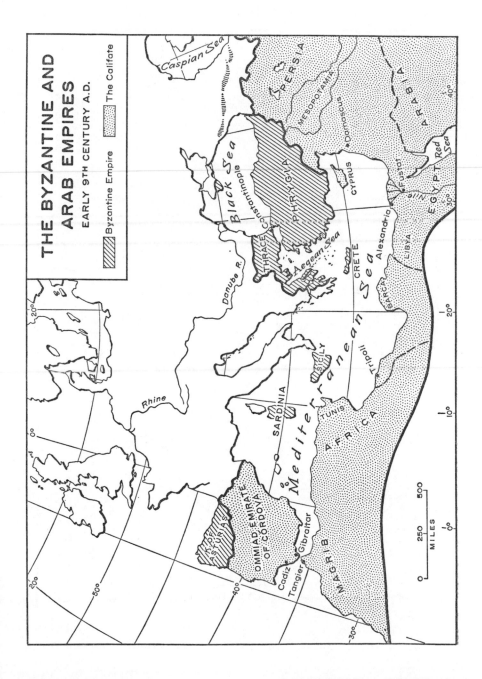

THE BYZANTINE AND
ARAB EMPIRES
EARLY 9TH CENTURY A.D.

Byzantine Empire    The Califate

Caspian Sea

Black Sea

PERSIA

MESOPOTAMIA

THRACE  Constantinople

PHRYGIA

Damascus

CYPRUS

ARABIA

EGYPT  Red Sea

Fustat

Cairo

Alexandria

LIBYA

BARCA

CRETE

Aegean Sea

Danube R.

Mediterranean Sea

Tripoli

SICILY

SARDINIA

TUNIS

AFRICA

Rhine

K. OF
ASTURIAS

OMMIAD EMIRATE
OF CORDOVA

Cadiz

Tangier

Gibraltar

MAGRIB

MILES

0    250    500

THE MONGOL AND
MING EMPIRES

——— Mongolian Empires, 14th Century A.D.
///// Ming Empire, 15th Century A.D.

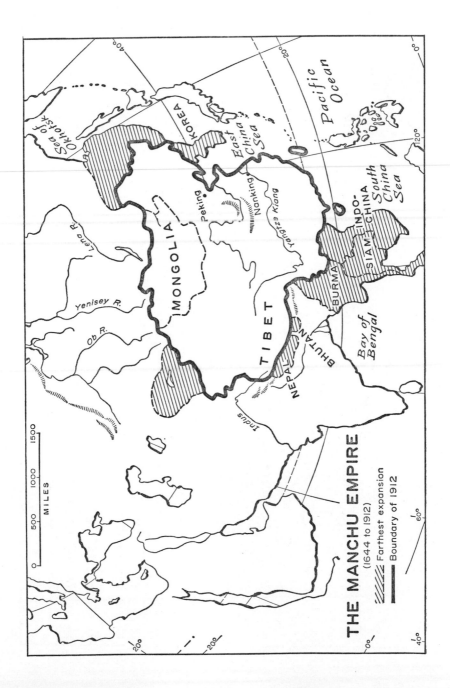

THE MANCHU EMPIRE
(1644 to 1912)

///// Farthest expansion
——— Boundary of 1912

MILES

0    500    1000    1500

Sea of Okhotsk

Lena R.

KOREA

East China Sea

Pacific Ocean

Peking

Nanking

Yangtze Kiang

MONGOLIA

Yenisey R.

Ob R.

TIBET

NEPAL

BHUTAN

Indus

Bay of Bengal

BURMA

SIAM

INDO-CHINA

South China Sea

# I / INTRODUCTION

Since the birth of civilization, the empires created by man have arisen and fallen, the cycles of their destiny dominating the history of man. In ancient times these empires included the Egyptian and Hellenistic (300-ca. 30 BC) the Roman (27 BC-AD 476), and Sassanid Persian (226-AD 650), as well as Maurya (327-236 BC) and Gupta (320-495 AD) in India. In the medieval period there appeared the Byzantine Empire (330-1453 AD) and the Arab Caliphates, followed by the Ottoman Empire which survived until 1918. Only in China did the imperial institution span the millennia from antiquity to the early twentieth century. These empires provided the most massive and enduring form of government man had known prior to the modern period. The most durable of all—the Chinese Empire—flourished for about two thousand years; (206 BC-AD 1912) the Roman Empire, about five hundred years; the Byzantine Empire, about a millennium.

But if these empires provide a picture of massivity, stability, and endurance, the picture also has overtones of long declines and, sometimes, precipitate falls. This paradoxical combination of power and frailty has naturally provoked the interest of historians and philosophers of history from antiquity to modern times. One of the earliest known attempts to analyze this problem was made by Polybius (208-123 BC) in *The Histories*. The great Arab historian, Ibn Khaldun (1332-1406), devoted large parts of his work to a search for the laws that, he believed, determine the rise and fall of dynasties and states. Among the first modern historians to treat this problem was Edward Gibbon (1737-94), who sought, in tracing the decline and fall of the Roman Empire, to discern the nature and the major trends of European civilization.

Later, man's concern with the decline of empires became a part of modern historical research. Although most historians, both ancient and modern, were greatly interested in the play of individual forces—the personalities of the rulers, or such significant historical events as mass migrations and external invasions—most of them also looked for some more basic reason—social, political or cultural—for the disintegration of each of the empires.

This search for more fundamental causes can also be found in the more recent works of leading historians: Jones and Boak, who have dealt with the decline of the Roman Empire; Lewis, who has analyzed the decline of the Ottoman Empire; Ostrogorsky, who has analyzed the history of the Byzantine Empire; or Cahen, who has written on the social history of Islamic Middle Ages (see the bibliography for the works of these scholars).

Although each of these writers has addressed himself to the problems of the specific society he studied, some common themes seem to run through their work. Jones, for example, finds that among the major reasons for the decline of the Roman Empire were the deterioration of civic spirit, the growing spiritual emphasis which deflected energies from the political scene, the continuous expansion of the bureaucracy, the shrinkage of the area of cultivation, the shortage of manpower, and the development of a parasitic landed-rentier class.

Similarly, Lewis, in his discussion of the decline of the Ottoman Empire, stresses the detrimental effects of the large and inefficient bureaucracy, the heavy burden of a growing rentier class, the decline of commerce, and the alienation of the non-Muslim merchant classes—an alienation which, in the changing circumstances of the eighteenth and nineteenth centuries, stifled all possibility of initiative and adjustment to change.

Pursuing this general theme, Cahen comments on the importance of the "feudalization" of the bureaucracy and the growing political apathy of the different religious groups as significant factors in the decline of the Abbaside Caliphate.

Ostrogorsky's analysis of Byzantine economic and social history focuses on the struggle between the forces of centralized polity and those of the aristocracy, with the rulers attempting to promote an independent peasantry which could provide a source of both military manpower and revenue, and the aristocracy continuously attempting to thwart this effort (and ultimately succeeding).

The fact that similar causes for the respective declines of different empires have been found by various historians gives rise to an important question: Are there similarities in the basic features of the social structure of these empires?

The answer suggested here, which forms the main theme of the discussion, is that—despite the great difference in cultural background—most of these empires have shown similar characteristics, and that these characteristics provide the key to an understanding of the processes of their decline.

The major common characteristic shared by these empires was the combination of traditional and relatively nontraditional elements and orientations within the political framework. Between these elements and orientations there existed potential contradictions, and only insofar as such contradictions were not allowed to manifest themselves could these empires subsist. To understand the nature of these political systems and their inherent contradictions, we must understand the process by which they came to be established.

The initiative for the establishment of these polities, in all cases, came from new rulers—emperors, kings, or the members of a ruling élite. Most of these rulers were either members of established upper-class families or lower-class usurpers attempting to establish new dynasties. In some cases they were conquerors who attempted to establish their rule over new territories. In most cases such rulers came to power in periods of unrest, or during the decline of the existing political system. Usually their aim was the re-establishment of peace and order. They did not, however, attempt to restore the old order in its entirety although, to further their own personal ends, they sometimes used the idea of such a restoration as a political ideology or slogan. They always had some distinct political vision, and specific goals: political unity, and territorial expansion. Their aim was to establish a more centralized polity in which they could monopolize the decision-making process and the determination of political goals without being bound by various traditional élite groups. Even the conquerors among them had such a vision and attempted to transmit it, in part at least, to the conquered population.

These goals very often encountered the opposition of the various social and political groups they were designed to circumvent. However great the turmoil and internal strife in a particular state may have been, there always existed some groups which either benefited from the dissension or hoped to re-establish the old order, in which they had held positions of power and influence. These groups—usually composed of aristocratic, patrician, or cultural élites—usually felt themselves menaced by the trend toward political centralization, and they were not willing to help in its implementation. Therefore they frequently attempted to obstruct the new rulers' resources and support, plotting and working against the realization of their goals.

The new rulers were consequently compelled to seek allies in the internal struggle against these élite groups. They had to weld together the various resources—economic, military, and political—required for the implementation of their programs. The rulers tried, naturally, to find these allies among those elements of the population whose interests were opposed to those of the aristocratic groups and who could benefit from the establishment of a more unified polity. These elements usually fell into one of two categories: the first included the more active (mostly urban) economic, cultural, and professional groups who, by virtue of their origins and/or their social interests and orientations, were opposed to the aristocratic groups; the second included the larger, though politically and socially more passive, lower-class groups (especially the peasants) who could benefit, even if only indirectly, from the weakening of the aristocratic forces and the establishment of a general order.

It was from these groups that the rulers hoped to mobilize the support they needed. But, in order to mobilize these resources and to implement their policies, the rulers also had to forge political and administrative instruments on which they could rely and through which they could provide various services to their potential allies or supporters. Hence they tended to develop new organs of centralized administration supervised directly by them, staffed by new people, and largely independent of the more traditional aristocracy.

But, despite their opposition to the Aristocracy, the new rulers were nonetheless greatly interested in maintaining many traditional orientations and patterns of life in their new domains. Their own claims to power and legitimacy were based on the great traditions of the society and its prevailing religion, and they certainly did not want to provide the opportunity for broader active participation in the political decision-making process. Hence, the rulers could not entirely reject the support of the traditional élite—and had even, to some extent, to encourage, or at least accommodate, them. The coexistence of opposing social elements within the same institutional frameworks gave rise to the problem of maintaining an equilibrium among them. Thus, from the very beginning, the new rulers were caught in a web of political and social conflicts.

Thus, the survival of the political system of these empires depended largely on the continuous existence of a certain balance between the political activity and involvement of some parts of the population and the political noninvolvement or apathy toward central political issues of the greater part of the population. The limited political involvement of some segments of the populace provided the ruler with a source of flexible political support, while the apathy of the majority was necessary to his retention of power.

It was only insofar as the ruler could maintain such a balance that the political system he instituted could prevail. Under certain conditions, this very delicate balance could be imposed and maintained, but such conditions were not assured. And any disruption of the balance of forces and interests could set off chains of events that would eventually lead to the decline of the empire.

# 1 / GENERAL OBSERVATIONS ON THE FALL OF THE ROMAN EMPIRE IN THE WEST / EDWARD GIBBON

*The following selection presents some of the thoughts of Edward Gibbon, the first modern European historian to concern himself with the problems of the decline of empires.*

The Greeks, after their country had been reduced into a province, imputed the triumphs of Rome, not to the merit, but to the *fortune,* of the republic. The inconstant goddess, who so blindly distributes and resumes her favors, had *now* consented (such was the language of envious flattery) to resign her wings, to descend from her globe, and to fix her firm and immutable throne on the banks of the Tiber. A wiser Greek, who had composed, with a philosophic spirit, the memorable history of his own times, deprived his countrymen of this vain and delusive comfort by opening to their view the deep foundations of the greatness of Rome.* The fidelity of the citizens to each other, and to the state, was confirmed by the habits of education and the prejudices of religion. Honor, as well as virtue, was the principle of the republic; the ambitious citizens labored to deserve the solemn glories of a triumph; and the ardor of the Roman youth was kindled into active emulation, as often as they beheld the domestic images of their ancestors. The temperate struggles of the patricians and plebeians had finally established the firm and equal balance of the constitution; which united the freedom of popular assemblies with the authority and wisdom of a senate and the executive powers of a regal magistrate. When the consul displayed the standard of the republic, each citizen bound himself, by the obligation of an oath, to draw his sword in the cause of his country, until he had discharged the sacred duty by a military service of ten years. This wise institution continually poured into the field the rising generations of freemen and soldiers; and their numbers were reinforced by the warlike and populous states of Italy, who, after a brave resistance, had yielded to the valor, and embraced the alliance, of the Romans. The sage historian, who excited the virtue of the younger Scipio and beheld the ruin of Carthage, has accurately described their military system; their levies, arms, exer-

Reprinted from Edward Gibbon, *The History of the Decline and Fall of the Roman Empire,* Vol. III (Philadelphia: Claxton, Remsen and Haffelfinger, 1872), pp. 633-43.

* Polybius, especially in his Book 6 (Ed.).

cises, subordination, marches, encampments; and the invincible legion, superior in active strength to the Macedonian phalanx of Philip and Alexander. From these institutions of peace and war, Polybius has deduced the spirit and success of a people incapable of fear and impatient of repose. The ambitious design of conquest, which might have been defeated by the seasonable conspiracy of mankind, was attempted and achieved; and the perpetual violation of justice was maintained by the political virtues of prudence and courage. The arms of the republic, sometimes vanquished in battle, always victorious in war, advanced with rapid steps to the Euphrates, the Danube, the Rhine, and the ocean; and the images of gold, or silver, or brass, that might serve to represent the nations and their kings, were successively broken by the *iron* monarchy of Rome.

The rise of a city, which swelled into an empire, may deserve, as a singular prodigy, the reflection of a philosophic mind. But the decline of Rome was the natural and inevitable effect of immoderate greatness. Prosperity ripened the principle of decay; the causes of destruction multiplied with the extent of conquest; and, as soon as time or accident had removed the artificial supports, the stupendous fabric yielded to the pressure of its own weight. The story of its ruin is simple and obvious; and, instead of inquiring why the Roman Empire was destroyed, we should rather be surprised that it had subsisted so long. The victorious legions, who, in distant wars, acquired the vices of strangers and mercenaries, first oppressed the freedom of the republic, and afterward violated the majesty of the purple. The emperors, anxious for their personal safety and the public peace, were reduced to the base expedient of corrupting the discipline which rendered them alike formidable to their sovereign and to the enemy; the vigor of the military government was relaxed, and finally dissolved, by the partial institutions of Constantine; and the Roman world was overwhelmed by a deluge of barbarians.

The decay of Rome has been frequently ascribed to the translation of the seat of Empire, but this history has already shown that the powers of government were *divided* rather than *removed*. The throne of Constantinople was erected in the East; while the West was still possessed by a series of emperors who held their residence in Italy and claimed their equal inheritance of the legions and provinces. This dangerous novelty impaired the strength, and fomented the vices, of a double reign; the instruments of an oppressive and arbitrary system were multiplied; and a vain emulation of luxury, not of merit, was introduced and supported between the degenerate successors of Theodosius. Extreme distress, which unites the virtue of a free people, embitters the factions of a declining monarchy. The hostile favorites of Arcadius and Honorius betrayed the republic to its common enemies; and the Byzantine court beheld with indifference, perhaps with pleasure, the disgrace of Rome, the misfortunes of Italy, and the loss of the West. Under the succeeding reigns, the alliance of the two Empires was restored; but the aid of the Oriental Romans was tardy, doubtful, and ineffectual; and the national schism of the Greeks and Latins was enlarged by the perpetual difference of language and manners, of interest, and even of religion. Yet the salutary event approved in some measure the judgment of Constantine. During a long period of decay, his impregnable city repelled the victorious armies of barbarians, protected the wealth of Asia, and commanded—both in peace and war—the important straits which connect the Euxine and Mediterranean seas. The foundation of Constantinople more essentially contributed to the preservation of the East than to the ruin of the West.

As the happiness of a *future* life is the great object of religion, we may hear, without surprise or scandal, that the introduction, or at least the abuse, of Christianity had some influence on the decline and fall of the Roman Empire. The clergy successfully preached the doctrines of patience and pusillanimity; the active virtues of society were discouraged; and the last remains of the military spirit were buried in the cloister; a large portion of public and private wealth was consecrated to the specious demands of charity and devotion; and the soldiers' pay was lavished on the useless multitudes of both sexes, who could only plead the merits of abstinence and chastity. Faith, zeal, curiosity, and the more earthly passions of malice and ambition kindled the flame of theological discord; the church, and even the state, were distracted by religious factions, whose conflicts were sometimes bloody, and always implacable; the attention of the emperors was diverted from camps to synods; the Roman world was oppressed by a new species of tyranny; and the persecuted sects became the secret enemies of their country. Yet party-spirit, however pernicious or absurd, is a principle of union as well as of dissension. The bishops, from 1800 pulpits, inculcated the duty of passive obedience to a lawful and orthodox sovereign; their frequent assemblies, and perpetual correspondence, maintained the communion of distant churches: and the benevolent temper of the Gospel was strengthened, though confined, by the spiritual alliance of the Catholics. The sacred indolence of the monks was devoutly embraced by a servile and effeminate age; but, if superstition had not afforded a decent retreat, the same vices would have tempted the unworthy Romans to desert, from baser motives, the standard of the republic. Religious precepts are easily obeyed, which indulge and sanctify the natural inclinations of their votaries; but the pure and genuine influence of Christianity may be traced in its beneficial, though imperfect, effects on the barbarian proselytes of the north. If the decline of the Roman Empire was hastened by the conversion of Constantine, his victorious religion broke the violence of the fall, and mollified the ferocious temper of the conquerors.

This awful revolution may be usefully applied to the instruction of the present age. It is the duty of a patriot to prefer and promote the exclusive interest and glory of his native country; but a philosopher may be permitted to enlarge his views, and to consider Europe as one great republic, whose various inhabitants have attained almost the same level of politeness and cultivation. The balance of power will continue to fluctuate, and the prosperity of our own or the neighboring kingdoms may be alternately exalted or depressed; but these partial events cannot essentially injure our general state of happiness, the system of arts, and laws, and manners, which so advantageously distinguish, above the rest of mankind, the Europeans and their colonies. The savage nations of the globe are the common enemies of civilized society; and we may inquire, with anxious curiosity, whether Europe is still threatened with a repetition of those calamities which formerly oppressed the arms and institutions of Rome. Perhaps the same reflections will illustrate the fall of that mighty Empire, and explain the probable causes of our actual security.

I. The Romans were ignorant of the extent of their danger, and the number of their enemies. Beyond the Rhine and Danube, the northern countries of Europe and Asia were filled with innumerable tribes of hunters and shepherds, poor, voracious, and turbulent; bold in arms, and impatient to ravish the fruits of industry. The barbarian world was agitated by the rapid impulse of war; and the peace of Gaul or Italy was shaken by the distant revolutions of China. The Huns, who fled before a victorious enemy, directed their march toward the West; and the torrent was swelled by the gradual accession of captives and allies. The flying tribes who yielded to the Huns assumed, in *their* turn, the spirit of conquest; the endless column of barbarians pressed on the Roman Empire with accumulated weight; and, if the foremost were destroyed, the vacant space was instantly replenished by new assailants. Such formidable emigrations can no longer issue from the north; and the long repose, which has been imputed to the decrease of population, is the happy consequence of the progress of arts and agriculture. Instead of some rude villages, thinly scattered among its woods and morasses, Germany now produces a list of 2300 walled towns; the Christian kingdoms of Denmark, Sweden, and Poland have been successively established; and the Hanse merchants, with the Teutonic knights, have extended their colonies along the coast of the Baltic, as far as the Gulf of Finland. From the Gulf of Finland to the Eastern Ocean, Russia now assumes the form of a powerful and civilized empire. The plough, the loom, and the forge, are introduced on the banks of the Volga, the Oby, and the Lena; and the fiercest of the Tartar hordes have been taught to tremble and obey. The reign of independent barbarism is now contracted to a narrow span; and the remnant of Calmucks or Uzbecks, whose forces may be almost numbered, cannot seriously excite the apprehensions of the great republic of Europe. Yet this apparent security should not tempt us to forget that new enemies, and unknown dangers, may *possibly* arise from some obscure people, scarcely visible in the map of the world. The Arabs or Saracens, who spread their conquests from India to Spain, and had languished in poverty and contempt, until Mohammed breathed into those savage bodies the soul of enthusiasm.

II. The Empire of Rome was firmly established by the singular and perfect coalition of its members. The subject nations, resigning the hope, and even the wish, of independence, embraced the character of Roman citizens; and the provinces of the West were reluctantly torn by the barbarians from the bosom of their mother country. But this union was purchased by the loss of national freedom and military spirit; and the servile provinces, destitute of life and motion, expected their safety from the mercenary troops and governors, who were directed by the orders of a distant court. The happiness of an hundred millions depended on the personal merit of one or two men, perhaps children, whose minds were corrupted by education, luxury, and despotic power. The deepest wounds were inflicted on the Empire during the minorities of the sons and grandsons of Theodosius; and, after those incapable princes seemed to attain the age of manhood, they abandoned the church to the bishops, the state to the eunuchs, and the provinces to the barbarians. Europe is now divided into twelve powerful, though unequal, kingdoms, three respectable commonwealths, and a variety of smaller, though independent, states; the chances of royal and ministerial talents are multiplied, at least with the number of its rulers; and a Julian, or Semiramis, may reign in the north, while Arcadius and Honorius again slumber on the thrones of the south. The abuses of tyranny are restrained by the mutual influence of fear and shame; republics have acquired order and stability; monarchies have imbibed the principles of freedom, or, at least, of moderation; and some sense of honor and justice is introduced into the most defective constitutions by the general manners of the times. In peace, the progress of knowledge and industry is accelerated by the emulation of so many active rivals: in war, the European forces are exercised by temperate and undecisive contests. . . .

III. Cold, poverty, and a life of danger and fatigue fortify the strength and courage of barbarians. In every age they have oppressed the polite and peaceful nations of China, India, and Persia, who neglected, and still neglect, to counterbalance these natural powers by the resources of military art. The warlike states of antiquity—Greece, Macedonia, and Rome—educated a race of soldiers; exercised their bodies, disciplined their courage, multiplied their forces by regular evolutions, and converted the iron which they possessed into strong and serviceable weapons. But this superiority insensibly declined with their laws and manners; and the feeble policy of Constantine and his successors armed and instructed, for the ruin of the Empire, the rude valor of the barbarian mercenaries. The military art has been changed by the invention of gunpowder, which enables man to command the two most powerful agents of nature: air and fire. Mathematics, chemistry, mechanics, architecture have been applied to the service of war; and the adverse parties oppose to each other the most elaborate modes of attack and of defense. Historians may indignantly observe that the preparations of a siege would found and maintain a flourishing colony, yet we cannot be displeased that the subversion of a city should be a work of cast and difficulty, or that an industrious people should be protected by those arts which survive and supply the decay of military virtue. Cannon and fortifications now form an impregnable barrier against the Tartar horse, and Europe is secure from any future irruption of barbarians, since, before they can conquer, they must cease to be barbarous. Their gradual advances in the science of war would always be accompanied, as we may learn from the example of Russia, with a proportionable improvement in the arts of peace and civil policy, and they themselves must deserve a place among the polished nations whom they subdue.

Should these speculations be found doubtful or fallacious, there still remains a more humble source of comfort and hope. The discoveries of ancient and modern navigators, and the domestic history, or tradition, of the most enlightened nations, represent the *human savage,* naked both in mind and body, and destitute of laws, of arts, of ideas, and almost of language. From this abject condition, perhaps the primitive and universal state of man, he has gradually arisen to command the animals, to fertilize the earth, to traverse the ocean, and to measure the heavens. His progress in the improvement and exercise of his mental and corporeal faculties has been irregular and various, infinitely slow in the beginning, and increasing by degrees with redoubled velocity; ages of laborious ascent have been followed by a moment of rapid downfall; and the several climates of the globe have felt the vicissitudes of light and darkness. Yet the experience of four thousand years should enlarge our hopes, and diminish our apprehensions; we cannot determine to what height the human species may aspire in their advances toward perfection, but it may safely be presumed that no people, unless the face of nature is changed, will relapse into their original barbarism.

The improvements of society may be viewed under a threefold aspect: 1. The poet or philosopher illustrates his age and country by the efforts of a *single* mind; but these superior powers of reason or fancy are rare and spontaneous productions, and the genius of Homer, or Cicero, or Newton, would excite less admiration if they could be created by the will of a prince or the lessons of a preceptor.

2. The benefits of law and policy, of trade and manufactures, of arts and sciences, are more solid and permanent; and *many* individuals may be qualified, by education and discipline, to promote, in their respective stations, the interest of the community. But this general order is the effect of skill and labor, and the complex machinery may be decayed by time or injured by violence.

3. Fortunately for mankind, the more useful, or, at least, more necessary arts can be performed without superior talents or national subordination; without the powers of *one* or the union of *many*. Each village, each family, each individual, must always possess both ability and inclination to perpetuate the use of fire and of metals, the propagation and service of domestic animals, the methods of hunting and fishing, the rudiments of navigation, the imperfect cultivation of corn or other nutritive grain, and the simple practice of the mechanic trades. Private genius and public industry may be extirpated, but these hardy plants survive the tempest, and strike an everlasting root into the most unfavorable soil. The splendid days of Augustus and Trajan were eclipsed by a cloud of ignorance, and the barbarians subverted the laws and palaces of Rome. But the scythe, the invention or emblem of Saturn, still continued annually to mow the harvests of Italy: and the human feasts of the Læstrygons* have never been renewed on the coast of Campania.

Since the first discovery of the arts, war, commerce, and religious zeal have diffused, among the savages of the Old and New World, those inestimable gifts: they have been successively propagated; they can never be lost. We may therefore acquiesce in the pleasing conclusion that every age of the world has increased, and still increases, the real wealth, the happiness, the knowledge, and perhaps the virtue, of the human race.

* Fabulous cannibals described in Homer's *Odyssey* (Ed. [of Gibbon]).

## II / THE BASIC COMMON CHARACTERISTICS
## OF THE EMPIRES


## BASIC POLITICAL ORIENTATIONS / INTRODUCTION

*In the following chapters we shall present essays dealing with the nature of the political orientations developed by these empires and with some of their basic structural and organizational characteristics: Ostrogorsky tells us about the nature of the concept of empires and imperial power in relation to the cosmic and cultural order developed by the Byzantine emperors; Han Shu and Wilson show us how imperial power as conceived in the cosmic order developed in China and in Egypt; Khadduri emphasizes the strong religious roots of the Islamic state.*

*In spite of the obvious differences in the specific contents of these conceptions, a common characteristic stands out: in all these cases, the political order is very closely interwoven with the cosmic, religious, and cultural order; the political center is seen as a focus of the cosmic order, and its legitimacy is based on its maintenance of this order.*


## 2 / AUTHORITY AND LAW IN ANCIENT EGYPT
### JOHN A. WILSON

Any brief characterization of a history covering three thousand years will of necessity have to deal rather brusquely with the complexities of a changing organism. Further, the statement which follows may have certain dicta which seem to be competitive or mutually contradictory, such as the argument that the king of Egypt, as a god, was the sole source of law and authority, yet relied upon other gods for oracular direction and delegated great legal responsibility to the vizier and other officials. If such statements are paradoxical, it is because the Egyptian state retained the paradox of a dogma which insisted upon the divine absolutism of the monarch, along with a practice of government which utilized a

Reprinted with permission from John A. Wilson, "Authority and Law in Ancient Egypt," *Journal of the American Oriental Society, Supplement,* 74, No. 3 (1954), 1-7.

number of responsible agents. Finally, the attempt to understand another culture in its own terms always has a semantic difficulty in the inexactness of the translation of concepts from one culture to the other.

## I. Authority Within the State

The basic proposition with regard to authority and the source of law in ancient Egypt is that the king of Egypt was a god. This may have been expressed in different ways in the course of Egyptian history, and this official dogma may have been imperfectly carried out in different periods, but there is abundant evidence from the beginning of the dynasties down to the Roman emperors that the central dogma of the state was that the ruler of Egypt was no representative or servant of the gods, did not rule by a divine right which came to him with his throne, but ruled because he was born a god, with the divine function of rule inherent in his physical and spiritual being. In the very first dynasty inscriptions designate the king as the god Horus, and some of the pyramid texts which exhibit an archaic type of writing and which apparently refer back to a predynastic situation insist upon his divine nature.

As the god who alone possessed and directed the state, the king of Egypt had certain divine attributes of rule. The most common are two, *hu* and *sia, or* sometimes three, *hu, sia,* and *ma'at.* We shall translate *hu* as "authoritative command," *sia* as "perception," and *ma'at* as "justice"; in other words, *hu,* the divine ability to create or recreate a situation by speech, *sia,* the divine recognition and understanding of situations, and *ma'at,* the maintenance of a divine order within society. All three attributes were deified by the Egyptians, Hu and Sia as gods and Ma'at as a goddess. To the king it was said: "Authoritative command is in thy mouth, perception is in thy heart, and thy tongue is the shrine of justice." [1] Elsewhere, the king was said to have carried off authoritative command by conquest, to have gained control of perception.[2] The first two, the ability to see and know a situation and the ability to meet that situation by command, are divine attributes which by themselves might work for good or evil; the third, justice or order or truth, is an attribute which imposes responsibilities upon the king, since it involves conformance with principles of the universe which come down from the creation or it involves right-dealing among humans. This *ma'at* is the most important of the divine attributes of the king, and we shall return to it later. Here it should be added that *ma'at,* in its sense of truth, order, or regularity, belonged to the world which the gods set up at the creation.

---

[1] Kuban Stela of Ramses II, l. 19: C. E. Sander-Hansen, *Historische Inschriften der 19. Dynastie,* I (Bruxelles, 1933), pp. 31 ff.

[2] K. Sethe, *Die altägyptischen Pyramidentexte,* I (Leipzig, 1908), § 300c; cf. § 307a-b.

Therefore, as the coronation of each king was a re-creation for Egypt, the coronation texts insist that *ma'at* has been restored through the effective arrival upon earth of this eternal yet new god, the incoming king.[3]

Nevertheless, the role of the king was not as arbitrary as most of the texts seem to claim. His brother gods recaptured a considerable share of the direction of specific acts of government. At the beginning of the Fifth Dynasty, the apparently unlimited authority of the king was checked by the abrupt rise in power of the sun-god Re. We cannot tell at what point in Egyptian history the gods began to express their desires through various kinds of oracles, but this agency becomes increasingly clear as time goes on. The king himself, as a priest of all the gods, might visit a temple and lay a proposition before a god, as Ramses III sought the approval of Amon-Re for military campaigns. Thus the communication was directly between the god and the god-king. However, in other instances the god seems to have acted independently in affairs of the state, as when the god Amon-Re in sacred procession sought out an unimportant prince and indicated that this young man was to be the king whom we call Thut-mose III.[4] Again, Hatshepsut refers to the dark period when Egypt lay under the foreign domination of the Hyksos conquerors: "They ruled without Re, and he did not act by divine command down to (the reign of) my majesty." [5] That is, since the barbarian Hyksos did not use the sun-god in their government, that god refused to give oracular direction to the state throughout their rule and even later.

This brief notice of oracles is all that will be said here as an indirect reference to the authoritative role of the priests within the state. Their agency did not appear in the expressed dogma of the state, but it may nevertheless have been very effective.

The most important "civil" official in the sacred state of Egypt was the vizier, who at first had been selected from the king's family, but by the Fifth Dynasty might be unrelated to the king. From the same dynasty on, he enjoyed a subsidiary title, or perhaps an epithet, "the Prophet of *Ma'at*," that is, the priest who might speak for the goddess Truth or Justice. One official tells us of his appointment to be Prophet of *Ma'at*, with the proud boast: "I was a noble, the second of the king, the fourth of him who judged the Pair." [6] This is remarkable language for one who

[3] E.g., a hymn celebrating the accession of Mer-ne-Ptah in A. Erman, *The Literature of the Ancient Egyptians* (London, 1927), pp. 278 ff.; see also H. Frankfort, *Kingship and the Gods* (Chicago, 1948), p. 150.

[4] From the temple of Karnak; J. B. Pritchard (ed.), *Ancient Near Eastern Texts relating to the Old Testament* (Princeton, 1950 [hereafter abbreviated as *ANET*]), p. 446.

[5] From the Speos Artemidos in Middle Egypt; *ANET*, p. 231.

[6] From the autobiography of the eighteenth dynasty vizier Rekh-mi-Re; *ANET*, p. 213.

was not a god: he claimed to be a partner of the king, as well as a partner of the god Thoth, who judged the pair of contesting gods, Horus and Seth. This is the clearest possible statement of the independent responsibility of this highest magistrate in the land, even though the accompanying text is careful to emphasize that this vizier acted only in strict conformance with the principles which the king had laid down for his office.

Those principles of just procedure and attitude will not be detailed here, but two points might be noted. First, in addition to the regular and formal hearing in his audience hall, when appellants might present their formal pleas, the vizier had to walk forth every day, so that poor or timid people might also have a chance to appeal to him for justice. Second, the king's charge to the vizier is very detailed, insists upon the strictest impartiality, and also directs that all of the vizier's judicial activity be carried out "in conformance with the regulations and that everything be done in conformance with the precedent therefor." [7] This sounds as though the vizier had very little personal discretion, as though he had to be scrupulous in maintaining justice according to known law, but essentially was merely the mouth-piece or the prophet for justice. The king uses the curious words to the vizier: "The place of refuge for the official is to act in conformance with the regulations." [8] Despite the very sweeping range of functions laid upon the vizier, his individual authority was thoroughly limited by known precedents and procedures from the past. Perhaps, after all, only the king, who was a god, could dispense justice in terms of ethical principles rather than customary procedures.

The Egyptian texts often relate how the king called together his counselors and sought their advice. This turns out to have no legislative force, since such a consultative assembly appears only in contexts where the king uses them as a sounding-board for his own ideas, or where the officials give a timorous advice which the king brusquely rejects in favor of his superhuman wisdom.[9] This, to be sure, is a device of propagandistic literature, in order to emphasize the higher qualities of the pharaoh, but it does indicate that the voice of the majority had no such weight in Egypt as it had in Mesopotamia.

Egypt is a land six hundred miles long, and the sole ruler could not exercise personal authority everywhere at all times. An elaborate bureaucracy was constructed, which dispensed justice and carried out administration in the king's name. As a matter of practical necessity, this included

[7] From the regulations for Rekh-mi-Re's activity; *ibid.*

[8] *Ibid.*

[9] For example, Ka-mose's attack upon the Hyksos (*ANET*, p. 232); *Thut-mose* III's advance upon Megiddo (*ANET*, pp. 235 f.).

considerable local responsibility and therefore authority. The autobiographies of officials frequently assert this provincial independence in the claim that a noble has undertaken forthright action to keep his province free from disaster or that he had judged his people with impartiality. Thus, although the king was theoretically the sole source of law and authority, in practice he sought the backing of the gods, delegated a heavy responsibility to the vizier, and also delegated much local autonomy to the nobles in their own home districts.

The king was the god who dispensed rule, and the people were his materials to be ruled. He had a responsibility to maintain *ma'at* in his realm, and he had a proprietary responsibility to maintain his flock in a prosperous condition. But the people were only mortals, and they had no inherent right to justice. They could only be humbly grateful if they were nurtured toward prosperity and did receive an impartial and paternalistic justice. At one period in Egyptian history, the troubled times between the Old and Middle Kingdoms, there was a debate as to whether an ordinary Egyptian had a right to demand justice,[10] but the normal situation in Egypt was that *ma'at*-justice was the king's offering to the gods, rather than a debt which the king owed to his subjects.

## II. The Laws of the State

Egypt had neighbors in Asia who wrote down laws, arranged in such a systematic way and having such comprehensive coverage that it is customary to speak of codes of law in the Asiatic cultures. Despite all the written documents which have come down to us from ancient Egypt, we possess neither a body of law which is comparable to the Asiatic codes, nor any textual references to such laws elsewhere, nor even a later tradition about a king or official who was a law-giver or law-codifier until one comes down to the late tradition about King Bocchoris, who reigned about 700 BC.[11] We do have legal documents, such as testaments and transfers of property, as well as abbreviated records of court proceedings.[12] These give us information about legal procedure but nothing about law. We do have specific legal regulations issued to cover specific situations, such as decrees exempting individual temples from the obligation to supply forced labor for the state, or a decree banishing a disloyal priest from his post.[13] But these are decrees rather than law.

[10] Most specifically stated in the protests of the Eloquent Peasant (*ANET*, pp. 407 ff.), also implied in the Admonitions of Ipu-wer (*ibid.*, pp. 443 ff.).

[11] Diodorus, 1, 79.

[12] E.g., *ANET*, pp. 214-17. Cf. A. Scharff and E. Seidl, *Einführung in die ägyptische Rechtsgeschichte* . . . I, Aegyptologische Forschungen, Heft 10 (Hamburg, 1939).

[13] E.g., *ANET*, p. 212; *JNES* 6 (1947), pp. 219 ff.; J. H. Breasted, *Ancient Records of Egypt* (Chicago, 1906), I §§ 773 ff.

It is necessary to remove from consideration the former understanding of one Egyptian scene, with its accompanying text. When the Egyptian vizier sat in judicial hearing, forty objects were spread out on four mats in front of him, and it was formerly assumed that these were forty scrolls of law. The Egyptian word for these forty objects has now appeared in other contexts, and it seems that they were instruments used in punishment, such as leather straps.[14] These then would be symbols of the punishing power of the state, and not the written, impersonal law toward which an appellant might stretch out his hand in supplication.

Since Egypt was blessed by having on earth a god as king, law proceeded from his mouth, always vitally renewed, and no codification was necessary or even proper. Of course legal procedure was followed in Egypt, but the specific practice must have stemmed from the customary law of the land before there was a unified state. It is even possible that such customary law differed in different parts of Egypt; that could well be within the divine understanding of the king as to what was good for his people.

Egypt had a word for a specific regulation or the law to cover a single situation, *hap*, but it had no word for law in general. The all-embracing term which applied to legal procedure and the spirit in which legal procedure was undertaken was *maʿat*, which in different contexts may mean "order, right, right-dealing, rightfulness, righteousness, truth, justice." There was no distinction between "truth" and "justice," both were covered by the term *maʿat*. Thus *maʿat* as "truth" involved right relations to "facts" as they were understood in a sacred society, and *maʿat* as "justice" involved right relations between the governor and those who were governed as this was understood in a sacred society. The concept of *maʿat* definitely belonged to the religious order; it was the substance upon which gods fed; it was the daily offering of the king to the gods.[15] It was thus a spirit which properly pervaded the civil carrying out of government and justice for the ends of religion.

The ancient Egyptians always shrank from the finality of carrying a series of concepts or a series of experiences on to their logical conclusions. They preferred to compromise or conciliate, to work things out on a topical basis, rather than to systematize experience into a set of working principles for the future. Crisis could be met with flexibility of action, if one were not obligated to follow written principles such as lie behind a code of law. Further, each king was a newly reborn god, a new source of

[14] P. E. Newberry *The Life of Rekhmara* (London, 1900), p. 23; N. de G. Davies, *The Tomb of Rekh-mi-Re at Thebes* (New York, 1944), I, pp. 31 ff.; ANET, p. 213.

[15] R. Anthes, *Supplement No. 14 to JAOS* (1952), pp. 3-7.

verbal law, and it would be unbefitting if he were to be made the heir to a long-standing code which came from outside of him.

Thus the picture which we get is that of a somewhat pragmatic order, governed only by the large and general principle of *ma'at,* which combined "truth," "justice," and "order." Certainly there was a recognition of the necessity and obligation for good management, but apart from that it is impossible to claim that ancient Egypt formulated any ethical basis for government and law. This "lawlessness" permitted a kind of flexible strength in allowing a dogmatically traditional society to meet the new situations of changing times. But it was also as inherent weakness of the society, and when the king ceased to function as a god and became the tool of priests, officials, and foreign rulers, Egyptian culture gradually disintegrated.

# 3 / ON THE DESTINY OF KINGS / *PAN PIAO*

The following essay was written by Pan Piao (AD 3-54) of the Latter Han to expound his theory of the divine election of rulers. It was on the basis of this conception of the divine election of Han Kao-tsu (Liu Chi) and his family as founders of the dynasty that Pan Piao and his son, Pan Ku, set about to continue and rewrite the *Shih chi* or *Records of the Historian* by their predecessor Ssu-ma Ch'ien. This resulted in the first of the so-called dynastic histories, the *Han shu* or *History of the Former Han Dynasty.*[1]

When Emperor Yao abdicated, he said to his successor: "Ah, Shun! The Heaven-appointed succession now rests in you." Shun used the same words in transmitting his mandate to Yü.

At this time Chi and Hsieh served as ministers to Yao and Shun, bringing light to all the world, and their virtue was borne down the countless generations to their respective descendants, T'ang *(founder of the Shang dynasty)* and Wu *(founder of the Chou)* so that they were able to rule over the empire. Thus though they encountered troubles in their own times and their lines of succession were different, yet in responding to the will of Heaven and according with human kind, they followed the same principle.

In the same way the family of Liu *(Han dynasty)* inherited the blessing of Yao, as we see from its genealogy written in the *Spring and Autumn Annals.* Yao ruled by the virtue of fire, which was handed down to the Han. When the future emperor, Kao-tsu, first arose in the Marsh of

---

Reprinted with permission from Han shu, "On the Destiny of Kings" (100 A:8a), in Theodore DeBary ed., *Sources of Chinese Tradition* (New York: Columbia University Press, 1960), pp. 192-96.

[1] From *Han shu,* 100 A:8a; *Wen hsüan,* 52.

P'ei, the spirit of the old woman appeared weeping in the night as a sign from the Red (*Fire*) Emperor.

For this reason we say that, in order for a man to enjoy the blessing of rulership, he must possess not only the virtue of shining sageliness and apparent excellence, but he must be heir to a patrimony of abundant merit and favor long accumulated. Only then can he, by his pure sincerity, communicate with the divine intelligence and extend his grace to all living men. Then will he receive good fortune from the spirits and gods, and all people will come to his rule. There has never been a case of a man who, the successive generations having passed without showing signs of his destiny or recording the merit and virtue of his family, has been able to rise to this position of eminence. The mass of people see that Kao-tsu arose from among the common men and they do not comprehend the reasons for his rise. They believe that, happening upon a time of violence and disorder, he was able to wield his sword, as the wandering political theorists compare the conquest of the empire to a deer chase in which success goes to the luckiest and swiftest. They do not understand that this sacred vessel, the rule of the empire, is transmitted according to destiny and cannot be won either by craft or force. Alas, this is why there are so many rebellious ministers and evil sons in the world today. To be so mistaken, one would not only have to be blind to the way of Heaven, but totally unobservant of human affairs as well!

Now when famine comes and the people wander from place to place, the starving and cold fill the roads. They think only of getting a coarse coat to cover themselves and a measure of grain to nourish life. Their desires go no further than a few coins, and yet they die and end tumbled in a ditch. If in this way even poverty and misery are meted out by destiny, how much more so the honor of the throne, the riches of all within the four seas, and the blessing of the gods. How could one recklessly try to arrogate to oneself such a position? True, there are some who, happening upon an age of trouble and peril, by bravery, like Han Hsin and Chi Pu; by their powerful situation, like Hsiang Yü and his uncle, Hsiang Liang; or by luck, like Wang Mang, manage to seize authority for a time. Yet all must end cast into the cauldron or bowed beneath the stroke of the ax, boiled alive, or struck down and quartered. How much more damned would be a mean and insignificant man who could not match even these and yet in his blindness hoped to contend for the throne of the sovereign? As a man cannot ride a thousand-mile journey on a crippled jade, as the little swallows and sparrows cannot soar with the great-winged flocks, as the timbers used for corbels and joists cannot bear the weight of beams and ridgepoles, no more can any mere dullard shoulder the burden of imperial rule.

The *Book of Changes* says: "If the leg of the cauldron is broken, the lord's porridge will spill out." That is, the pot is not fit for the purpose.

At the end of the Ch'in Dynasty, the strong men in power joined in urging upon Ch'en Ying the title of king. But Ying's mother pressed him not to accept, saying: "From the time I came as a bride into your father's house, I have known only the poverty and lowliness which have been with your family for generations. Now if you were to rise too suddenly to wealth and honor, I fear it would be unlucky. It would be better to take your forces and place them under the command of another. If you are successful you may receive somewhat less profit, but if things go badly then the misfortune will fall on someone else." Ch'en Ying followed her counsel and assured the safety of his family.

The mother of Wang Ling, in like manner, perceived that the Hsiang family would perish and the Liu family rise to power. At this time Wang Ling was a general of the Han forces (*Liu family*) but his mother was held captive by Ch'u (*Hsiang forces*). An envoy came from the Han camp and the mother of Ling addressed him in these words: "I beg you to tell my son that the King of Han is a superior man and will surely become ruler of the Empire. My son should serve him with all diligence and not be of two minds on my account." Then before the envoy of Han she stabbed herself and died, to urge her son on the course he should follow. Later, when it turned out that the Han was victorious, Wang Ling became prime minister and was enfeoffed as a marquis.

Now if a common woman's perception can deduce the course which events will take and can search out the beginnings of good and bad fortune and insure the perpetuation of her family so that the memory of her deeds is handed down in the pages of history, how much more should a great man be able to do? Therefore, though failure and success rest ultimately with destiny, yet it is up to men to choose between the lucky and unlucky. Ch'en Ying's mother understood what would decline, Wang Ling's mother perceived what would prosper. By judging of these, the disposition of the rulership can be determined.

There were five indications of Kao-tsu's rise to the throne. First, he was a descendant of Emperor Yao. Second, his body and face showed many strange markings. Third, there were omens testifying to his divinely inspired conquest. Fourth, he was liberal and of a keen mind, humane and merciful. Fifth, he understood men and knew well how to use their services. In addition, he was trustworthy and sincere, a good strategist who knew how to listen to others. When he saw what was good, he strove for it; when he employed others, he used them as he would himself. He complied with good advice as a boat follows the current, and responded to his opportunities as an echo answering a sound. [*There follows a list of references to Kao-tsu's wise and good acts, and the wonders and prodigies accompanying his rise to power.*]

If one adds up the successes and failures of history, examines the victories and defeats in the course of human affairs, perceives how the throne has passed from family to family through the generations, and ponders what is meant by the five signs of Kao-tsu's good fortune enumerated above; and if his character does not come up to the requirements for the highest position, and omens and signs do not appear as they did for Kao-tsu, and yet he tries unjustly to seize power and profit, recklessly violating the proper order, failing to weigh external circumstances and in his heart to comprehend the commands of destiny, then must he bring destruction upon the household he should guard, and lose the years Heaven has granted him; his will be like the misfortune of the cauldron with the broken leg and he will go down beneath the punishment of the ax.

But if brave and ambitious men have sincere understanding and awareness; if they fear and heed the warnings of disaster and use transcendent vision and profound judgment; if they employ the perception of Wang Ling and Ch'en Ying and avoid the overblown ambitions of Han Hsin and Chi Pu; [if they] rid themselves of the blind notion that the mandate of Heaven can be pursued like a deer in chase and realize that the sacred vessel of rule must be given from on high; if they do not covet that which they could never hope for, in a way that would draw ridicule even from the two simple country women, the mothers of Ch'en Ying and Wang Ling, then will fortune and blessing flow to their sons and grandsons, and the rewards of Heaven will be with them to the end of their days.

## 4 / THE BYZANTINE EMPEROR AND THE HIERARCHICAL WORLD ORDER * / GEORGE OSTROGORSKY

The political ideas of the Byzantines have only recently become the subject of more detailed study and of a deeper contemplation among historians. The research work done in this field in the course of the last few decades has for the first time revealed the substance and peculiarities of the Byzantine theory of imperial authority and established it as the mainspring of the Byzantine political ideology. Among the most outstanding studies, the following may be mentioned: the penetrating researches of A. Alföldi on the formation of Roman court ceremonial

Reprinted with permission from George Ostrogorsky, "The Byzantine Emperor and the Hierarchical World Order," *The Slavonic and East European Review*, 35 (1956), 1-8, 13-14.

* Lecture given at King's College, London, and at the University of Edinburgh on January 12 and 18, 1956, respectively.

and on the insignia and robes of the Roman emperor;[1] the very vivid and interesting work by A. Grabar on the emperor in Byzantine art;[2] the fundamentally important work by O. Treitinger on imperial court ceremonial as an expression of the Byzantine idea of emperorship and empire;[3] numerous very instructive papers by F. Dölger on the relations between the Byzantine Empire and contemporary foreign powers in the light of the Byzantine theory of imperial authority.[4] And already since 1936 I myself have been attempting to outline the Byzantine interpretation of the idea of empire and the Byzantine conception of the world order, to which I gave the name of the Byzantine hierarchy of states.[5] I should like to follow up these trends of thought today and to summarize them in a more coherent manner.

Although the destinies of the Byzantine Empire varied a great deal and the character of its state policies was apparently heterogeneous, the basic idea underlying these policies, the idea of emperorship, was firmly upheld through the ages, in spite of all divergencies. Like all other elements of fundamental significance for the development of the Byzantine state, this idea is traceable to Roman and Hellenistic sources. And, like everything else in Byzantium, it emerges here in a christianized version, in which the original pagan concept has been little by little overshadowed by the power of Christian ideas.

It is well known that the pagan concept of the god-emperor represented the crucial stumbling-block for Christians and that their refusal to worship the emperor as a god was the main reason for the persecution of Christians in the ancient Roman Empire. Nevertheless, the transition from pagan to Christian empire was completed without any outward distortion of the concept of imperial authority in the time of Constantine. The sovereign's power preserved its divine character, and thus the Roman-Hellenistic cult of the sovereign lived on in the Christian Byzantine Empire in all its ancient glory. This would not have been possible if the idea of emperorship had not gained a deeper sense even in the pagan world. The idea of the divine origin of the sovereign's power was gradually built up around the original naïve concept of the god-emperor. The Christian Byzantine Empire accepted this conception, for nothing

[1] A. Alföldi, "Die Ausgestaltung des monarchischen Zeremoniells am römischen Kaiserhof," *Mitt. d. Deutschen Archäol. Inst.*, Röm. Abt. 49 (1934), 1-118; "Insignien und Tracht der römischen Kaiser," *ibid.*, 50 (1935), 1-176.

[2] A. Grabar, *L'empereur dans l'art byzantin* (Paris, 1936).

[3] O. Treitinger, *Die oströmische Kaiser- und Reichsidee nach ihrer Gestaltung im höfischen Zeremoniell* (Jena, 1938).

[4] Reprinted in F. Dölger, *Byzanz und die europäische Staatenwelt* (Ettal, 1953).

[5] G. Ostrogorsky, "Die byzantinische Staatenhierarchie," *Seminarium Kondakovianum*, 8 (1936), 41-61.

could appear more natural to Christians than to see in the Christian emperor a sovereign appointed by God's will. Moreover, belief in its divine vocation accorded to the Christian emperorship a sacred character that made possible the maintenance of old forms of rites and even gave them a natural appearance.[6]

The Christian subjects of the Emperor Constantine firmly believed that he had been called to rule by the Christian God, and he himself ordered an effigy to be struck on a gold medallion representing the hand of God placing the imperial crown on his head.[7] Many works of art belonging to a later epoch reproduce a similar motif—the crowning of the emperor by Christ, who is seen setting the crown on the sovereign's head with His own hand.[8]

The emperor is the Chosen of God, he is called to rule by Divine Providence and fulfills the Divine Will in his quality of sovereign of the empire protected by God. This idea dominates the minds of all the Byzantines, from the emperor to the last of his subjects. They are constantly reminded of it both in speeches and in written documents. It emanates incessantly from monuments with which public buildings and streets are adorned, from seals and coins circulating from hand to hand. It is shown to them in a particularly striking manner in all the rites of the imperial court ceremonial which are emphasized by an exuberance of symbols, with the sacred figure of the emperor in the center.

It would be a mistake to consider the Byzantine court ceremonial as a stiff system of effete formalities. It was, in fact, a carefully elaborated system of rites aimed at the glorification of the emperor and of his Empire. And these rites were used for the implementation of a political and religious cult of a peculiar nature.

The learned Emperor Constantine VII Porphyrogenitus wrote a book containing a detailed description of the imperial court ceremonial. Such a subject, as he himself admits in the preface, was dearer to his heart than any other, because "through the praiseworthy system of court ceremonial the imperial power is displayed in great beauty and magnificence, thus filling with admiration both foreign nations and our citizens".[9] He describes the rites to be observed on the occasion of church and state celebrations with great affection and care. Each act of ceremony, gesture,

---

[6] Cf. J. A. Straub, *Vom Herrscherideal in der Spätantike* (Stuttgart, 1939). W. Ensslin, "Gottkaiser und Kaiser von Gottes Gnaden," *Sb. d. Bayer. Akad. d. Wiss.*, 1943, Heft 6 (München, 1943). N. H. Baynes, *Byzantine Studies and Other Essays* (London, 1955), pp. 168 ff., 343 ff.

[7] Alföldi, "Insignien . . . ," *op. cit.*, pp. 55 f. and Fig. 6.

[8] Grabar, *op. cit.*, pp. 112 ff.

[9] *De caerimoniis*, ed. Bonn., p. 3 sq.

word, acclamation, and hymn is recorded in detail, for every detail has an underlying symbolic meaning—the outcome of a coherent ideology, and everything points toward one single aim: the mystical glorification of the emperor.

Everything that surrounds the emperor inspires awe. The palace itself in which the Christ-loving emperor lives is under divine protection, and his subjects consider it to be a holy place; the same solemn stillness reigns in it that was once observed in the presence of Divus Augustus, the Roman god-emperor. Everything is performed in awe-inspiring silence, not a single superfluous word is spoken, no unnecessary noise is allowed to break the solemnity of the moment when the emperor appears before his people.[10]

Every time the emperor appears, his subjects throw themselves to the ground and touch it with their brows. This is the custom of prostration (προσκύνησις) that was taken over by the Byzantine ceremonial, together with many other forms of ritual, from the Roman-Hellenistic cult of the sovereign.[11] All the emperor's subjects, including even the highest dignitaries of the empire and the members of the imperial family greet the emperor by prostration, because all of them without distinction are his slaves (δοῦλοι).

Although all the subjects are considered slaves of the emperor, this does not mean that they are equals among themselves. According to their respective official positions, some of them have a higher station than the others, or, which is the same and constitutes the most important point, they stand nearer to the sacred person of the emperor. This gave rise to the formation of a hierarchical order of ranks which is specifically characteristic of the Byzantine state.

The imperial insignia and robes are invested with sacred meaning. Constantine Porphyrogenitus affirmed that the crowns and festive robes of the emperor were not made by the hand of man; according to old scripts, an angel brought them to Constantine the Great with the command that they should be kept in the cathedral of St. Sophia and worn only on the most solemn occasions.[12] The color of the emperor's robes is normally crimson, and they are heavily ornamented with gold. With these robes the emperor wears a diadem, which is the main symbol of imperial dignity, and crimson shoes. The symbolism of colors is a very important aspect of the Byzantine cult of the emperor. During his public appearances on solemn occasions, the emperor never stands on the floor, but is placed on a special stool, upholstered with crimson stuff,

[10] Treitinger, op. cit., pp. 52 ff.

[11] Treitinger, op. cit., pp. 84 ff. Alföldi, "Zeremoniell . . . ," op. cit., pp. 46 ff.

[12] De adm. imp., ed. Moravcsik-Jenkins, cap. 13, 1. 28 sq.

on a podium, or on high marble steps. The emperor's hands may touch only crimson stuff or porphyry.[13]

Theocratic tendencies become more and more apparent in the life of the imperial court. Not only the church but also the state celebrates a special liturgical service on every holiday. The court, all the government and military officials, the representatives of the people, praising the emperor with ceremonious acclamations, take part in this sumptuous mystery-play. This empire desires to be a reflection of the kingdom of God. The emperor takes Christ as a model and emulates his example, going even so far as to represent him at many church celebrations, at which Christ's life on earth is evoked.

According to a tradition which is recorded about 900, the emperor used to invite twelve guests to a meal on Christmas Day "following the example of the twelve apostles." [14] In an Easter Day procession described in Constantine VII's Book of Ceremonies, "the magisters and patricians take the places of apostles, while the emperor, so far as possible, imitates Christ." [15] In later times, the emperor performs the ceremony of the washing of feet on Maundy Thursday.[16] Just as Christ had washed the feet of his disciples, so the emperor washes the feet of twelve poor men from his empire. The fact that poor men were selected for this tended to emphasize the Christian humility of the emperor. And this humility represented a new and most powerful source of spiritual elevation, for it was more important than all earthly grandeur that the emperor should follow the example of the Son of God, who became man, and imitate His humility.

The particular nearness of the emperor to God and the divine origin of his sovereignty imply the concentration of all authority in his hands. As the emperorship was an emanation of divine power, it was bound to gather up the whole power on earth, and its authority could not be impaired by any other inner or outer force. Thus the absolute power of the Roman emperor was further increased with the advent of Christian ideas.

For we should not forget that the Christ-loving sovereign of Byzantium was a Roman emperor, and the empire that God had called him to rule was the Roman Empire. The name *Byzantine* is an expression coined in later times which was not known to those whom we now call *Byzantines*. They have always, quite consciously, called themselves *Romans;* their

[13] Cf. R. Delbrück, *Antike Porphyrwerke* (Berlin-Leipzig, 1932), pp. 11 ff., 27 ff. Treitinger, *op. cit.*, pp. 58 ff. Alföldi "Insignien . . . ," *op. cit.*, p. 51.

[14] *Kletorologion of Philotheos,* ed. Bury, pp. 157, 12.

[15] *De caerimonis, op. cit.,* pp. 638, 3.

[16] *Pseudo-Codinus,* ed. Bonn., p. 70, 10 sq.

capital was for them the new Rome; their emperors were the successors of Roman emperors. Throughout its history, the Byzantine Empire holds on obstinately to its right of succession to Rome. The inheritance of Rome, like the belief in the divine origin of imperial power, represents a special source from which the conception of the absolute power of Byzantine emperors and their high claims on the world beyond the borders of their empire is derived.

The emperor and omnipotent ruler of the Romans will be the leader of all the world and the guardian and protector of the Christian faith, because he is the only legitimate emperor on earth, being the Chosen of God and the successor of Roman emperors. The idea that there may be only one single legitimate empire is the basic principle, the alpha and omega of all Byzantine political doctrines. To the Byzantines, and also to all those living in the Middle Ages, this seemed as natural and incontestable as the belief that there could be only one true Christian church.

Like the Roman Empire, the Byzantine Empire was at first a universal power, and since the time when the Romano-Byzantine domination of the world was shaken by the barbarian invasions, the empire struggled (and this constitutes the most fundamental aim of the state policies of the early Byzantine Empire and the focal point of the attempt at restoration made by Justinian) first for the preservation and then for the reestablishment of its position as a universal power. All the countries that had once belonged to the Roman *orbis,* and later joined the Christian Church, were considered by the Byzantine emperors as their everlasting and incontestable possession. The real developments however undermined the validity of this proud claim. The world empire was in fact crumbling away, and its former components gradually acquired independence and tended to shake off the guardianship of the Roman successors in Constantinople. Political independence did not however mean equal standing with the empire. From the legal and ideological point of view, the Byzantine Empire, as the sole legitimate empire on earth, had a more elevated position than all other countries, even when these enjoyed political independence and were growing more powerful than the empire itself. And so great was the suggestive power of the Romano-Byzantine ideas that even rulers of independent countries recognized for a long time the ideal supremacy of the Byzantine emperor. They liked to have the Byzantine court titles which they obtained from Constantinople. They were thus incorporated in the Byzantine hierarchy, in which some of them held a higher and others a lower rank. The medieval countries were part of a complicated hierarchy of states: at the summit of this hierarchy stood the Byzantine sovereign, both in his quality of Roman emperor and as the head of Christendom. Just as in the earlier stages the Byzantine Empire struggled to uphold its position as a universal power, so in later times it strove to maintain this ideal supremacy.[17] For soon insubordination began to creep in.

With the further shifting of the balance of power, the ideal supremacy of the Byzantine Empire was also jeopardized. Fully conscious of their power, other nations began to claim priority. The crowning of Charles the Great as emperor was the heaviest blow to the prestige of the Byzantine hierarchy of states.[18] This action, which seemed to have upset the balance of the traditional hierarchy of states, was considered in Constantinople as the usurpation of the inherited right of the Byzantine Empire. After some futile resistance Byzantium succumbed to the overpowering superiority of the adversary, and already in 812 recognized the imperial status of Charles the Great. Although this was a very high distinction and a tremendous concession on the part of the Byzantine Empire, the imperial status of Charles the Great still appeared to the Byzantines as having a significance limited territorially and, in the long run, of transitional character, as opposed to their own universal Roman Empire, which never surrendered in principle its claim to world sovereignty, and whose mission it was to reunite all Christian states in response to God's command. It is most significant that ever since the recognition of the imperial title of Charles the Great, the Byzantine emperors began more and more frequently and with more and more ostentation to call themselves not merely *emperors,* but *emperors of the Romans,* thus indicating the difference between the status of their empire and that of the West.[19]

The medieval idea of imperial authority is, however, in essence connected with the claim to the Roman succession, and while Charles the Great himself, consciously trying to avoid the emphasis on the Roman character of his emperorship, contented himself with the title *Imperium Romanum gubernans,* the later Western emperors insisted most emphatically on the Roman origin of their imperial status, thus entering into open conflict with the Byzantine Empire.[20] The twofold question— to whom did the imperial status actually belong and who was entitled to inherit Rome—divided minds for centuries in East and West and gave rise to many desperate conflicts. In these circumstances, the Byzan-

---

[17] Cf. Ostrogorsky, *op. cit.,* pp. 41 ff.

[18] On this most discussed problem, cf. especially Dölger, "Europas Gestaltung im Spiegel der fränkisch-byzantinischen Auseinandersetzungen," in *Byzanz . . . , op. cit.,* pp. 282 ff.

[19] Cf. E. Stein, "Zum mittelalterlichen Titel 'Kaiser der Römer,'" *Forschungen und Fortschritte* (1930), pp. 182 f. Dölger, *op. cit.,* pp. 305 ff.

[20] Cf. P. E. Schramm, *Kaiser, Rom und Renovatio,* I (Leipzig, 1929), pp. 12 ff. 83 ff.

tines often contested even the claim of the Western emperors to the title of emperor in general, particularly as the breakup of the kingdom of the Carolingians helped to commit the earlier explicit recognition to oblivion. In fact, the Western rulers were never recognized by the Byzantines as Roman emperors proper. This was, however, the main issue in the struggle for the leading position in the hierarchy of states, as only the Roman emperor had a claim to universality.

Already at the beginning of the tenth century the hierarchical order of Christian states defended by the Byzantine Empire suffered a new blow. It was the turn of the Bulgarian ruler Simeon (893-927), who had grown extremely powerful. He stretched out his hand for the imperial crown, claiming the leading position in the hierarchy of states. For Simeon, who had grown up in Byzantium and whom the Byzantines called a half-Greek, was also absolutely convinced that there could exist only one single empire—the universal Roman Empire. He aimed, accordingly, not at founding a national Bulgarian Empire alongside Byzantium, but at substituting a new empire of universal significance for the old Byzantine Empire.[21] His daring claim was not limited to the title of *Basileus of the Bulgarians*; he demanded the status of *Basileus of the Romans* either with or without the addition of *and of the Bulgarians*.[22] In spite of the tremendous pressure which he brought to bear, Byzantium did not recognize his claim; it could not do so, as it did not wish to surrender. In 927, however, the Byzantine government, forced to make concessions, ceded, with the hand of a Byzantine princess, the title of *Basileus of the Bulgarians* to Simeon's more tractable son Peter. This was, once more, a very considerable concession, which meant great promotion for Bulgaria in the hierarchy of states. The Byzantine Empire managed however to defend its supremacy against the powerful Bulgarian Empire, because the territorially limited Bulgarian kingdom lacked the main characteristic of a true empire, viz. the universality inherited from Rome.

A similar crisis in the Byzantine idea of emperorship arose in the fourteenth century, when the predominance in southeastern Europe of the Serbian ruler Stephen Dušan (1331-55) began to make itself felt. Like Simeon of Bulgaria, Stephen Dušan also lived in the Byzantine world of ideas, and his political thinking was also based on the theory of a single world empire. This is why he too did not strive for the

[21] Dölger "Bulgarisches Zartum und byzantinisches Kaisertum" in *Byzanz* . . . , *op. cit.*, pp. 140 ff. Ostrogorsky, "Die Krönung Symeons von Bulgarien durch den Patriarchen Nikolaos Mystikos," *Bull. de l'Inst. archéol. bulgare* 9 (1935), 275 ff. and "Avtokrator i samodržac," *Glas Srpske akad. nauka*, 164 (1935), 121 ff.

[22] T. Gerasimov in *Bull. de l'Inst. archéol. bulgare*, 8 (1934), 350 ff., has published a seal of Simeon with the significant legend: Συμεὼν ἐν Χριστῷ βασιλεὺς Ρομέων,

foundation of a Serbian Empire beside the Byzantine Empire, but wished to replace it by a Greco-Serbian Empire of his own creation. He was also not content with the title of *Serbian emperor*, but assumed the prodigious title of *Emperor and Sovereign of Serbia and Romania.*[23] The wars that this powerful Serbian ruler waged in order to strengthen his claim brought the Byzantine Empire to the verge of ruin, but again the old empire held out and overcame the grave crisis without abandoning its high ideals.

The most striking and, perhaps, the most significant aspect of this struggle for spiritual and political supremacy was the fact that both the attacking young powers and the old empire on the defensive were imbued with the same theology. For neither the Roman emperors of the German nation nor the South Slavonic tsars had ever opposed the principle of the hierarchy of states. This principle remained inviolable also for them, and the rival rulers actually fought for a higher position within the same hierarchy, in the first place for that of emperor.

In reality, however, this struggle for the highest position led to the division of the Christian world and also, however much it was contrary to the political ideology of all the participants in this struggle, to the formation of separate empires. On the one hand, the old Byzantine Empire would not let the competing powers merely push it out of the way, and on the other hand, it no longer had the possibility of hindering the rise of new empires governed by independent rulers. . . .

One of the most beautiful illustrations of the hierarchy of rulers is provided by a contemporary description of the solemn entry of the emperor Manuel I into subjugated Antioch in 1159. The emperor, adorned with all the imperial insignia, was riding on horseback, and at a considerable distance the king of Jerusalem followed him, also on horseback, but without any adornment. The prince of Antioch walked on foot near the mounted emperor, holding on to the emperor's stirrup.[24] It could not be explained more clearly that there was a greater difference between the Byzantine emperor and the prince of Antioch, his vassal, than between the same Byzantine emperor and the king of Jerusalem, who was a "crowned head"; and yet in this case too there existed an important and obvious difference of rank.

So, according to Byzantine conceptions, some rulers held a higher and others a lower rank within the hierarchy of rulers. But the highest rank was held by the Roman emperor in Constantinople, as the bearer of the highest title of sovereign, as the head of the oldest Christian empire,

[23] Cf. M. Dinić, "Dušanova carska titula u očima savremenika," *Zbornik u čast šeste stogodišnjice Zakonika cara Dušana* (Beograd, 1951), pp. 87 ff.

[24] *Cinnamus,* ed. Bonn., p. 187 sq.

and as the father of all Christian peoples and the head of the family of rulers.

## 5 / NATURE OF THE ISLAMIC STATE / MAJID KHADDURI

Ever since the word *theocracy* was coined by Flavius Josephus (AD 37-100) to characterize the type of the Israelite state which existed in the first century of the Christian era, the term has gained currency among publicists and was applied to all states governed by religious codes or states whose religious and political institutions presented a unity.[1] The Islamic state was no exception to the rule and, therefore, has been classified, from the point of view of the incidence and exercise of authority, as a theocracy.[2] A careful examination of the nature of the Islamic state shows, however, that it was not a theocratic state but falls under a different category of states. The writer has briefly touched on this point elsewhere,[3] but it is possible now, within the space allowed in this review, to treat the subject more adequately.

## I

The principles of Muḥammad's . . . ideal state are to be found in the *Qur'ān* (which he probably contemplated, had he lived longer, to translate into a reality).[4] It is true that the term *state (dawlah)* is neither used in the *Qur'ān* nor was it in vogue at Muḥammad's time, but the essential elements that constitute a state were referred to in the *Qur'ān* which clearly indicate that the concept, if not the term, *state* was specifically meant in the *Qur'ān*.

The *Qur'ān* often refers to organized authority, divine and unlimited, which belongs to *Allah*.[5] The sovereignty of the Islamic state resides, therefore, with *Allah*. The exercise of that ultimate authority or sover-

Reprinted with permission from Majid Khadduri, "Nature of the Islamic State," *Islamic Culture*, 21 (1947), 327-31.

[1] See J. C. Bluntschli, *Allgemeine Statslehre* (Stuttgart, 1875), pp. 390, 397-99; Fritz Kern, *Kingship and Law in the Middle Ages,* trans. S. B. Chrines (Oxford, 1939), pp. 27-34; F. G. Wilson, *The Elements of Modern Politics* (New York, 1936), pp. 87-88.

[2] See J. Wellhausen, *The Arab Kingdom and its Fall,* trans. M. G. Weir (Calcutta, 1927), pp. 5, 8; T. W. Arnold *The Preaching of Islam,* 3rd ed. (London, 1935), p. 32; Muhammad Hamidullah, *Muslim Conduct of State* (Lahore, 1945), pp. 74, 180.

[3] See my *Law of War and Peace in Islam* (London, 1941), pp. 6-7.

[4] Very few publicists have argued that Muḥammad's mission, like that of Christ, aimed at the propagation of a new faith rather than the setting up of a state. See Ali Abd-ul-Raziq, *al-Islam wa Usul al-Hukm* (Cairo, 1925), pp. 64-89. For criticism of Raziq's theory, see A. Sanhoury, *Le Califat* (Paris, 1926), pp. 45-48.

[5] *Qur'ān*; XXIX, 75; CXIV, 2-3.

eignty was delegated to the Prophet Muḥammad, or *Allah's* vicegerent on earth, who was instructed to rule with justice.[6] *Allah,* accordingly, was regarded in Islam as the (*titular*) *head,* not the direct ruler or king of the Islamic state, while His vicegerent on earth was advised to rule in accordance with divine laws communicated to him in the form of *commands.* The citizens of the Islamic state were *Allah's* subjects . . . , and its laws were divine laws, because they emanated from *Allah,* [and were] not enacted or legislated by man. Divine law, as such, is infallible and man can only obey, because *Allah* knows better than any other authority what His ignorant subjects need. In his attempt to consummate his obedience to law, man realizes his religious ideal. Law in Islam, accordingly, has the character of a religious obligation; at the same time it constitutes a political sanction of religion.[7]

Upon the death of Muḥammad (P.B.O.H.), communication with *Allah* became impossible, because there was no other prophet and Muḥammad was the last, "the seal of the Prophets." [8] It was tacitly understood by the Muslims, however, that *Allah* had delegated the exercise of His sovereignty, after the death of Muḥammad, to the Muslim community, which immediately elected a successor to Muḥammad, not in the capacity of a prophet but as a *caliph,* or successor, to Muḥammad's position as a vicegerent of *Allah.* In theory, therefore, sovereignty, as the ultimate divine authority in Islam, remained in *Allah's* hands, but its exercise was delegated to the people of the Islamic state. In practice, however, the caliphate, which was inherently an elective position, had become virtually hereditary, though consent . . . of the people was required for every new *caliph.*[9]

[6] *Qur'ān;* XXXVIII, 25. "O David! verily We have made thee Our vicegerent upon earth. Judge therefore between men with truth, and follow not the passion, lest they cause thee to err from the way of *Allah.* . . ." States have crumbled to pieces because its rulers have failed to abide by the divine law. Moses and his brother went to Pharaoh because he "transgressed [the bounds of law]," and had become a "tyrant in the land" (*Qur'ān;* V, 84; XX. 25). See H. K. Sherwani, "The Origin of Islamic Polity," *Islamic Culture,* X (October, 1936), 538.

[7] M. Khadduri, *Law of War Peace in Islam,* pp. 7-8, 9-10; Abdur Rahim, *The Principles of Muḥammadan Jurisprudence* (Madras, 1911), pp. 48 ff.; N. P. Aghnides, *Mohammadan Theories of Finance* (New York, 1916), pp. 23-29; D. B. Macdonald, *Development of Muslim Theology, Jurisprudence, and Constitutional Theory* (New York, 1903), pp. 65 ff.; I. Goldziher, *Le Dogme et la loi de L'Islam* (Paris, 1920), pp. 27 ff.

[8] *Qur'ān,* XXXIII, 40.

[9] Practice had much deviated from theory in the exercise of the caliphate. The caliphs indeed had monopolized all the powers of Caesar, and some of them, in the Abbasid period, even claimed that they directly represented *Allah* on earth. On the origins and use of the divine rights of the caliphs, see Ignaz Goldziher "Ombre de dieu, Khalife de dieu," *Revue de l'Histoire des Religions* XXV (1897), 331-38. See also Ibn-Jama'a *Tahrir al-Ahkam fi Tadbir Ahl al-Islam,* in *Islamica,* VI (1934), 355-56.

## II Could Such a State Be Called a Theocracy?

Any definition of the term *state* should take into consideration the incidence and exercise of political authority as a criterion of its nature and character. A state is called *monarchical* or *oligarchical* (in the Aristotelian sense) if its ultimate authority is entrusted, by force or reason, to one or the few; it is *democratic* if ultimate authority is regarded flowing from, and by the consent of, the people. A state is *theocratic* if it "claims to be governed by a god or gods." [10] The *Oxford [English] Dictionary* defines it as "a form of government in which God (or a deity) is recognized as the king or immediate ruler." [11]

In its origin, the term *theocracy* was coined by Flavius Josephus to characterize the type of Israelite state which existed in the first century of the Christian era.[12] Tailliar is of the opinion that Judaism, Christianity and Islam were all theocracies.[13] Wellhausen, however, maintains that Jewish theocracy existed only in theory; that is, an ideal representation at the time of Jewish decline.[14] Christianity, on the other hand, was not originally associated with politics, since Jesus Christ had declared "My kingdom is not of this World." [15] From the time of St. Paul to that of Emperor Constantine, the tradition was laid down in Christianity that every power possessing authority in the state ought to be recognized

[10] C. Ryder Smith, "Theocracy," *The Encyclopedia of Religion and Ethics,* Vol. XII, pp. 287-289.

[11] See also Georg Jellinck, *Allgemeine Statslehre,* 3rd ed. (Berlin, 1919), p. 289.

[12] "There are innumerable differences," says Josephus, "in the particular customs and laws that are among mankind; some have entrusted the power of their states to monarchies, some to oligarchies, and some to democracies; but our legislator had no regard to any of these forms, but ordered our government to be what I may call by a strained expression a *theocracy,* attributing the power and the authority to God" (translated from the Greek and cited by J. Wellhausen, *Prolegomena to the History of Israel,* trans. R. F. Black and A. Menzies [Edinburgh, 1885], p. 411n.).

[13] M. Tailliar, *Essai sur l'Histoire des Institutions de Principaux Peuples* (Douai, 1843); *Précis de l'histoire des Institutions de l'Europe Occidentale an Moyen-Age* (Saint Omer, 1845), passim.

[14] "In Ancient Israel," says Wellhausen, "the theocracy never existed in fact as a form of constitution. The rule of Jehovah is here an ideal representation; only after the exile was it attempted to realize in it the shape of a Rule of the Holy with outward means" (J. Wellhausen, *op. cit.,* p. 411).

[15] John, XVIII, 36. "His kingdom," says Tellenbach, "was a supernatural power working in the world and remaining for all others a matter of hope and expectation. Out of Christ's attitude to the world, there arose among the early Christians a tendency to withdraw from temporal affairs and to concentrate on the kingdom of Heaven" (Gerd Tellenbach, *Church, State and Christian Society at the Time of the Investiture Contest,* trans. R. F. Bennett [Oxford, 1940], p. 25).

as a divinely ordained authority.[16] When the state adopted Christianity the sanction of the church became necessary for political authority, and the aim of the state had become, in the words of Kern, to "put God's law into practice." [17] At that stage Christianity and the state had come so near to one another that the Christian religion had rather become Christendom.[18]

It is to be noted that God (*Allah*) has never been regarded, as stated above, the *immediate* ruler in Judaism, Christianity, or Islam; only his representatives on earth were the real executives. It was therefore the *divine law,* or the sacred code, regarded as the source of governing authority, which was the essential feature in the process of control under such systems. This is what we call a *divine nomocracy*. The *Oxford [English] Dictionary* defines it as "a system of government based on a legal code; the rule of law in a community." "Nomocracy," says Quincy Wright, "exists if a supreme law regarded as of divine or natural origin is the source of governing authority." [19] In Judaism, Christianity, and Islam, the immediate rulers were not regarded as legislators, but were, together with their subjects, bound by the divine law. The *Shari'a,* or the sacred code, was the source of the governing authority; only its execution was entrusted to the Prophet or his successors.[20]

## III

Christendom and Islam may be regarded as universal nomocratic states, while Judaism was a parochial nomocratic state. Christianity and Islam, it is true, had emerged in countries dominated by parochial traditions and local particularism, but they arose in protest to these conditions and, accordingly adopted universal concepts and ideals current in the Hellenistic world, for the trend of thought, since Alexander the Great advocated his revolutionary ideas of "the unity of Mankind," [21] began gradually

[16] Math. XVII, 21: "render to Caesar the things that are Caesar's; and to God, the things that are God's." See also Fritz Kern, *op. cit.,* p. 27.

[17] Fritz Kern, *op. cit.,* p. 28. See also Tellenbach, *op. cit.,* pp. 26-27.

[18] The principal Biblical verses for the so-called theocratic idea in Christendom are: Mark; IX, 35 X, 42; Math; XX, 26 sq; Luke; XXII, 26.

[19] Quincy Wright, *A Study of War* (Chicago, 1942), Vol. II, p. 968.

[20] Theocracy exists only where God is regarded as the immediate ruler. At present it exists where the Lama rules (in Tibet) or, under Shintoism, in Japan. See D. C. Holtom, *The Political Philosophy of Modern Shinto* (Chicago, 1922).

[21] See W. W. Tarn, *Alexander the Great and the Unity of Mankind.* Proceedings of the British Academy, Vol. XIX (London: Humphrey Milford, 1933). See also T. J. Haarhoff, "Alexander's Dream: The Unity of Mankind," *The Contemporary Review* (July 1942), 48-50.

to turn from parochial to universal values.[22] The Stoics carried further Alexander's ideas and expressed their philosophy in terms of universal concepts and values. The Romans translated Alexander's ideas and the Stoics' philosophy into an organized system of life.[23] Both Christianity and Islam developed under the impact of these ideas. Thus Islam was bound to be a universal religion and, especially after the great Arab conquest, the Muslims became completely Hellenized.[24] Judaism, which appeared and developed before such concepts were accepted, was naturally parochial and the Jews were regarded as God's chosen people; their state, therefore, was national and not a universal state.

The universality of Islam, as preached by the Prophet Muḥammad did not necessarily carry with it the conception of a universal or world-state. But the legal prerequisites were already existing, such as the universal conception of religion, equality of races before *Allah* and law, and common allegiance to one head of the state. Thus in theory, as well as in practice, Islam presented a type of universal nomocratic state since the Abbasid period.

The universal nomocracy of Islam, like the *Respublica Christiana* in the West, assumed mankind to constitute one community, bound by one law and governed by one ruler.[25] The nature of such a state is entirely exclusive; it does not recognize, by definition, the coexistence of a second universal state. It is true that Islam tolerated Christianity as a religion, but Christendom, as a universal state, was always, in the words of H. A. R. Gibb, "The sworn foe of Islam." [26]

The Islamic nomocracy, however, in contrast to the *Respublica Christiana,* presented, in its legal theory at least, a real unity in the religious and political aspects of the state. Thus the Islamic state spared itself the internal conflict between church and state which was so characteristic

[22] Alexander may have been influenced by Buddhism or may have had developed his ideas independently under the influence of the practical considerations of his great military achievements which he thought could only be maintained by the unity of the various races in his new empire. Cf. Arnold J. Toynbee, *A Study of History* (London, 1939), Vol. I, p. 86.

[23] Ernest Barker, "The Conception of Empire," in Cyril Bailey (ed.), *The Legacy of Rome* (Oxford, 1923), pp. 46, 51-54. It was the policy of the Roman senate to confer Roman citizenship upon the conquered populations and to incorporate their territories into the Roman Empire. See speech of Claudius in the senate in Tacitus, *The Annals* (Everyman's ed., 1934), pp. 306-307.

[24] For the controversy [over] whether Islam was preached by the Prophet as a national or universal religion, see my *Law of War and Peace in Islam,* pp. 4-6.

[25] *Qur'ān;* XXI, 23: "If there were two gods, the universe would be ruined." But see M. Hamidullah, *Muslim Conduct of State* (Lahore, 1945), p. 74.

[26] H. A. R. Gibb (ed.), *Whither Islam?* (London, 1932), p. 24.

between the pope and the emperor.[27] The caliph in Islam was the head of both the church and the state, as one institution, monopolizing, at the same time, all the powers of Caesar.[28]

## CENTRALIZED ADMINISTRATION / INTRODUCTION

*The essays on the following pages discuss another crucial characteristic of these empires: political and administrative centralization. The excerpts from Edgerton, Berkelbach Van der Sprenkel, and Beyer emphasize the administrative and political aspects of centralization, but they also indicate its broader social and political implications, and the important role it has played in the social and political framework of these empires. They show how the administrative service constituted a major channel of social mobility and provided contacts between the major groups and strata in the empires.*

*The excerpt from Balazs, which deals with China as a bureaucratic society, reflects this general sociological theme and points out the specific characteristics and problems not only of bureaucratic administration but also of a bureaucratic society.*

## 6 / THE GOVERNMENT AND THE GOVERNED IN THE EGYPTIAN EMPIRE [1] / WILLIAM F. EDGERTON

English and American Egyptologists have long given the name "the empire" to a period of five centuries from the accession of Ahmose I about 1580 BC to the accession of Ḥeriḥor about 1085 BC.[2] These five cenurties are a well-defined epoch in Egyptian history. The epoch begins with the expulsion of the Hyksos and the reunification of all Egypt under the princes of Thebes. It ends with a new division of Egypt into two

[27] In Christendom the spiritual and the temporal rulers were separate authorities. There were three theories as to the relation between the spiritual (the pope) and the temporal (the emperor) powers. The first advocated the necessary superiority of the spiritual over the temporal powers; the second, the superiority of the temporal; and the third, the equality of the two powers. Even the extreme papal party admitted in practice the principle of the separation of powers. See Otto Gierke, *Political Theories of the Middle Ages*, trans. F. W. Maitland (Cambridge, 1900), p. 12.

[28] Al-Mawardi, *Kitab al Ahkam al Sultaniyah* (Cairo, 1909), pp. 3, 4; T. W. Arnold, *The Caliphate* (Oxford 1924), pp. 47-49; H. K. Sherwani, *Studies in Muslim Political Thought and Administration* (Lahore, 1945), pp. 117-20.

Reprinted with permission from W. F. Edgerton, "The Government and the Governed in Egyptian Empire," *Journal of Near Eastern Studies*, 6 (1947), 152-60.

[1] Presidential address delivered before the Middle West Branch of the American Oriental Society at Ann Arbor, April 18, 1947. I am grateful to George G. Cameron, Keith C. Seele, and John A. Wilson for helpful criticisms.

[2] Naturally there is some variation in the precise dates chosen.

independent principalities, a southern principality under Ḥeriḥor with his capital in Thebes, and a northern principality under Smendes and his wife Tentamun with their capital in Tanis. It includes the period of Egypt's greatest power and wealth and magnificence—"that golden age of empire when Egypt ruled the East" in the words of Steindorff and Seele—and it ends, as it began, in a long period of powerlessness and relative inertia, associated with internal division.

The immense national effort of expelling the Hyksos gave the Egyptian armies a momentum which carried them to the northern end of Syria. As far as we know, these armies of the early Eighteenth Dynasty consisted almost entirely of native Egyptians. The conquering Pharaohs, during that initial period of imperial expansion, rewarded their more outstanding veterans with lands, with captive slaves, and with other forms of booty. They also gave lands, slaves, and booty to the temples of the chief national gods, and this practice of giving rich endowments to the temples continued throughout our period.

For their military and police forces, the later Pharaohs of the Empire came to rely more and more on foreigners, especially Nubians and Libyans, though the Egyptian element remained very important in the armed forces. Some foreigners rose high in the government service, and in the period of disorder at the end of the Nineteenth Dynasty a Syrian adventurer actually was able to seize the throne for a brief period.

Thus, out of the relatively homogeneous Egypt which expelled the Hyksos, there developed during our period a number of more or less distinct and powerful classes with potentially conflicting interests. We may single out particularly the civil service, the priesthoods (especially those of the great temples), the professional Egyptian army officers, and the foreign mercenaries. All these groups overlapped more or less with one another, for the professions of civil servant, army officer, and priest were by no means mutually exclusive.

We know from the so-called "school texts" of the Nineteenth Dynasty that the civil servants (the clerks and executives in government offices, sometimes called bureaucrats) looked down on both the military and the priesthoods. These men, or some of them, therefore, were certainly conscious of having class interests different from the class interests of the army and the priesthoods. It is at least a reasonable assumption that the army and the priesthoods reciprocated, and it would seem strange, a priori, if struggles for power did not sometimes occur among the three groups. But the existing evidence of such struggles is so slight, and so much colored by propaganda, that we may easily make the most extraordinary mistakes in trying to interpret it.

We have recently had a very striking illustration of this danger. The founder of the Twenty-first Dynasty, the Pharaoh Ḥeriḥor, whose accession about 1085 BC marks the formal close of the period of the empire which we are studying, had been high priest of Amun for a number of years before taking the royal titles. When he did ascend the throne, Ḥeriḥor actually adopted the title "High Priest of Amun" as his royal prenomen, placing it in his first cartouche, with his personal name Ḥeriḥor and the epithet "Son of Amun" in his second cartouche. And earlier, while he was high priest of Amun and not yet king, Ḥeriḥor had dared to represent himself on temple walls as of equal dignity with the reigning King Ramesses XI, an almost unprecedented piece of impudence. These and other indisputable facts seemed to prove beyond question that Ḥeriḥor's elevation to the throne was a triumph for the Karnak priesthood of Amun, and all Egyptologists had so regarded it— until 1936, when Hermann Kees showed that the true explanation is exactly the opposite.[3] Ḥeriḥor was not primarily a priest at all, but probably an army officer. His assumption of the office of high priest of Amun in the latter part of the reign of Ramesses XI represented a crushing defeat for the priestly party,[4] and his coronation as Pharaoh a few years later was no priestly triumph. Ḥeriḥor assumed the very powerful secular offices of viceroy of Nubia and vizier of Upper Egypt at about the same time as the high priesthood. He may later have transferred the office of vizier to another official (doubtless a loyal follower of his own party), but there can be no doubt that his subsequent seizure of the Pharaonic crown rested on military rather than on priestly power. He emphasized his relationship to Amun and the Amun priesthood for the same reason for which Queen Hatshepsut emphasized her miraculous birth—in order to give an outwardly respectable but completely false theological coloring to his usurpation. This direct reversal of a view which used to seem both obvious and certain may perhaps help us to guard against dogmatism in interpreting the undercurrents of ancient Egyptian politics.

As for the organization and powers of the government, everyone knows that the Pharaoh was an absolute monarch and that his authority rested theoretically on his supposed divinity. He is constantly called "the good god." One of his most frequent titles designates him as the son of the sun-god Re, and we know that this claim of divine parentage was not a mere figure of speech: it was meant to be taken literally.

[3] Kees, "Herihor und die Aufrichtung des thebanischen Gottesstaates," *Nachrichten von der Gesellschaft der Wissenschaften zu Göttingen,* phil.-hist. Kl., Neue Folge, Fachgruppe I, 2. Band (1936-38), pp. 1-20.

[4] Or at least a defeat for the previous high-priestly family. That family itself probably had no very deep roots in the priesthood.

The court scribes tell us that the divine Pharaoh personally did everything needful for the welfare of Egypt, with that unlimited personal ability which properly characterizes a god. They tell us that he personally mowed down his enemies by tens of thousands on the battlefield, personally discovered what was wrong throughout his empire, and personally devised the necessary laws and regulations to set everything right. They tell us that foreign kings came spontaneously from their distant lands, bearing their tribute on their backs and begging Pharaoh for the breath of life which he alone could give. And they tell us many other things equally incredible.

The autobiographical inscriptions of officials and priests are usually as boastful, on their own level, as are the court eulogies of the Pharaoh. It is usually easy to learn that So-and-So was a paragon of virtue and skill, but our information about what So-and-So actually did is usually limited to a list of his titles, and titles may not always mean exactly what they seem to us to say.

Actual information about how the Pharaonic government functioned, and what effects it produced on the lives of its subjects, is unfortunately very scanty. Many of the relevant documents can be interpreted in more than one way, and the resulting picture necessarily includes much which is uncertain.

There is no doubt that the Pharaoh's rule was absolute in the strictest sense of that word. The law was merely his formally expressed will. If the law was codified,[5] it is clear that any provision of the code could be changed or rescinded by the reigning Pharaoh at any time. Among the very few records of judicial proceedings which have come down to us

[5] As Seele points out to me, Davies, *The Tomb of Rekh-mi-rēᶜ at Thebes* (New York, 1943), pp. 31-32 and 50, n. 24, has argued vigorously that the forty *šsm* (with "skin" determinative) on the floor of the Vizier's Hall are not forty leather rolls bearing the text of the law code but "probably flexible rods cut from a thick hide" (p. 50, n. 24), "batons of authority put into the hands of the district functionaries as an authorization to execute the law, as with the tipstaff of the English bailiff. As actual instruments of correction they are seen in use in the hands of the ushers close by" (p. 31). "Actual instruments of correction" *as such* would scarcely receive the prominence which is accorded to the forty *šsm* both in the picture and in the text, and the perfectly simple form of the forty objects seems to me difficult to reconcile with "batons of authority put into the hands of the district functionaries." I see no difficulty in the view that a word *šsm* meaning primarily "thong" or "band" or the like came to mean both "lash" (as in "he is beaten with fifty lashes," *Revue d'Égyptologie*, I [1933], 63) and one of a specific group of leather manuscripts. English *code* (ultimately from Latin *codex, caudex*, "trunk of a tree" "block of wood," "writing tablet") often means "systematic compilation of laws" or even a specific compilation of laws, e.g., that of Justinian. As for the long, thin shape of the forty objects, the unreliability of proportions in Egyptian pictures is well known. The absence of cords around them may actually be a bit of realism, the roll being perhaps united for ready reference. But the existence of a Pharaonic law code should no longer be treated as a known fact unless new evidence can be produced.

from our period of five centuries, there is only one which directly cites a rule of law by way of authority, and in this one case the citation is introduced by the simple words "Pharaoh has said." [6] The few actual laws which have come down to us, such as the Edict of Harmhab[7] and the Nauri Decree of Seti I,[8] reflect the same legal theory. The text of the Nauri Decree begins: "His Majesty hath commanded," and the Harmhab text begins: "The King himself hath said." What Pharaoh has said *is* the law.

Theoretically, of course, the Pharaoh's right to rule rested on his divinity. He was begotten by the sun-god Amen-Re, who took the form of the previous king for this purpose, and Amen-Re with the enthusiastic approval of the other gods placed him on the throne and decreed a long and brilliant reign for him. No doubt these theological fictions helped to strengthen the Pharaoh's position. But the really solid basis of his power was his control of the machinery of government, including the army and the police. The usurper Hatshepsut, after serving several years as regent for the legitimate but immature Pharaoh Thut-mose III, pushed the legitimate Pharaoh into the background when she felt herself firmly established in control of the government, and the legitimate Pharaoh remained in the background while Hatshepsut lived. Because she already controlled the government, Hatshepsut was able also to proclaim herself a child of Amen-Re. Certainly no one publicly denied her claim to divinity while she lived—but one wonders how many of her contemporaries actually believed it. The legitimate Pharaoh Thut-mose III finally succeeded in seizing the throne, not because of his superior claim to divinity but because Hatshepsut's death removed the very real human obstacle from his path. Still more striking is the case of the royal revolutionist Akhnaton, who was able to abolish the traditional polytheistic theology, altering his own title to divinity almost beyond recognition, but who continued to rule until his death. Clearly the fact was that the Pharaoh's divinity rested on his power to rule, though the official theory was exactly the reverse of this.

Side by side with the divine Pharaoh, whose real power rested on the civil service, the army, and the police, there were, of course, a large number of other gods in Egypt, and some of them (or their priesthoods) took part in the government of Egypt from time to time by promulgating

---

[6] Pap. Turin 2021, 3, 4, published by Černý and Peet, *JEA*, Vol. XIII (1927), Pl. XIV and p. 32. Cf. Seidi *Einführung in die ägyptische Rechtsgeschichte bis zum Ende des Neuen Reiches* Vol. I: *Juistischer Teil* ("Ägyptologische Forschungen," Heft 10 herausgegeben von Alexander Scharff [Glückstadt and New York, 1939]), p. 20.

[7] Latest edition by Pflüger, *JNES*, V (1946), 260-76.

[8] Published by Griffith, *JEA*, Vol. XIII (1927), Pls. XXXVII-XLIII and pp. 193-206.

oracles which seem to have had practical legal consequences. I shall return to this subject a little later. But the real part played by oracles in the government of the empire was a minor one, and I want first to discuss the purely human elements in the government.

*Legislation* seems to have been a function of the Pharaoh alone; he does not appear to have delegated it to any other person or group.

The Pharaoh's *administrative* and *judicial* work was delegated to a very large and elaborately organized body of officials. The Egyptians were perfectly aware of the difference between administrative and judicial functions, but under the empire it seems that judicial functions were usually performed incidentally, by men whose primary duties were administrative.

The delegation of both administrative and judicial power was of course strictly authoritarian, from the top downward, from the Pharaoh to the highest officers of the state and from them to their subordinates.

The government service was divided in two ways, by type of activity and by geography. On the one hand, there were departments of the central administration such as the royal treasury and the royal granary which operated throughout Egypt proper and perhaps throughout the empire. On the other hand, the country was divided into administrative districts, each of which had its own organs of local government, though these were subordinate to the central government in every respect.

During the empire there was usually no single officer under the Pharaoh who exercised authority in all parts of the country and in all departments of the government at the same time. In the Old and Middle Kingdoms the vizier had been such an officer. But in the empire there were regularly two viziers, one for Upper Egypt and one for Lower Egypt. Each vizier in his own region probably directed all public activities, being subordinate only to the Pharaoh. It is not at all certain that either vizier exercised any general authority in Nubia (where a viceroy ruled and was perhaps responsible directly to the Pharaoh) or in Asia. We may suspect that the Pharaoh's of the empire intentionally avoided letting any one subject represent the royal authority everywhere and in every respect.

In every large town there was a loosely organized group known as *the council* (*k̲nbt*), and over these there were two "Great Councils" in Thebes and Heliopolis[9] presided over by the two viziers, respectively. It is not certain whether these councils as such directly performed any administrative functions, but they certainly sat as courts of law in both civil and criminal cases, and in some cases they certainly dealt in a

[9] Gardiner, *The Inscription of Mes* (Leipzig, 1905), pp. 33-38; Seidl, *op. cit.*, pp. 32-33.

judicial capacity with administrative questions. The individual members of the councils, for the most part, were men whose principal duties were administrative. Thus the councils must have tended in some degree to cut across the dividing lines between the administrative departments.

When the names of the members of a council are listed, the list is often headed "the council of this date" as if the composition of the council changed from day to day. In one judicial hearing, which perhaps involved interests of the Temple of Mut at Karnak,[10] the council is presided over by the high priest of Amun and consists entirely of priests of the different Karnak temples excepting the recorder, who bears the title "record-scribe of the Council of Thebes." Other councils are found consisting entirely of lay officials or of priests and lay officials together.

It seems to me that the temples of the gods should be regarded as departments of the royal administration. Theoretically, it was the Pharaoh in person who performed the regular daily ritual in each and every temple throughout Egypt. The priest who actually performed the ritual each day did so as the Pharaoh's representative. The temple endowments existed ostensibly for the purpose of supporting this ritual— the perpetual service which the divine Pharaoh rendered to his divine fathers and mothers, the great gods and goddesses of the empire. The priests and other temple functionaries were as truly the Pharaoh's agents as the army officers or the tax-collectors. As far as I can judge, the Pharaoh had the same power of appointment and removal in the priesthoods as in other departments of the public service. It is true that priests were often able to hand on their offices to their sons after them, but this was equally true in other government departments. It is true that the wealthiest priesthoods—especially the Karnak priesthood of Amen-Re-King-of-the-Gods—were a potential danger to a weak Pharaoh —but so was the army, and so indeed was the Pharaoh's own household. A strong Pharaoh normally controlled the priesthoods as completely, and by essentially the same methods, as he controlled his household or his army.

It is well known that the Pharaohs of the Eighteenth, Nineteenth, and Twentieth Dynasties gave enormous endowments to the temples of their gods, and above all, to the great temple of Amen-Re-King-of-the-Gods at Karnak. These endowments included agricultural land, gold mines, and other types of real estate; slaves in vast numbers who were captured in war or taken from conquered countries; great herds of livestock of all kinds; boats on the Nile and on the sea; temple furniture, cloth,

---

[10] Pap. Berlin 3047, published by Erman, *ÄZ*, Vol. XVII (1879). Pl. 1 and pp. 71-76; cf. Seidl, *op. cit.*, p. 33.

grain, wine, beer, and movable property of every description; and workshops in which multifarious articles were manufactured. It is perfectly clear that Amen-Re-King-of-the-Gods must have been the wealthiest property owner in Egypt, with the single exception of the Pharaoh, throughout our period.

It is often stated or implied by modern scholars[11] that all temple property in Egypt was exempt from all taxation. I am not sure that this was true at any period whatever, and Papyrus Wilbour[12] gives us positive evidence that it was not true in the reign of Ramesses V (ca. 1150 BC, a date when current Egyptological literature might lead one to suppose that the royal government was rapidly losing its grip over the great priesthoods or had already lost it).

The royal decrees granting administrative privileges and immunities to specific temples prove, by their very existence, that there was no general law granting similar privileges and immunities to all temples. Only one such decree of privilege and immunity has come down to us in good preservation from the period of the empire. This is the Nauri Decree of Seti I (ca. 1300 BC) protecting the Nubian interests of a particular temple at Abydos. I am not sure that this long and elaborate document even mentions taxation. It certainly does not absolutely forbid the conscription of temple personnel for the *corvée*. It forbids the *arbitrary* seizure of temple personnel and *carrying them from one district to another district* for the purpose of forced labor. It also forbids royal officers to rob the temple of its livestock, to commandeer the temple's boats on the Nile, or to interfere with the temple's laborers and other personnel in the performance of their duties. In short, the Nauri Decree undertakes to protect a particular temple organization against a specified list of arbitrary and oppressive acts, against which modern civilized governments protect *all* organizations and *all* citizens or subjects without exception. What the Nauri Decree brings home to us is not the weakness of the royal government but its strength and its sometimes arbitrary character. It is clearly implied that those who were *not* specifically protected by such a decree might expect to have not only their livestock and

---

[11] E.g., Eduard Meyer, *Geschichte des Altertums*, II, 1, 2nd ed. (Stuttgart and Berlin, 1928), pp. 73-74; not quite so sweepingly Kees, *Kulturgeschichte des alten Orients, Erster Abschnitt: Ägypten* (München, 1933), pp. 255-56. Contrast Otto, *Priester und Tempel im hellenistischen Ägypten*, II (Leipzig and Berlin, 1908), 43, n. 2. It would be possible to argue from P. dem Ryiands IX, 6, 13—7, 6 that the "great temples" were normally exempt from taxation in late times (Twenty-fifth and Twenty-sixth dynasties?), but the conclusion would seem to me to lack confirmation.

[12] *The Wilbour Papyrus*, ed. Alan H. Gardiner, Vol. I (plates) (Oxford, 1941). See my review in *JAOS*, Vol. LXII (1942), 206-207.

their boats but even their own persons arbitrarily seized by the king's officers and carried off for indefinite periods, perhaps to distant parts of the empire, either for agricultural labor or for military service or for any other purpose which any petty representative of the crown might direct.[13]

On the other hand, there is very definite evidence to show that the Pharaoh and his vizier and other officers exercised some degree of control at least over the economic affairs of temples, and the government unquestionably made appointments in some cases both to the highest and to the lowest priestly offices.

I said earlier that I would return to the subject of oracles. By way of illustration, let us take two specific oracles, one on an administrative question of the highest public importance, the other in a very minor case of theft.

Ramesses II in the first year of his reign had to choose a new high priest of Amun of Karnak—a new incumbent for the most important priesthood in all Egypt. According to his own statement,[14] Ramesses laid before the god the names of all officials of the royal court, the commander of the militia ($r_3$ $hry$ $n$ $mnfy[t]$), and the chief priests and other notables of Amun's own temple ($pr$), and Amun himself chose a certain Nebwenenef, who was not even a member of the Theban priesthood but was high priest of Ḥatḥor of Dendera, high priest of Onuris of This, and overseer of priests of all the gods between This and Thebes, offices which his father had held before him. Ramesses therefore proceeded to install this Nebwenenef as high priest of Amun of Karnak, instructing him to install his son in the other priesthoods which had previously been in the family. In this case there can be no reasonable doubt that the king who installed the new high priest of Amun also selected him. The oracle was doubtless no more difficult to arrange than a modern plebiscite.

The other of our two examples comes from the middle of the Twentieth Dynasty, more than a hundred years later than the first.[15] Five garments had been stolen from a servant named Amenemuia. The injured servant appealed to a minor Theban deity called Amun of Pekhenty to reveal the name of the thief. The god having consented to do this, the servant Amenemuia recited to him the names of all the inhabitants of the village. When the farmer Peteumdyamun was named, the god

[13] I intend to discuss the Nauri Decree more fully in a forthcoming number of this *Journal.*

[14] See Sethe, "Die Berufung eines Hohenpriesters des Amon unter Ramses II," *ÄZ*, Vol. XLIV (1907), 30-35 and Pls. I-III.

[15] See Dawson and Blackman *JEA*, Vol. XI (1925), 247-55, and Pls. XXXV-XXXVIII, and Černý, *JEA*, Vol. XXIII (1937), 60 and 188-89.

nodded,[16] as much as to say, "He stole them." Then the farmer Peteum-dyamun said to the god, "(That is) false, I did not steal them." Then the god became very angry.

On a later occasion, the accused farmer Peteumdyamun appealed to another minor Theban god, but this god also nodded, as much as to say, "He took them." Once more the farmer said, "(That is) false." And this god, like the first one, became very angry that a man whom the god had declared to be a thief should have the impudence to assert his innocence.

Then the accused farmer stood again before Amun of Pekhenty, the god of his own village, the one who had accused him in the first place, and the farmer appealed to the god saying, "Come to me, Amun of Pekhenty, my good and beloved lord! Did I take the garments?" (Or perhaps "I did not take the garments!") Then the god nodded a great deal, as much as to say "He took them."

The remainder of the record is not at all clear to me. Perhaps the accused farmer confessed the theft as Blackman and Černý believe.[17] At any any rate, he was almost certainly punished for it. But I cannot doubt that he was innocent. The assertion of the farmer's guilt, put into the mouth of Amun, was actually made, of course, by a priest or a group of priests. There is nothing to suggest that the priests had any knowledge of the matter. There seems to have been no evidence of any kind which would be admitted by a modern court. On the contrary, the farmer be-haves like a man whose conscience is clear. If he did finally confess, he must have done so under a kind of psychological third degree.

These two oracles, taken together, seem to me to illustrate very neatly what the power of the oracles was and what it was not during the Nine-teenth and Twentieth dynasties. An oracle might actually be decisive in a minor case, involving only the interests of humble men. But where in-terests of state were involved, the Pharaoh doubtless "arranged" the oracle as a matter of course, just as naturally as he incorporated the most imaginative fiction in the official records of his reign.

For ambitious Egyptians of the empire, apparently the only satisfying fields of activity lay in the various branches of the public service—the

---

[16] I keep the traditional translation *nod* for *hnn, hn,* though nodding was probably not the actual method by which the god expressed affirmation. See Černý, *Bulletin de l'Institut français d'archéologie orientale,* Vol. XXXV (1934), 56-58.

[17] *ꜣIwf ꜣintf* and *ꜣiwf ꜣirt* (verso 6 and 7) translated by Blackman as narrative, may possibly, I think, be future and continue the priestly interpretation of the oracle: "He shall take him and inflict chastisement on him in the presence of the townspeople, and he shall pronounce an oath in the god's presence saying 'It is I who took them.'" It is a suspicious circumstance that the god (and no human witness) "testified to the people of the towns, saying: 'Behold, the man acknowledges the garments of Pharaoh, saying: "I have them, I will (?) give them back."'" Seidl (*op. cit.,* p. 39) has rightly pointed out that the god betrays an uneasy conscience at the end.

civil administration, the priesthoods and other temple services, and the army. We have no knowledge of careers based on private wealth[18] or professional skill outside the public service.

Private property in some sense certainly existed, though we cannot define its limitations. Cattle, slaves, and land were bought and sold by private individuals—even by individuals of very humble station, such as the herdsman Mesy in the reigns of Amenhotep III and IV—and slave-owners were able to rent out the services of their slaves to others.[19] The herdsman Mesy evidently passed for a man of property among his neighbors—a man who had cattle for sale and who probably increased his wealth from year to year by shrewd bargaining. Clearly the seeds of private enterprise were there, but the seeds seem not to have developed during the empire. Between the productivity of the individual household, on the one hand, and the large-scale activities of temples and other government departments, on the other hand, I have the impression that little room was left for private enterprise in commerce or industry. But the paucity of documents precludes certainty here.

In addition to individuals like the herdsman Mesy who bought and sold for their own account, there were "traders" who carried on commercial activities as agents of great religious foundations.[20] Not much is known about these "temple traders" beyond the fact of their existence. In some cases, apparently, their trade was international in scope.[21]

In other cases we read of "traders" without knowing whether they traded for their own account or for some temple or government department. So, e.g., Papyrus Boulaq No. 11,[22] a leaf from an Eighteenth Dynasty account book, records deliveries of meat, wine, and cakes to "the merchant Min-nakht" and to "the merchant Sherybyn." The merchant Min-nakht received supplies on at least ten different occasions in a period of fourteen days. The amounts received are always small, such as could easily be disposed of by a very small shopkeeper or even by a peddler carrying his wares from door to door. The articles sold (meat, wine, cakes)

[18] There is reason to believe the lands involved in the lawsuit of Mes constituted a fortune for the successful litigant. There is also reason to believe that the successful litigant was a "goatherd" during the lawsuit and a "scribe of the treasury" afterward (see Gardiner, *The Inscription of Mes,* p. 20, n. 54, and p. 25). This change of titles in association with sudden affluence is very striking, but no general theories can be built on it, since it is (*a*) uncertain and (*b*) unique.

[19] See Gardiner "Four Papyri of the 18th Dynasty from Kahun," *ÄZ*, Vol. XLIII (1906), 27-47 and Pls. I-II.

[20] E.g., Pap. Harris 46, 2.

[21] Nauri Decree 40, *šwytw n ḫ3st* ("foreign traders," Griffith), not necessarily of foreign origin or nationality but trading with foreign lands.

[22] *Revue de l'Égypte ancienne,* Vol. I (1927), Pls. III and IV.

suggest that our merchants intended to sell to the more prosperous class in the population—at any rate, not to the poorest!

Some agricultural land was owned by private individuals and could be transferred from one individual owner to another either by inheritance or by sale. Such land, of course, paid taxes to the crown, but I cannot see that any other public obligation, such as *corvée* or military service, was necessarily connected with landownership as such. We do not know whether the amount of land in private ownership during the empire was large enough to be of great economic importance.

Vast tracts of land were owned by the crown and by the great temples. Crown lands and temple lands were commonly parceled out to high officials, either of the royal government or of a temple administration, for management. In some such cases, the responsible official lived at a great distance from the land. Such a piece of land, then, had first an absentee owner (Pharaoh or god) and second an absentee manager, the high official to whom the land was assigned. If all went well, the absentee manager doubtless expected to make a handsome profit over and above the amount of grain required by Pharaoh. But sometimes, it seems, the laborers ran away to avoid mistreatment by their immediate boss[23] and sometimes they might be conscripted for government work elsewhere, even in another part of Egypt.[24] What happened then, we are left to imagine.

In brief, the government of the Egyptian Empire was an autocratic bureaucracy, highly centralized in principle and to a great extent centralized in practice. Conflicts of interest certainly existed among different elements in the bureaucracy, and there are indications that the Pharaohs consciously utilized these conflicts in order to strengthen whatever dynasty happened to be ruling from time to time. The priestly and military classes, both of which became very important in the following centuries, can be seen developing in embryo, and during the last half-century of the empire, both of these classes were involved in serious disturbances which contributed to the downfall of the Twentieth Dynasty and the collapse of the empire.[25] The common man, I think, had scarcely begun to emerge

[23] P. Bologna 1094, 3, 1-5 (Gardiner, *Late Egyptian Miscellanies* ["Bibliotheca Aegyptiaca," Vol. VII (Bruxelles 1937)] p. 3).

[24] Implied by its prohibition in the Nauri Decree.

[25] Hans-Wolfgang Helck in his stimulating and valuaable book *Der Einfluss der Militärführer in der 18, ägyptischen Dynastie* ("Untersuchungen zur Geschichte und Altertumskunde Ägyptens," Vol. XIV [Leipzig, 1939]) finds that conflicts of interest between military and nonmilitary elements in the royal service were of great importance in the Eighteenth Dynasty and especially in the Amarna period. Although impressed by Helck's collection and analysis of the evidence, I am not convinced that the evidence suffices fully to establish his conclusions.

as an element whose wishes required serious consideration in political or economic life.

# 7 / CIVIL SERVICE OF THE ANCIENT WORLD / W. C. BEYER

## Ancient Rome

When Rome emerged from the prehistoric period, late in the sixth century BC, it was a small city-state, comparable in size to ancient Athens. By AD 300, when it reached the height of its territorial conquests, it had expanded into an immense empire exceeding in extent that of Alexander the Great.

Along with this territorial expansion had come profound political changes. When Rome first appeared upon the stage of history, about 500 BC, it was a patriarchal monarchy; from 500 to 27 BC it was an oligarchical republic; from 27 BC to AD 285, the period of the Early Empire, it was a limited monarchy; and from AD 285 to the end of the Western Empire in AD 476, the period of the Late Empire, it was an absolute monarchy. During the Late Empire, the imperial bureaucracy was in its most highly developed state, though the period ended with Rome's fall.

### Administrative Structure of the Empire

With the general organization of the Late Roman Empire, too, it will be assumed that the reader is familiar, and we shall proceed at once to sketch the administrative structure of the central government. This consisted of (1) the emperor's domestic household, which also played an important role in the affairs of the state, (2) the imperial council, which deliberated on general questions of administration and assisted the emperor in his judicial functions, (3) the executive departments, and (4) the judicial administration.

Our concern is primarily with the executive departments, of which there were five, each headed by an appointee of the emperor and assisted by a numerous staff. In modern parlance, we may speak of them as the departments of administration, interior, finance, justice, and war. It is in these departments that we find the bulk of the imperial bureaucracy, though the high officials of the administrative districts and provinces of the empire were also appointees of the emperor and, therefore, together with their staffs, a part of the imperial bureaucracy.

Reprinted from W. C. Beyer, "The Civil Service of the Ancient World," *Public Administration Review*, the journal of the American Society for Public Administration, 19 (1959), 247-49, by permission of the publisher.

## Internal Characteristics of the Bureaucracy

Even in the days of the republic, the Roman civil service was structured along class lines, with most of the magistracies reserved for the patricians; but under the empire this stratification was carried further and made more pronounced. The imperial service was divided into three distinct divisions, each recruited from a particular class: (1) the upper division, comprising the top posts in the imperial service, from the senatorial class; (2) the intermediate division, including the high offices next in rank, from the equestrian class; and (3) the lower division, embracing the numerous minor positions and employments, from the humbler citizens, the freedmen, and slaves. Under the Late Empire the senatorial and equestrian classes became more or less merged, but they continued in their virtual monopoly of the higher positions. Both classes were open only to full citizens whose property holdings reached a prescribed minimum.

In ancient Rome, both under the republic and the empire, the state did not concern itself with primary and secondary education. In nonprofessional university education, it participated only to the extent of supporting a few chairs of philosophy or rhetoric in leading cities, and the city of Rome had a university of sorts. There were, however, special schools attached to governmental offices in which new appointees received instruction in their own work. These were of two kinds: one, providing a general literary education for the upper-grade office workers, and the other, instruction in routine for the lower office personnel. For the higher posts in the imperial service, a law education was required.

Under the republic only the lower-ranking government workers other than freedmen or slaves were paid for their services, the magistrates being required to serve without pay other than expenses. Under the empire, however, salaries were extended to all citizen officeholders regardless of rank. The salaries, moreover, were graded, and officials of different rank were placed in different salary grades, much as is done under our modern classification and compensation plans. Officeholders also were exempted from certain taxes and received retirement allowances.

Career opportunities and promotions under the Late Empire, being closely related to the standardization of positions and salaries, were handled in the same systematic manner. The imperial service offered three distinct careers, coinciding with the division of the service along class lines: the senatorial, the equestrian, and the lower. Each of these divisions was subdivided into salary grades which formed rungs on a promotion ladder. Normally promotions were confined to divisions, but there was some movement from the lower to the higher divisions, just as there had been in recent years in the British civil service, which is organized somewhat along imperial Roman lines. The method of normal promotion was by seniority, but there is reason to believe that departures therefrom were not infrequent.

Members of the civil service were appointed by the emperor and served during his pleasure. The actual practice varied from one emperor to another, but, as H. Mattingly has put it, "The better administrators seem to have made a point of allowing considerable terms of office." Legally, too, all appointments made by an emperor terminated upon his death. His successor could, if he wished, replace all existing officeholders with appointees of his own. Here, again, the practice varied with the emperors. Some made wholesale removals upon their accession to office while others made scarcely any. Diocletian, for example, though he wrought a revolution in the character of the imperial government, converting it from a limited into an absolute monarchy, made relatively few immediate changes in its personnel. Generally speaking, while the Roman civil servant did not have the protection of tenure laws, he probably had a high degree of actual security in practice.

### Appraisal and Comment

The Roman civil service developed into a truly magnificent professional body for administering the affairs of the state. In its organization, competence, and magnitude it partook of the grandeur of the empire itself—indeed, formed a part of that grandeur.

Like the ancient Egyptians, the Romans had a penchant for system and order, and this imparted to their civil service a degree of standardization in positions, titles, and salaries approaching that of a military organization. This standardization, in turn, not only made for orderly administration of personnel affairs but also enhanced the dignity and prestige of the service.

For its prestige, however, the Roman civil service was indebted more importantly to other considerations. One was the manning of the higher administrative posts with members of the senatorial and equestrian classes, which was begun by Augustus and continued by the later emperors. The other was the fact that the Roman civil servant, like his Egyptian counterpart, was the representative of an autocratic power and, as such, was both respected and feared.

Notwithstanding its own lapses from rectitude, the imperial civil service proved a great improvement upon the corrupt and rapacious officialdom by which the Roman world was governed during the latter days of the republic. This was true particularly in the administration of the provinces, more especially in the levying and collecting of provincial taxes, which formerly had been done on a contract basis. After the amount of taxes to be collected from a community had been determined, the task of collecting it was turned over to a company of *publicani*, who then proceeded to extract from the taxpayers a much larger amount than the levy, retaining the difference as profit. This method resulted in great abuses in which provincial officials became involved. Under the empire, the collection of taxes was taken over by salaried public servants and the gouging of the taxpayers for personal gain was greatly mitigated, to the great joy of the provincials.

In common with the Egyptian bureaucracy, the Roman civil service finally became oppressive and burdensome. It, too, engaged in excessive regulation of the economic life of the people and subjected them to heavy taxation to support a growing army of imperial agents. Under this dual frustration, the Roman citizenry suffered the same breakdown of spirit as did their Egyptian predecessors under the Ptolemics. Industry and agriculture languished, population declined, even the army became so weakened that it could no longer hold back the barbarians who were pressing upon the nation's borders. In a very real sense, the Roman civil service, which at the outset had been the empire's chief instrument for bringing peace and prosperity to the Roman world, in its latter stages became one of the principal causes of the empire's fall.

# 8 / THE CHINESE CIVIL SERVICE
### OTTO P. N. BERKELBACH VAN DER SPRENKEL

The size of the civil service in the Chinese Empire was surprisingly small, especially in view of the vast extent of the empire it administered and the wide variety of its functions. Under the Sung, in the middle of the eleventh century, the total number of serving officials was probably under 13,000. For the heyday of the Ming, in Galeote Pereira's time for example, a contemporary source puts the establishment at 24,683 officials: of whom 1416 staffed the ministries at the northern capital, Peking; another 558, those of the southern capital, Nanking; while the rest, amounting to 22,709, served in various capacities in the provinces, prefectures, and districts into which the empire was administratively divided.[1] These figures should not be taken to imply that any distinction was made be-

Reprinted with permission from Otto P. N. Berkelbach van der Sprenkel, "The Chinese Civil Service," *The Nineteenth G. E. Morrisson Lecture in Ethnology* (Canberra: The Australian University, 1958), pp. 8-21.

[1] For the Sung, see E. A. Kracke, *Civil Service in Early Sung China*, Harvard-Yenching Institute Monograph Series XIII (Cambridge, Mass.: 1953, p. 55. The Ming figures are given in Wang Ch'i, *Hsü wên hsien t'ung k'ao*, Chap. 84, 46b.

tween the civil servants who worked in the capital and those whose posts were in the provinces. There were never two services. On the contrary, every civil service career included both provincial and capital postings, and usually several of each. From early times, the service was hierarchically ordered into ranks. During the T'ang dynasty (618-907) there were nine of these, each including two or four subdivisions. Later the nine ranks were restricted to an upper and lower division only, making effectively eighteen grades in all. Rank always attached to the man, and an official, holding at a particular stage in his career a certain rank, was liable to be assigned to any post whose established ranking was the equivalent of his own.

Entry into the civil service in traditional China was, in the fullest sense, entry into the ruling class; for the 25,000 or so officials who staffed the administrative machine were the whole government of the empire. The titular head was the emperor, who in theory announced his decisions to the highest officers of state at imperial audiences. In practice the emperor's role was normally restricted to the selection of his chief ministers from among the upper bureaucrats. These ministers, forming a collegium of from two or three to perhaps as many as ten persons (though usually swayed by only one or two powerful personalities) were, as long as they enjoyed the sustaining support of the monarch, the real architects of policy and controllers of the governing apparatus.

There was therefore, in the Chinese system, no real distinction, either in terms of status or of function, between what we should call "higher civil servants" and "politicians." The great officials, the heads of the imperial chancellery and the imperial secretariat, the presidents of the various ministries, both were, and behaved as if they were, politicians. They had their organized cliques of supporters; they promoted their friends and did what they could to embarrass their enemies; made political alliances with and against other civil service cliques; advocated and opposed particular policies. Even when the reigning Son of Heaven was an energetic and dominating personality, like Wu Ti of the Han or T'ai Tsung of the T'ang, the position was not so much changed as simplified by the descent into the arena of the First Civil Servant of them all. In more usual times—and Chinese imperial families were not much more prolific of great men than the royal families of other countries—the Chinese system had the interesting and instructive result that a high official who had advocated and successfully secured the adoption of a political program would normally find himself charged with the responsibility of putting it into operation—with the fate of his own career dependent on the outcome. To bolder spirits, to men like Wang An-shih of the Sung for example, this was both a stimulus and a challenge: more often its effect was to discourage innovation and reinforce the compulsion of precedent.

The functions undertaken by governments in traditional China in some fields exceeded, in others fell short of, those normally performed by governments in the West. Chinese rulers, though always paternalist, have usually taken the view that well-brought-up children can, for the most part, be trusted to behave themselves without too much policing, and that parental intervention should be used sparingly and only when the circumstances genuinely warrant it. It is a mistake—perhaps a Western mistake—to think that, because the Chinese people have for so long been governed by a bureaucracy, they have therefore been governed too much. "Governing a country," to quote an ancient Chinese philosopher, "is like cooking a small fish: neither should be overdone." Confucianism, though in Han times it came to terms with the legalist doctrine of rewards and punishments, still laid major emphasis on education by example and on the power of moral exhortation and persuasion. China was never a police state in the sense that the Mauryan Empire in India as revealed to us in the Arthasastra, or the Tokugawa state in Japan with its ubiquitous *metsuke,* were police states. Local self-government was encouraged at the village level; and the empire was essentially a vast aggregation of villages. No centrally appointed officials were ever provided for any local government area smaller than a *hsien,* a county with perhaps several tens of thousands of inhabitants. Civil disputes were as far as possible left to be arbitrated and settled by the families concerned or by the larger kinship group of the clan. Recourse to the courts was discouraged. Commercial cases were more often decided by private tribunals established by craft guilds and merchant associations than by the courts, which indeed often referred such cases, when brought before them, back to these extra-constitutional bodies for decision. For the common people it was both easier, cheaper, and less dangerous to use a middleman or go-between to arbitrate a dispute than to invoke the majesty of the law. As a general rule the courts, presided over with awe-inspiring ceremony by the local mandarins in their special capacity as judges, were reserved for major crimes against public order and for cases which had proved recalcitrant to less formal modes of treatment.

Among the tasks which Chinese governments, in common with those of other countries, were regularly called upon to discharge were internal security and external defense, and the assessment, collection, and disbursement of the public revenue. To ascertain the country's taxable capacity, since the Chinese economy was predominantly agricultural, it was necessary for the Board of Revenue (the *Hu Pu*), to carry out periodic cadastral surveys, mapping the cultivated land and classifying the fields according to their productivity. The main source of the government's income was the land tax which, until comparatively recent times, was paid in kind. Since this "tribute grain" was delivered locally, the government was obliged to erect and maintain storage facilities, and make arrangements for its transport, often over considerable distances, to nourish the seat of government and the defense forces on the frontiers. The further existence of the poll tax and the corvée, which were taxes on people rather than on produce, meant that the board of revenue was also charged with the taking of censuses. The first Chinese census for which we have detailed figures was taken in AD 2. In its institution of decennial censuses, China antedates the West by several centuries.[2]

Of considerably greater importance for the light it throws on the formation and development of the Chinese bureaucratic state is another governmental function, typical for China, though with little, if any, parallel in the practice of the West. I refer to the government planning and implementation of large-scale public works, especially in the fields of flood control and irrigation.

It is important that the nature, and also the social and political repercussions, of this characteristic Chinese institution should be made clear. The sinologist who has done most to explore and illuminate the determining role of large-scale public works in the history of Chinese society is K. A. Wittfogel, who in a series of publications, extending from his magistral *Wirtschaft und Gesellschaft Chinas* (Leipzig, 1931) to his recently published volume on *Oriental Despotism* (New Haven, 1957), has conclusively demonstrated the connection between bureaucratic political forms and what he calls the "hydraulic agricultural" economy.

Wittfogel distinguishes three kinds of agriculture: first, *rainfall agriculture,* which calls for no particular explanation or description here as it is the type most familiar to Europeans and Americans; second, *hydroagriculture,* which is farming based on small-scale irrigation, and which, though increasing the food supply, "does not involve the patterns of organization and social control that characterize hydraulic agriculture"; and third, *hydraulic agriculture,* which is agriculture involving the control of water on a large scale. The three main features of hydraulic agriculture are: that it both permits and demands very intensive cultivation; that it rests upon a specific type of division of labor (namely, between preparatory and protective operations on the one hand and pro-

---

[2] See H. Bielenstein, "The Census of China during the Period AD 2 to 742" in *Bulletin of the Museum of Far Eastern Antiquities,* Vol. XX (1947), 125-63. See also the present author's "Population Statistics of Ming China" in *Bulletin of the School of Oriental and African Studies,* Vol. XV (1953), 289-326.

ductive operations on the other) on a wide territorial basis; and that it involves social cooperation on a massive scale.

The terrain which saw the birth and early growth of Chinese civilization, if it did not absolutely determine, at least powerfully favored, the rise of an hydraulic type of agriculture. The Wei River valley, the great bend and lower course of the Yellow River, the North China Plain, with seventeen inches of annual rainfall, with summer floods and periodic river silting, provided a semiarid environment whose productive potentialities could only be adequately realized with the help of great public works for water control, designed at once to give protection against the danger of flood and to provide the fields with irrigation water.[3]

Wittfogel's thesis here—and in the Chinese context it is unanswerable —is that "the resulting regime [is] decisively shaped by the leadership and social control required by hydraulic agriculture." [4] He writes:

Irrigation farming always requires more physical effort than rainfall farming performed under comparable conditions. . . . If irrigation farming depends on the effective handling of a *major* supply of water,[5] the distinctive quality of water—its tendency to gather in bulk—becomes institutionally decisive. A large quantity of water can be channeled and kept within bounds only by the use of mass labor; and this mass labor must be coordinated, disciplined, and led. Thus a number of farmers eager to conquer arid lowlands and plains are forced to invoke the organizational devices which—on the basis of pre-machine technology—offer the one chance of success: they must work in cooperation with their fellows and subordinate themselves to a directing authority.[6]

But must this directing authority necessarily take the form of a state disposing of a complex bureaucratic apparatus? A little consideration of what the planning and performance of large-scale public works entails is enough to give the answer.

Most writers who mention the cooperative aspect of hydraulic agriculture think in the main of digging, dredging, and damming; and the organizational tasks involved in these labors [are] certainly considerable. But the planners of a major hydraulic enterprise are confronted with problems of a much more complex kind. How many persons are needed? And where can such persons be found? On the basis of previously made registers, the planners must deter-

[3] The importance of hydraulic operations in China was even noted by Burton (in his reading of Ricci). He writes: "Admirable cost and charge is bestowed" in China on "conduct and navigable rivers . . . and so likewise about corrivations of waters to moisten and refresh barren grounds." *Anatomy of Melancholy*, p. 78.

[4] K. A. Wittfogel, *Oriental Despotism* (New Haven: Yale University Press, 1957), p. 27.

[5] My italics.

[6] Wittfogel, *op. cit.*, pp. 17-18.

mine the quota and criteria of selection. Notification follows selection, and mobilization notification. The assembled groups frequently proceed in quasi-military columns. Having reached their destination, the . . . privates of the hydraulic army must be distributed in proper numbers and according to whatever division of operations (spading, carrying of mud, and so on) is customary. If raw materials such as straw, fagots, lumber, or stone have to be procured, auxiliary operations are organized; and if the work teams—in toto or in part— must be provided with food and drink, still other ways of appropriation, transport, and distribution have to be developed. Even in its simplest form, agro-hydraulic operations necessitate substantial integrative action. In their more elaborate variations, they involve extensive and complex organizational planning.[7]

Without a highly trained civil service these tasks could neither be planned nor carried out.

The existence of hydraulic public works, themselves required by the geographical setting of early Chinese civilization, was then the main factor determining the appearance and growth of the mandarinate. The particular form which this finely tempered instrument finally took must be accredited both to historical circumstances, such as the suppression in the third century BC of the feudal aristocracy and its replacement by a gentry class whose members eventually formed the social reservoir from which the bureaucracy was drawn; and to the inventive genius of the Chinese, illustrated in the ingenious institutional devices by which their officials were selected, trained, and controlled.

With the experience acquired in mobilizing and organizing vast labor forces for hydraulic public works, it was possible for Chinese governments to extend the range of their enterprises into other fields with only a peripheral relation, or no relation at all, to water control. Such were, for example, defense structures like the Great Wall, and navigation canals like the eight-hundred-mile long Yün Ho, connecting the political centers of the North with the fertile rice-producing provinces of the lower Yangtse. This canal, on which a million workers at a time are said to have been employed, if superimposed on a map of Europe, would reach from Hamburg to Rome; in American terms it would link New Orleans with Chicago; in Australian, Darwin with Alice Springs. Other enterprises included the construction and embellishment of a number of capital cities: magnificent and spacious examples of town-planning whose influence is traceable in many lesser cities all over China and in foreign capitals such as Nara and Heian in Japan. The establishment and maintenance of a network of imperial highways, and of a posting system with its necessary horses, relay stations, and rest houses, are further examples.

[7] *Ibid.*, p. 26.

Large-scale works for irrigation, flood control, and transportation already represented a massive intervention by government in the economic life of the community; and, the precedent once set, it is not surprising that the Chinese civil service found itself, to an ever-increasing extent, involved in economic activities which in the West, at least until very recently, have commonly been regarded as falling within the proper province of private enterprise. The so-called "ever-normal granaries," designed both to facilitate the control of agricultural prices and provide emergency stocks for the relief of local famines; government monopolies such as those controlling the production and sale of salt, iron, and tea; government-operated factories, especially for the manufacture of military supplies; government printing and publishing, as of the official almanacs which told the farmer the proper dates for beginning and ending the various operations of the agricultural year, and of simply written illustrated handbooks on rice-cultivation, sericulture, spinning, and weaving: these were but some of the tasks which tradition and the received Confucian orthodoxy prescribed as the rightful concern of the bureaucracy.

The personal quality of the civil service was necessarily a matter of the first importance to the empire, and successive dynasties were unremitting in their efforts to secure and maintain a high standard in their administrative personnel. At least as early as the Han, officials serving in the provinces were required to recommend likely candidates for the public service, and these were then given an oral examination at the capital to test their suitability for office. From such beginnings grew up the system of open competitive state examinations as we find it, already well developed, under the T'ang in the seventh century.

Two strongly opposed views have been canvassed about the effect of the examination system on the character of the Chinese civil service. Both state extreme positions, and neither can be fully justified. One sees the examination system as throwing wide the doors of the civil service to merit—wherever it might be found. The other, in full reaction against this, denies any vestige of democracy to the Chinese system, and claims that in practice it was virtually impossible for other than members of well-established gentry families to enter the service. A classical education was a necessary condition of examination success, and only wealthy families could provide a classical education for their children. Although state schools existed in most periods of Chinese history, they catered to only a very small fraction of the population. Wolfram Eberhard in his *Toba-Reich Nordchinas* instances the Wei Dynasty law of 466, which called for the establishment of a school in every district (*chün*) of the empire. The schools in large districts were to accommodate up to one hundred pupils; in medium districts, up to sixty, in small districts forty.

At this time Ch'ang-shan *chün*, in Hopei, which would rank as a large district, had a population of 56,890 families. Less than one family in five hundred, therefore, would have been able to send a child to the district school; and as if this in itself were not enough to rule out poor families, the law actually laid it down that pupils should, wherever possible, be taken from *kao mên*—i.e., wealthy upper-class families. Private tutors, who played by far the most important role in gentry education, were usually themselves of good family, and seldom took pupils whose family connections were inferior to their own. Eberhard, in the study already referred to, also points out that of the 135 *po-shih* (scholars of wide learning) mentioned by name in the *Wei History* about whose family relationships something is known, 107 (or 80 per cent) belonged to Great Families of the upper gentry, and the rest, with one exception (and he was a professor of geomancy) to other well-to-do gentry families.[8]

While these figures are correct, their relevance to other and later periods of Chinese history is open to doubt. The Toba Wei was a barbarian dynasty which ruled (387-557) during the Age of Division, before the reunification of the empire under the Sui and T'ang, and before the effective establishment of the examination system. Though the gentry class continued to provide the overwhelming majority of civil service examination candidates, it was both a numerous class and an expanding one. Information on social mobility in China is difficult to obtain and even more difficult to evaluate; but the gentry was never a completely closed group. There was always a seepage of families into and out of it. The gradual integration of the southern provinces into the Chinese culture complex immediately before and during the T'ang significantly enlarged the ranks of the gentry. Moreover the higher reaches of the bureaucracy, which at first were almost the private preserve of the great upper-gentry families, were increasingly invaded by new men drawn from the middle and lower layers of the gentry class. It is clear, for example, during the Northern Sung, when printing came into general use, making education easier and less expensive, that the social reservoir from which the bureaucracy was recruited underwent considerable growth. This process, interrupted under the alien rule of the Mongol Yüan, went forward once more, and at an accelerated rate, in the Ming period, and again in the Ch'ing. The Chinese mandarinate, therefore, although it had a strongly marked class character, was never an hereditary corporation. Its techniques of selection, posting, and promotion were indeed incompatible with the hereditary principle, as was shown by the failure of Japanese attempts, in the Taika Reforms of the seventh century, to in-

[8] See Wolfram Eberhard, *Das Toba-Reich Nordchinas: eine soziologische Untersuchung* (Leiden 1949), pp. 138-40.

troduce a Chinese-style bureaucratic administration while simultaneously retaining within it privileged status for a class of hereditary aristocrats.

The social role of the examination system in traditional China was extremely complex. Its first and most obvious function was to insure a supply of highly trained candidates for the public service. Through the establishment of provincial quotas for the *chin-shih* or doctoral degree, it was also used to secure an acceptable regional balance in the civil service establishment, since it was held undesirable that any province should be either grossly over- or underrepresented in the governing apparatus. That this danger existed was due to the fact that certain provinces, like Kiangsu and Chekiang in the southeast, had for hundreds of years been centers of learning, had a deeply rooted scholastic tradition, and were much better provided with libraries, literary academies, and private teachers than, for example, the provinces of the west and southwest. These regional advantages were inevitably reflected in the examination results, as Etienne Zi's analysis of the local provenance of the scholars winning the first three places in the successive doctoral examinations of the Ch'ing period brings out.[9] Out of a total of 321 first, second, and third places, scholars from Kiangsu gained 116, or over a third of the whole, and scholars from Chekiang seventy-four; while the western provinces of Shansi, Shensi, Szechwan, Kweichow, Kwangsi and Yünnan could only muster thirteen successes between them. The adoption of provincial quotas in the examinations offered a simple way of reducing the effect of these regional differences.

Another and extremely persistent type of regionalism which, as it affected postings and promotions within the service rather than entrance to it, was less easy to control, arose from the tendency of high officials to favor the careers of members of their own kinship group or of persons who, though not related to them, were fellow provincials and came from their native district. For example, out of the 350 highest ranking officials in 1893, the province of Hunan, with considerably less than the provincial average of examination successes, accounted for fifty-eight, almost double the total of any other province. This is a striking testimony to the influence of the Hunanese Tsêng family, and in particular to the prestige of the great statesman Tsêng Kuo-fan. It may be added, as a notable example of continuity in Chinese political practice, that at the present moment seven out of the seventeen members of the Communist Party Political Bureau, and twenty-seven out of the ninety-seven members of the Central Committee, are natives of Hunan. This province,

[9] Etienne Zi, *Pratique des examens littéraires en Chine,* Variétés Sinologiques No. 5 (Shanghai 1894), Appendix II.

with about 7.5 per cent of the population, has almost four times its proportionate share in the supreme directing organs of the Party and the People's Republic: a situation which is not unconnected with the fact that the Head of the State, Mao Tse-tung, is himself a Hunanese.[10]

In traditional China the examination system, apart from its main task of selecting from the educated gentry an élite of scholar-officials, also functioned as an efficient instrument of social control over the gentry class itself. Since status, power and prebend were the prizes of examination success, the social goals of the gentry group were inevitably set by the examination system, while the classical Confucianist curriculum which the candidates had to prepare just as certainly determined the content of gentry education. Preoccupation with successive examinations to enter the bureaucracy, and then with the further written tests on which promotion within the service largely depended, effectively checked the expression of nonconformist ideas. Through the examination system the conservative acceptance of an orthodox ideology was institutionalized; and the *literati*, so often a potential source of danger to the established order, became instead its prop, and a principal support of things as they were. This happy result was not, of course, achieved without price paid: the price being the discouragement of original thinking. In its favor it can be said that the ideal inculcated by the official Confucianism of the empire, that of the "moral man," was no mean one.

The examination life of the typical gentry member began in earliest childhood with the study of the Classics in Chu Hsi's commentaries, and of the Histories. A variegated and pedestrian literature of handbooks, abridgments, model examination essays, books of classified quotations, rhyming dictionaries, and the like, catered to the requirements of the student. The examinations themselves were taken at three levels. The first tier, held in the district cities and presided over by the local magistrate, did little more than qualify the successful candidates, known as *hsiu-ts'ai*, to compete in the examinations of the next level. These were held in the capital cities of the various provinces, and were conducted by specially appointed provincial examiners. Those who passed them were awarded the title of *chü-jên*, and were already eligible for appointment to the lower ranks of the civil service. More commonly the *chü-jên* proceeded directly to the third round of the examinations, which were held every third year at the imperial capital. Success in this metropolitan examination was crowned with the award of the coveted *chin-shih* or doc-

[10] See Franklin W. Houn, "The Eighth Central Committee of the Chinese Communist Party: A Study of an Elite," in *American Political Science Review*, vol. LI (1957), 392-404. I owe this reference to the kindness of my colleague, Mr. S. Encel.

toral degree. In most settled dynastic periods, the possession of a *chin-shih* degree was almost indispensable to anyone wishing to embark on an official career.

Every precaution was taken to insure that the examinations were fairly conducted. The questions were set and marked by officials of the Board of Rites, a different ministry from the one that supervised the civil service and was responsible for appointments to it. At the end of the tenth century the Sung revived and extended the practice, briefly experimented with under the T'ang, of insuring the anonymity of candidates by substituting a number for the candidate's name on the examination paper. In order to exclude the possibility of a candidate being identified from his calligraphy, all papers were recopied in the Bureau of Copyists before being submitted to the examiners. Every examination paper was read independently by two examiners, and a third examiner received their sealed reports, verified them, and if necessary reconciled their marks. That in spite of these measures abuses sometimes occurred is clear, both from the accounts in satirical novels like Wu Ching-tzu's *Ju lin wai shih* (recently translated into English under the title of *The Scholars*) and from the scandals, court cases, and severe punishments that followed when flagrant breaches of the regulations were discovered. These last, however, at least underline the honesty of purpose that informed the administration, and it is perhaps also relevant that Wu Ching-tzu, himself an able scholar, had been embittered by repeated failure to pass the examinations he ridiculed.

Competition in the examinations was severe. The number of those who passed was seldom as high as 10 per cent—and often a much lower fraction—of those who sat. There was no limit of age, and no restriction on the number of times a candidate could present himself for the same examination. The number of doctoral degrees awarded bore, of course, some relation to the needs of the service; though many holders of the *chin-shih* degree, either from their own volition or from some other cause, failed to enter upon a civil service career. During the first century of the Northern Sung 18,125 *chin-shih* degrees were given—an annual rate of 181. During the Ming, the annual rate rose gradually from about 50 to 140. In the Ch'ing, the annual average for the whole dynastic period was 118.

There were, as well as the road which led by way of the examinations, other ways of entry into the bureaucracy. The two most important of these "irregular" routes were: first, by transfer, either from the military establishment or from the subordinate and "unclassed" clerical services; and second, through the so-called *yin* privilege. This, which already existed under the T'ang, empowered certain categories of high officials to nominate for entrance into the civil service one or more of their sons, and, on occasion, even dependants not related by blood. Though entrants under the *yin* privilege were not particularly numerous, and did not share the prestige of their degree-holding colleagues, the practice was nevertheless contrary to the spirit of the merit system and probably harmful to the morale of the service as a whole. Recruitment by transfer, on the other hand, had this to be said of it, that it gave men who had neither a technical education in the classics nor the advantages of wealth and family influence a chance of entering the service which they otherwise would not have had. In the main, however, it was the officials who had won the entrance through the hard test of the open competitive examinations who formed the mainstay, and set the tone, of the Chinese civil service.

## 9 / FEATURES OF THE CHINESE SOCIAL STRUCTURE
### E. BALAZS

Now, it seems to me that the only valid method for letting light into this solid mass of historical fact is to seek out the causes of continuity—that is, try to discover the specific and significant features of Chinese social structure. I shall have to confine myself to discussing the social structure of imperial China, for it would take me far beyond the limits of the present essay to make comparisons with earlier periods, however interesting and instructive that might be. And I can only point out the more striking of its distinctive features, since anything approaching a complete description of the social structure of imperial China would require not an essay but several large tomes.

What, then, were its most striking features?

1. In the first place, China was a large *agrarian* society, highly developed but using traditional techniques, and established on a subcontinent that lacks any marked geographical articulation. Its cells, scattered over an immense territory whose main arteries were a system of waterways, existed in an economic autarchy that made each of them an individual unit, and isolated each unit from every other. These cells were the peasant families that composed the overwhelming majority of the population. They were self-sufficient; but without the system of economic exchanges and the organizational framework imposed from above, they would have disintegrated irremediably into their component particles, into an anarchy that would have made impossible not only the distribu-

Reprinted with permission from E. Balazs, "China as a Permanently Bureaucratic Society," *Chinese Civilization and Bureaucracy* (New Haven: Yale University Press, 1964), pp. 15-19.

tion, but also the production of goods, and indeed the maintenance of life itself. It was, in other words, a pre-industrial, nonmaritime society, based on a peasant subsistence economy.

2. This society was *bureaucratic* because the social pyramid—which rested on a broad peasant base, with intermediate strata consisting of a merchant class and an artisan class, both of them numerically small, lacking in autonomy, of inferior status, and regarded with scant respect— was capped and characterized by its apex: the mandarinate.

3. The class of *scholar-officials* (or mandarins), numerically infinitesimal but omnipotent by reason of their strength, influence, position, and prestige, held all the power and owned the largest amount of land. This class possessed every privilege, above all the privilege of reproducing itself, because of its monopoly of education. But the incomparable prestige enjoyed by the intelligentsia had nothing to do with such a risky and possibly ephemeral thing as the ownership of land; nor was it conferred by heredity, which after all can be interrupted; nor was it due solely to its exclusive enjoyment of the benefits of education. This unproductive elite drew its strength from the function it performed—the socially necessary, indeed indispensable, function of coordinating and supervising the productive labor of others so as to make the whole social organism work. All mediating and administrative functions were carried out by the scholar-officials. They prepared the calendar, they organized transport and exchange, they supervised the construction of roads, canals, dikes, and dams; they were in charge of all public works, especially those aimed at forestalling droughts and floods; they built up reserves against famine, and encouraged every kind of irrigation project. Their social role was at one and the same time that of architect, engineer, teacher, administrator, and ruler. Yet these "managers" before their time were firmly against any form of specialization. There was only one profession they recognized: that of governing. A famous passage from Mencius on the difference between those who think and those who toil perfectly expresses the scholar-officials' outlook: "Great men have their proper business, and little men have their proper business. . . . Some labor with their minds, and some labor with their strength. Those who labor with their minds govern others; those who labor with their strength are governed by others. Those who are governed by others support them; those who govern others are supported by them." [1]

4. Being specialists in the handling of men and experts in the political art of governing, *the scholar-officials were the embodiment of the state*, which was created in their image—a hierarchical, authoritarian state, paternalistic yet tyrannical; a tentacular welfare state; a totalitarian Mo-

[1] *Mencius* III A, 4; trans. James Legge, *Chinese Classics*, 2, 249-50.

loch of a state. The word *totalitarian* has a modern ring to it, but it serves very well to describe the scholar-officials' state if it is understood to mean that *the state has complete control over all activities* of social life, absolute domination at all levels. The state in China was a managerial, an interventionists state—hence the enduring appeal of Taoism, which was opposed to state intervention. Nothing escaped official regimentation. Trade, mining, building, ritual, music, schools, in fact the whole of public life and a great deal of private life as well, were subjected to it.

5. There are still other reasons for speaking of a totalitarian state. In the first place, there was a *secret-police atmosphere* of mutual suspicion, in which everyone kept watch on everyone else. Then there was the *arbitrary character of justice*. In the eyes of the authorities, every accused person was assumed to be guilty. Terror was instilled by the principle of *collective responsibility* (which, contrary to what one might suppose, had no connection with the Confucianist ideal of the family), making every subject shake in his shoes, and the scholar-officials most of all, for, although they ruled the state, they were also its servants. I should like to add that this last point is only apparently contradictory. The truth is that in all totalitarian societies it is a fundamental principle that public interest comes before private interests, and that reasons of state take priority over the rights of the individual human being. The inevitable corollary is that an official in his capacity as a representative of the state is sacrosanct, but as an individual he is nothing.

A final totalitarian characteristic was the state's tendency to clamp down immediately on any form of private enterprise (and this in the long run kills not only initiative but even the slightest attempts at innovation), or, if it did not succeed in putting a stop to it in time, to take over and nationalize it. Did it not frequently happen during the course of Chinese history that the scholar-officials, although hostile to all inventions, nevertheless gathered in the fruits of other people's ingenuity? I need mention only three examples of inventions that met this fate: paper, invented by a eunuch; printing, used by the Buddhists as a medium for religious propaganda; and the bill of exchange, an expedient of private businessmen.

In view of its contemporary relevancy, one additional feature of the bureaucratic state may be worth mentioning here: the panicky fear of assuming responsibility. To avoid getting into trouble was the Chinese bureaucrat's main concern, and he always managed to saddle his responsibilities on to some subordinate who could serve as a scapegoat.

6. The scholar-officials and their state found in the Confucianist doctrine an ideology that suited them perfectly. In ancient times, Confucianism had expressed the ideals of those former members of the feudal

aristocracy who had formed a new social stratum of revolutionary intelligentsia, but in Han times (206 BC-AD 220), shortly after the foundation of the empire, it became a state doctrine. The virtues preached by Confucianism were exactly suited to the new hierarchical state: respect, humility, docility, obedience, submission, and subordination to elders and betters. In comparison with the usefulness of virtues such as these, ancestor worship and the cult of the family were no more than additional, though welcome, features. Moreover, the new elite found it convenient to adopt the Confucian nonreligious, rationalist outlook. Mysticism was usually a cloak for subversive tendencies, and the scholar-officials, anxious above all to maintain the position they had won, felt that it was something to be guarded against. Prudence dictated that they should remain soberly realistic and down to earth. Prudence also dictated that the new Confucianism should be conformist and traditionalist in character: strict adherence to orthodox doctrines was the surest defense against the pressures of other social groups. Thus the contradiction between the rationalism of early Confucianism and the traditionalism of its later development created a tension within the mandarinate which can be explained by the play of interests—of vital interests—within the society as a whole. The conflict of interests also explains the contradiction between, on the one hand, the claims to be a democracy (claims real enough as far as internal relations within the group of scholar-officials were concerned), and, on the other, the actual existence of an oligarchy —the contradiction, that is, between the two poles of Confucianist political doctrine.

I do not wish, however, to go into the whole question of Confucianism, which is far too complex a matter to deal with in passing. The only point I want to make is that the continuity of Confucianism depended entirely upon the continued existence of the scholar-officials' centralized, hierarchical, and bureaucratic state. Whenever this state was at bay, whenever the scholar-officials had to let other actors take the center of the stage (never for long), the Confucianists went into retirement and kept quiet, taking cover in order to prepare a triumphant return.

# III / SOCIOPOLITICAL PROCESSES IN THE EMPIRES

## INTRODUCTION

*The essays in this section deal with the policies of the rulers as well as with the attitudes of the various social groups toward these policies. They indicate how the rulers were influenced by the interplay between traditional and nontraditional elements, and how there consequently developed some contradictions among their policies.*

*The rulers wanted, above all, to implement their own political goals, such as territorial expansion, and to maintain internal political control. They were also interested in promoting free resources (manpower, commodities, and political support uncommitted to any formal groups) and mobilizing them for their own use. Finally, they wanted to maintain their traditional legitimation and their symbols of status.*

*The rulers also attempted to limit the power of the aristocracy and to create new status groups, but they faced several obstacles. Regardless of the number of new titles they created, of the encouragement they gave to new groups, the status symbols they used were usually very similar to those borne by the landed aristocracy or the established religious élites. The creation of an entirely new secular aristocracy was either beyond their power or contrary to their basic interest, for it would necessarily involve an increase in political participation by such a group and, consequently, a growth in its influence.*

*Therefore, the ability of the rulers to appeal to the lower strata of the population was obviously limited. Even more important, the new urban middle-class groups and the bureaucracy itself tended to identify with the established élite and, consequently, to "aristocratize" themselves—i.e., to acquire land and other symbols of aristocratic status.*

*But, on the other hand, however tradition-bound the ruling élites may have been, their policies required the creation and propagation of more flexible "free" resources in various institutional fields. The propagation of such free resources gave rise to nontraditional religious, intellectual, and legal groups. Although in many cases these newer elements were very weak and subject to the influence of the ruling élite, they sometimes*

65

*developed into relatively independent concentrations of power, and their opposition to the rulers was only increased by the more conservative policies.*

*Similar contradictions developed in the economic sphere—and they were especially evident in conflicts between short-range problems and long-range aims. The continuous necessity to mobilize extensive resources for the implementation of various political goals—such as military expansion—could either exhaust the "free" economic resources, or conversely, strengthen those groups which produced these resources, make them too independent of the rulers and thus threaten the traditional basis of the political system. Hence, the rulers often had to turn back to the traditional aristocratic groups with whom they often felt a much greater social affinity.*

*A similar contradiction existed in the policies dealing with problems of administrative manpower. In many cases, because means of communication and technical facilities were inadequate, it was very difficult to supervise such personnel effectively. It then became necessary to delegate supervisory functions to local gentry and landowners, who gradually became aristocratized or independent feudal lords.*

*The best example of how the social groups created by the ruling élite came to oppose its aims and basic political premises is the development of the system of sale of offices. This system was usually introduced by the rulers as a means of solving their financial problems and admitting new, nonaristocratic elements into their service. But in time, the new bureaucrats came to regard their positions as possessions to be passed on to other members of their families or sold to the highest bidders. In this way, the rulers slowly lost control over the offices they had created.*

*The same types of problems were faced by the rulers of the different empires. The major differences arose from the extent to which the contradictions in policies were eliminated by the rulers, and the relative strength of the various groups that opposed them. It was these differences that were of crucial importance in the ultimate destiny of these empires.*

*The essays that follow deal with the sociopolitical processes in the Roman Empire, in the Byzantine Empire, and in Imperial China. They indicate how, in spite of the differences in historical setting, some processes were common to all these societies.*

*The excerpts by Jones, Boak, and Walbank discuss the fall of the Roman Empire, examining the problem of manpower shortage, the burden of an excessive bureaucracy, the shrinkage of free resources (especially of free peasantry), and the strengthening of the landed aristocracy.*

*A similar range of themes can be found in the essays dealing with the Byzantine Empire and Imperial China. The excerpt from Diehl's book describes the growth of administrative centralization in the Byzantine Empire and its effects. Charanis' essay analyzes the gradual weakening of the Byzantine administration, the strengthening of the aristocracy, and the concomitant decline of the free peasantry. Hucker analyzes the system of administrative centralization in China, while Balazs examines the economic controls over available free resources, which influenced the development of China. Balazs also describes the changes in landownership in China, and the continuous struggle of the peasants to retain some freedom. In the remaining essays, Strayer and Coulborn analyze the religious institutions in the Roman, Islamic, and Chinese empires, while Lotz discusses the "farming out" of public offices—a basic problem common to most of these empires.*

## 10 / THE SOCIAL, POLITICAL, AND RELIGIOUS CHANGES DURING THE LAST PERIOD OF THE ROMAN EMPIRE

### A. H. M. JONES

It is hardly possible to assign reasons for the mysterious changes which come over man's whole attitude to life from one age to another. The historian can do little more than register them. In the classical age of Greek and Roman civilization, when the city was the effective political unit, it was the city that dominated men's thoughts and emotions. Religion was in the main a communal activity, the worship by the citizens of the gods who protected their city. The virtues which were valued were the civic virtues: courage in fighting for one's city, wisdom and public spirit in guiding its policy, and open-handed generosity in contributing to its expenses. The average man seems to have found satisfaction in the service of his city: he had no hankering for personal immortality, being content to live on in the memory of his fellow citizens, and felt no need for personal communion with the divine powers. The political subjection of cities to kings and ultimately to Rome inevitably weakened civic spirit. Many of its outlets were cut off. As Plutarch regretfully remarks, under the all-embracing rule of Rome a man could no longer win glory by leading his fellow citizens to victory in war, nor by statesmanlike handling of a political crisis. Civic patriotism survived the political extinction of the city for a surprisingly long period, but, deprived of useful outlets, it was diverted into futile backwaters and ultimately sank into stagnation. Now that cities could no longer fight one another for freedom or empire, they carried on bitter feuds over questions of precedence and honorific titles, and view with one another in competitive building programs and games and festivals. Now that any challenge to the oligarchies which the Roman government supported was ruthlessly suppressed as sedition, internal politics degenerated into personal rivalries, in which, as Plutarch is forced to admit, ability or

Reprinted with permission from A. H. M. Jones, "The Decline and Fall of the Roman Empire," *History*, 40, No. 140 (October 1955), 210-20.

merit counted for little and the issue was decided by the wealth of the candidates and their willingness to spend it lavishly for the city's glory. This competition in extravagance between cities and between individuals was no doubt less destructive than the internecine wars and the party struggles which had been the bane of the sovereign city-state. But it was economically ruinous, and led to an increasingly strict surveyance by the imperial government of local administration, especially on its financial side, with a corresponding decay of civic initiative, and to a growing distaste for local politics on the part of the wealthy, who alone could take any active part in them. Local politics were not only losing their savor, now that the cities were mere cogs in the imperial administrative machine, but were becoming a positive nuisance, since they involved a heavy expenditure. Even the members of the governing oligarchies began to regard local office as a burdensome responsibility and to seek ways and means of evading it.

While civic spirit decayed, there was no growth of imperial patriotism. From the first, the imperial government had been regarded as an external power, at worst an oppressive tyrant, whose agents extorted taxes and levied recruits and exploited the provincials on their own account, at best a benevolent protector, which maintained armies to defend the provinces against the barbarians, and assured internal peace and order. The ideal relation of the cities of the empire to the imperial government was aptly expressed by the official cult of Rome and Augustus, whereby the provincial communities manifested their humble gratitude to the emperor and the eternal city for benefits received and prayed for their continuance for all time. The ordinary citizen's role was purely passive, being in practice in most cases limited to paying his taxes. He neither felt, nor was encouraged to feel, any sense of responsibility for the welfare, or even for the survival, of the empire. His loyalty was passive, not active.

The army which protected the empire had from the beginning of the principate, and indeed before, been a professional body, whose efficiency depended on its own traditions and *esprit de corps*. The various grades of the civil service which administered the empire were likewise in origin professional, or early became so. The senatorial order had, by the second century, become an aristocracy of service: in the third, it was increasingly superseded by the equestrian order, which had been professional from its origins: the lower grades of imperial slaves and freedmen and military clerks had always been professional. The strength and efficiency of the empire might therefore seem to have been independent of any sentiment of patriotism among its subjects. Nevertheless the decay of local civic spirit in the second and third centuries did seriously affect the efficiency of the imperial administration. In the early empire the central government depended largely on the cities for the execution of its orders. It was the city councils which were responsible for collecting the taxes, repairing the roads, levying recruits for the army, and furnishing the supplies requisitioned for its use, and so long as the cities performed these functions efficiently, the central civil service had only to regulate and supervise and could be kept small; its cost was therefore low, its quality could be maintained, and its abuses readily checked. This happy state of affairs, however, depended on the survival of civic spirit; the wheels would go round smoothly only so long as the upper classes in the cities were zealous to serve as local magistrates and councillors and to take their share in the administrative duties involved. As they became more and more reluctant to serve, and had, by the third century, to be unwillingly conscripted, more and more supervision and regimentation by the central bureaucracy was required to keep the administrative machine in motion. The bureaucracy was expanded in number, its quality inevitably sank, and it became increasingly difficult to control its abuses. Diocletian's administrative reforms mark a decisive stage in this process. By multiplying provincial governors, each with his staff of clerks, separating the military command in many provinces from the civil administration, and creating the dioceses with their *vicarii, rationales,* and *magistri,* and their staffs of clerks, he strengthened the administrative machine, with the result that it was able to dragoon the city councils into levying the recruits, labor and supplies that the imperial government required. But he only did so at the expense of imposing a scarcely tolerable burden on the empire. The expanded bureaucracy, though ill paid, involved a heavy charge in salaries—or, rather, rations and uniforms; and because it was ill paid and diluted in quality and difficult to control, it was inefficient, corrupt, and extortionate.

Concurrently with, and perhaps in compensation for, the decay of civic spirit there was a growth of personal religion. Its origin can be traced back to the Hellenistic age, in the rise of philosophic systems like Cynicism, Stoicism and Epicureanism, which sought to establish a standard of values and inculcate a way of life for the individual, isolated from his community. On a more emotional level it is expressed in the growing popularity of mystery religions, in which the individual worshipper sought communion with the divine, and was encouraged in hopes of individual survival beyond the grave. These two streams ultimately coalesced in the mystical Neoplatonism which dominated educated paganism from the third century onward. According to this creed the world of sense was illusory or evil, and the soul found fulfilment by shaking itself free from its earthly shackles and rising into the world of ideas with the ultimate goal of communion with the Absolute.

Christianity likewise inculcated indifference to the things of this world. The earliest generations of Christians, living in eager expectation of the Second Coming of the Lord, were naturally uninterested in the world around them. And as this hope became less vivid they concentrated on the life of the spirit and the world to come. There was a school of thought which regarded the empire as a satanic organization. Most Christians, however, were not positively hostile to the empire, and indeed regarded it as of divine institution. But even when it became Christian it inspired no sense of loyalty or devotion. Christians did not feel called upon to fight for its survival or to remedy its abuses, because their eyes were fixed on the salvation of individual souls. The calamities of the empire were regarded not as challenges to action but as tribulations sent by God to purify the righteous and call sinners to repentance.

This outlook on life not only bred a generally defeatist attitude to the problems of the time, which must have weakened the resistance of the empire, but produced specific movements which undoubtedly to some degree diminished its strength. Prominent among these is monasticism, the complete abandonment of this world for a life of spiritual contemplation. The movement reached vast proportions, especially in the East, and must have sterilized a significant proportion of the empire's failing manpower. For hermits and monks were, of course, lost as potential recruits to the army and the administration. The rare attempts of the imperial government to assert the claims of the public service were bitterly resisted by the church. When Emperor Maurice enacted that soldiers and civil servants might not enter the monastic life before their discharge, Pope Gregory the Great protested vehemently that a Christian emperor could in no circumstances deny his subjects the right of saving their own souls, and did his best by passive obstruction to prevent the enforcement of the decree.

Monasticism represents in its most extreme form the other worldly spirit, an utter condemnation of this world and an attempt to escape from its temptations and responsibilities and devote oneself entirely to the world of the spirit. Not all Christians were expected to follow this perfect way, but even those who remained in the world were strongly discouraged from the service of the state. Popes Siricius and Innocent I ruled that men who after baptism pursued the career of soldiers, civil servants, or lawyers were ineligible for holy orders, and Siricius issued a yet severer decree that those who, having done penance, like dogs and swine returning to their old vomit and wallowing place, sought anew a post in the imperial service or the pleasures of the theater or new marriages or forbidden intercourse

should be, though allowed to attend church, denied the sacrament. There survive a number of letters from the leaders of Christian thought urgently dissuading their correspondents from entering the imperial service, which they represent as tantamount to damnation. Some Christian writers denounced the brutality, corruption, and extortion of the imperial administration, but the church, so far from pressing for its reform, urged good Christians to avoid compromising their own salvation by taking any part in it. In this climate of opinion it is little wonder that the persistent efforts of the emperors to check abuses which seriously weakened the empire were always frustrated, for earnest and conscientious men who could have implemented the reforms were discouraged from serving them, and they were left with the less scrupulous members of society. Too many men of character and ability devoted their lives to the church for the good health of the state. Despite his great work as bishop of Milan, one may reasonably doubt whether a man of Ambrose's commanding character and high principles would not have served mankind more effectively had he, following in his father's footsteps, become praetorian prefect.

Another manifestation of the otherworldly ascetic spirit, celibacy, must have adversely affected the empire's manpower, which was one of its weakest points. The vogue for celibacy was immense, and affected not only professed monks and nuns and hermits. It was enforced with increasing strictness from the latter years of the fourth century on the clergy, more especially in the west under pressure from the Roman see, and it was practiced by many pious persons who did not aspire to the full rigors of monastic life. Celibacy not only reduced the gross total of the population, but may have had a dysgenic effect, since it was on the whole the more serious and conscientious who felt called upon to practice it.

I have dwelt somewhat long on these psychological factors because they have hitherto received too little attention. They help to explain some of the notable weaknesses of the later empire, the combined brutality and inefficiency of the administration, forced to rely, in the absence of any public spirit, on compulsion and regimentation, and the ineradicable corruption of the bureaucracy, as it grew in numbers and was diluted in quality, and came to be shunned by good men. They also help to explain the curious apathy, not to say defeatism, of the population in the face of barbarian invasion and occupation. Occasionally the citizens of a town would rally to defend the walls, but even such last flickerings of civic patriotism were rare. Normally if the imperial army failed to defend them, the population submitted passively; only the least civilized of the provincial communities, those of Britain and Armorica, are recorded to have organized their own defense. In general the provincials had so long been used to rely on the emperor with his professional army to protect them that they could not conceive of defending themselves. And above all they were not interested in preserving the empire; in their eyes the barbarian invasions were calamities sent by God to punish their sins and test their faith, and the duty of good Christians was not to resist but to repent and endure patiently.

The later empire also suffered from serious economic weaknesses. The decay of trade and industry, on which so much stress has been laid by some modern historians, was in my opinion a very minor matter, for even at their most prosperous they contributed a minimal fraction of the national income and of the imperial revenue. The Roman empire was to an overwhelming extent an agricultural state. The vast majority of its population were peasants. The wealthy derived their income almost exclusively from agricultural rents, and the state drew its revenue almost exclusively from taxes assessed on the land and on the agricultural population; from the scanty figures available it would seem that even in the East, where trade and industry still remained in a relatively prosperous condition, agriculture yielded more than twenty times as much revenue in direct taxation as they did when Anastasius finally abolished the only direct tax which fell upon them, the *collatio lustralis*.

It is evident that the cultivated area shrank under the later empire. *Agri deserti,* lands which had once been cultivated and paid tax but were now abandoned, were a constant trouble to the imperial government, which either sought, by temporary tax exemptions, to bring them under the plow again, or, by attaching them to productive land and making the owner of the latter responsible for them, secured that their taxes were paid. On these facts has been built a theory of soil exhaustion. This theory is unlikely to be true, for the problem of *agri deserti* seems to have been no less acute in the recently developed lands of northern Europe, and in Egypt, where the annual flood of the Nile renewed the soil each year, than in the areas where long cultivation might have caused a diminishing return. Moreover it is clear that most of the land continued to yield good profits: the emperors were continually besieged by applicants for grants of land which had in one way or another fallen in to the crown, and it must not be overlooked that the immensely wealthy senators of Rome derived their huge incomes from agricultural rents, that the revenues of the church came mostly from the same source, and the imperial *res privata* consisted of landed property.

It would seem that it was only land of marginal quality that fell out of cultivation, and that the main reason was the high rate of taxation, which was in most parts of the empire crudely assessed on simple categories—olives, vineyard, arable, pasture—without distinction of quality, and sometimes on area alone. In these circumstances landlords often were unable to find tenants who could pay a rent in addition to the taxes on land of inferior quality.

The other main economic problem of the later empire was a shortage of manpower. This evidently made itself felt in almost all the less attractive occupations, and led to the government's attempting—with only partial success—to tie various classes hereditarily to their tasks. The government was naturally mainly concerned with occupations immediately vital to the state—soldiers, lower-grade civil servants, miners, workers in the mints, in the state factories producing arms and uniforms and in the public transport service, and above all peasants, on whose labor the revenue depended. Landlords eagerly welcomed the legislation, which tied their tenants to their estates, and for tenants (*coloni*) it was rigorously maintained, and to a large extent enforced, while for peasant proprietors it fell into desuetude, partly perhaps because proprietors were less liable to leave their holdings than tenants, partly because there was no one with a direct interest in reclaiming fugitive freeholders. The shrinkage in agricultural manpower no doubt contributed to the abandonment of less fertile land; landlords seem always to have been ready to take on tenants from any source—vagrants, often fugitive *coloni* from the estates of others, sometimes urban workers who could find no employment in the decaying towns, or again barbarian prisoners distributed by the government.

A manpower shortage does not necessarily imply a fall in population, for it may be caused by an increase in the demand as well as by a decrease in the supply. There was a heavy demand for manpower in the later empire for the greatly expanded army, and for its ancillary services, the arms and clothing establishments, and for transport. The swollen bureaucracy also absorbed many men, and the Christian clergy produced a new demand, for there had been a few full-time professional pagan priests. The monastic movement, as mentioned above, withdrew many men from the market. Nevertheless it seems probable that the population on which these heavy demands were made was at any rate static, if not dwindling.

War and famine and plague no doubt played their part in producing this result, but the lack of resilience in the population is probably to be accounted for by the same fact as the decreasing area of cultivation— the heavy burden of taxation imposed on the peasantry, who formed the vast bulk of the population, on which was often superimposed the further burden of rent. A number of stories, from different periods and areas, strikingly illustrate the miserable condition to which the peasants were reduced. In bad seasons, we read, they came flocking into the towns for food, and there the granaries of the state and of the rich landlords contained grain with which to feed them. The state and the landlord extracted their dues, by the ruthless methods described in many contemporary sources, whether the crops were good or bad, and if there was not enough left to feed the peasant and his family they starved. The reaction of the peasantry to this treatment was singularly passive. No peasant revolts are recorded save those of the *Bacaudae* in Gaul and Spain, which persisted from the end of the third century till the fall of the empire. More usually peasants sought the protection, for which they had to pay, of some powerful patron, the commander of the local garrison or a great landlord; in the latter case their last state was worse than their first, for the price of protection was their land and often their liberty. But most commonly they had recourse to flight, becoming the vagrants so often alluded to in the Codes as potential recruits for the army or as being employed by landlords short of tenants, or in the last resort joining the bands of brigands which infested the provinces.

It is not surprising that in these miserable circumstances the peasantry did not rear enough children to maintain their numbers. But it may be asked why so heavy an economic burden was laid on them. The short answer to this is simple. The empire supported an excessive number of —economically speaking—idle mouths in relation to the number of producers, taking into account their low level of production. The empire had always had a large *rentier* class, ranging from senators with their vast estates scattered over many provinces to the thousands of more modest landowners who filled the councils of its cities. The area held by this class tended always to increase, as peasant freeholders from time to time fell into difficulties and were forced to mortgage and ultimately part with their land to their creditors. The reverse process of the breakup of great estates seems never to have taken place, for there were always rich buyers ready to snap up any land which came on the market. To private landlords were added in the later empire the churches and the monasteries, which from Constantine's reign onward rapidly built up from gifts and bequests of pious benefactors, great and small, large and ever-increasing endowments in land. The income of the church, it may be noted, at this time consisted almost entirely of agricultural rents, tithe not having been invented, and the offerings of the faithful being a relatively minor item. Monks were normally idle mouths; the Pachomian communities of Egypt, which worked their own land and produced a surplus for charity, were an exception.

In addition to this landlord class, which lived on rents, agriculture, through the land and poll tax, supported a large professional army, greatly increased in numbers if not in effectiveness since the principate, a vastly swollen administrative bureaucracy, the state transport service, whose heavy demands for fodder and remounts were a constant source of anxiety to the government, not to speak of the workers in the state arms factories and weaving and dyeing establishments. The universal corruption of the administration, the countless sinecure offices, the peculation of officials, and the mounting fees and commissions, at first illicit, but gradually recognized by custom, superimposed on the regular taxation, made the burden all the heavier. Despite the periodic efforts of reforming emperors to cut down superfluous expenditure, the burden steadily increased. To Lactantius the rate of taxation imposed by Diocletian seemed intolerable; it was leading, he declared, to a wholesale abandonment of the land. But we have a statement of Themistius that the standard rate had by gradual increases been doubled in the forty years preceding the accession of Valentinian and Valens in 364.

The Roman Empire, we must not forget, was technically more backward than the Middle Ages. In agriculture a two-field system of alternate crops and fallow was usually followed, and the potentially richest soils were little exploited. The horse collar had not been invented, so that oxen had to be employed for plowing and for carting. Water mills existed, but seem to have been relatively rare, and corn was generally ground by animals or by human labor in hand querns. Yet with this primitive technique, agriculture had to carry an ambitious superstructure far heavier than that of any medieval state. No medieval kingdom attempted, as did the Roman Empire, to support, as well as a landed aristocracy and the church, a professional standing army, and a salaried bureaucracy.

## 11 / MANPOWER SHORTAGE IN THE GOVERNMENT SERVICES OF THE ROMAN EMPIRE / A. E. R. BOAK

Next to be considered is the imperial civil service, the employees of which formed a large and important element in the population.[1] Unfortunately,

Reprinted with permission from A. E. R. Boak, *Manpower Shortage and the Decline of the Roman Empire in the West* (Ann Arbor: The University of Michigan Press, 1955), pp. 101-104.

[1] On the civil servants in general, see "Officium," *RE*, Vol. XVII, No. 2, 2045-46.

their total number has not been transmitted in our sources and cannot be estimated even approximately, but it was in no wise comparable to that of the armed forces. The civil service included the personnel, administrative and clerical, of the central government bureaus, the agents of these bureaus throughout the provinces, and also the office staffs of the provincial governors. As a class the civil servants enjoyed a highly favored position among the inhabitants of the empire. They were exempt from military service, enjoyed regular pay, perquisites, and promotion, and upon retirement after twenty-five years of service they received various titles, honors, and immunities. Theirs was a safe and regular career, in many respects the most peaceful and secure that one could follow in the days of the Late Empire. The only drawback was that, because their rate of pay was not sufficiently high, many of them were forced to resort to making use of their official position to practice extortion upon those whom they could oppress with impunity. In fact, as time went on, the civil service became more and more a highly desired haven of refuge for those who sought to escape from the hopelessness of the hereditary careers of the *curiales, corporati,* and *coloni.* Needless to say, the government took vigorous steps to block the admission of these deserters to any of the government offices and to recover for their landlords or corporate bodies those who managed by one means or another to worm their way into an official position. Under these conditions one would not expect the government to be faced with a shortage of personnel in its civil service bureaus, unless there was a serious numerical deficiency in those elements of the population which were legally eligible for admission to these offices. And yet, from the early fourth century at least, the sons of all civil servants were bound to enter their fathers' offices, and not merely the civil service in general. This obligation is stated clearly in laws of 329 and 331, but had been created by an earlier enactment of unknown date which is referred to in the law of 329.[2] Once entered on the roll of a government office, the employee was bound to remain in it until he had completed his term of service.[3] Although these regulations applied to all bureaus in the civil administration, they were aimed in particular at the so-called

[2] *Cod. Theod.* xii, I, 18, Section I (329); vii, 22, 3 (331). According to the former of these enactments, if a son reached age thirty-five and still refused to enter his father's office, he was to be assigned to a municipal *curia* as were the sons of veterans who were physically unfit for military service. Other laws implying the hereditary obligation are *Cod. Theod.* viii, 7, 3 (349); 15 (381); 19 (397); and *Nov. Theod.* vii, 2, 2 (447). The obligation probably goes back to Diocletian.

[3] See the laws cited in n. 1. Twenty years was the regular minimum length of service, cf. *RE*, Vol. XXI, No. 2, 2051.

*cohortales,* the employees in the lower-ranking offices, such as those of the provincial governors, who were excluded from admission to the more highly paid and honored staffs of the great palace officials. Far from suffering from a dearth of applicants for vacancies, these offices had long lists of supernumeraries eagerly awaiting to be enrolled.[4] Nevertheless, in spite of these exceptions this brief survey of the imperial civil service reveals that a shortage of available manpower was felt at least from the early fourth century and possibly from the late third. This led to the treatment of the civil servants in a manner paralleling that of soldiers serving in the armed forces.

More significant in this connection is the condition of the third class of government servants, those who were employed in the government factories of various kinds and in other undertakings which concerned state-directed production. These were the minters' (*monetarii*), the coin circulators (*collectarii* or *numularii*), the armorers (*fabricenses*), workers in the silk factories (*gynaeciarii*), weavers and garment makers in the shops which produced clothing of other materials (*linteones, linearii, linyficii, textores*), collectors of shellfish which furnished purple dye and those who made dyes therefrom (*murileguli, conchylileguli*), and workers in the government mines (*metallarii*). Along with these, I propose to consider certain employees of the government post and transport services (*bastagarii*).

The minters were the employees attached to the government mints, of which there were six in the western part of the empire: at Rome, Aquileia, Siscia, Lugdunum, Arles, and Treves.[5] In the Early Empire the important mint at Rome had been manned by imperial slaves and freedmen, but by the time of the Late Empire the minters were all free persons, some of whom even attained the property qualification of the class of *curiales.* Those employed in each mint formed a single guild or corporation. By 317 their duties were both obligatory and hereditary, and probably they had become so at a considerably earlier date.[6] With respect to the coin circulators, it is known that in the fourth and fifth centuries in Rome they formed a corporation subject to the city prefect. At Constantinople there was a similar corporation, but they are not heard of elsewhere. Their service was obligatory and their condition

---

[4] *RE,* Vol. XVII, No. 2, 2050.

[5] *Not. Dign. Occ.* xi, 38-44. For the minters, see Waltzing, *Étude historique sur les corporations professionelles chez les Romains,* II, 229-30.

[6] *Cod. Theod.* x, 20, I, which seems to imply that their status was already well established. Also *ibid.,* 20, 10 (380); 16 (428).

hereditary.[7] The date when these regulations were imposed is not known, but it is at least reasonable to think that it corresponds to the time when duties of the minters became obligatory.

In the Late Empire the government exercised a monopoly of the manufacture of the type of clothing that was reserved for the emperor and his house. Such were silk garments dyed purple or woven with gold threads or having gold borders.[8] In addition, the government maintained factories for the production of linen clothes which were supplied to the army. Both silk works and linen factories were found in the West. Seventeen of the former and two of the latter are known to have existed.[9] For the most part, they seem to have been operated by free labor, although there were also groups of slave workers among the employees.[10] The free *gynaeciarii* and *linteones* were organized in hereditary colleges from which they were not permitted to withdraw.[11] Here again, the date at which their condition became legally fixed is unknown. As in the case of the minters, the properties of the free garment workers had to be used for the maintenance of their trade and could not be transferred from the service of the corporation to which they belonged.[12] Once more the government policy indicates a dearth of skilled craftsmen available for what were regarded as essential occupations.

## 12 / SOCIAL STRUCTURE AND ECONOMY IN THE ROMAN EMPIRE / *F. W. WALBANK*

Government at Rome throughout the period of the republic was in the hands of an aristocratic clique whose wealth was derived from land and

[7] For Rome, Symmachus *Rel.* 29 (384/385); *Nov. Val.* iii, tit. 14, p. I (445). For Constantinople, *Cod. Theod.* xvi, 4, 5, Section I (404). In general, see Waltzing, *op. cit.*, pp. 230-32; V. Premerstein, "Collectarii," *RE*, Vol. IV, 376-77, who points out that they may have operated in all large cities.

[8] On the imperial silk monopoly, see R. Lopez, "Silk Industry in the Byzantine Empire," *Speculum*, Vol. XX (1945), 1-42, particularly pp. 1-4, 10.

[9] *Not. Dign. Occ.* xi, 45-60, 62-63. For the operatives in these factories, see Waltzing, *op. cit.*, pp. 232-34; Hug, "Lintearius," *RE*, Vol. XIII, 717 (collection of references only).

[10] *Cod. Theod.* x, 20, 2 (357); 3 (365); 9 (380).

[11] *Ibid.*, 6 (372); also I, 5 of the same year, 8 (374).

[12] *Ibid.*, 16 (426). Even if an individual was released from this service as a special favor upon the condition that he find a suitable substitute, he had to allow his estate to remain at the disposal of his corporation, and his family remained bound to the hereditary occupation.

Reprinted with permission from F. W. Walbank, *Decline of the Roman Empire in the West* (London: Cobett Press, 1946), pp. 25-27, 40-45.

which had debarred itself from commerce by a self-denying ordinance. This caste was the natural opponent of any economic improvement which challenged its own position. After the conquest of Macedonia in 168 BC, it closed down the Macedonian mines lest they should strengthen the commercial elements which would have worked them; and once current needs could be met from the Spanish mines, the senate practically stopped mining in Italy: "This maintained Senatorial authority beyond challenge, but it also checked the economic expansion which might have restored the balance in the country." [1]

It was this landed class which peopled the countryside of Italy and Sicily with the slave gangs which later threatened Rome's very existence in the revolt of Spartacus (73-71 BC). Meanwhile the towns and cities were filling up with eastern slaves, who not only undertook all kinds of manual work, but also acted as teachers, doctors, architects, and professional men. The consequence was that socially these activities were ill thought of. "The meaner sort of mechanic has a special and separate slavery," wrote Aristotle (*Politics*, I. 13. 13 1260*a*); and similarly the Romans despised the free artisan as one doing work proper to a slave. Thus the atmosphere was wholly unfavorable to technical progress in a field for which anyone of any consequence had nothing but contempt. When labor is cheap and worthless, why conserve it? So the classical world perpetuated that technical retardation which had been one of the most paradoxical features of the civilizations of the Nile and Euphrates—paradoxical because it was thanks to a unique crop of technical inventions—the plow, the wheeled cart, the sailing boat, the solar calendar, the smelting of copper ores, the use of the power of oxen and the harnessing of the winds with sails—that these civilizations had come into being. In both instances the cause of retardation was the same—the bisection of society into classes with contrary interests.

Economically, this division of society insured that the vast masses of the empire never tasted the fruits of their labor; and this meant a permanently restricted internal market. Because wealth was concentrated at the top, the body of society suffered from chronic underconsumption. Accordingly industry had to seek its market either in the limited circle of the middle and upper class, together with the army (which therefore had considerable economic significance), or else outside the empire, where of course there were even fewer markets for mass-produced goods. Consequently, the economic basis for industrialization was not to hand. The expansion of the empire brought new markets, which staved off the problem for a time; but, as we shall see, the effects of this expansion

[1] A. H. McDonald, *The Rise of Roman Imperialism* (Sydney, 1940), p. 12.

were soon cancelled out by the decentralization of production and were never radical enough to carry a large-scale industry, using all the resources of advanced technique and advanced forms of power.

On the other hand, because of the social structure, Greece and Rome never even considered the possibility of catering for the proletariat and peasantry, and so creating a deeper, instead of a wider, market. What expansion the empire brought proves on closer examination to be "a matter of greater extension, not of greater depth." The *pax Augusta* removed many handicaps and much wastage; goods circulated with greater ease and over wider areas. But there was no qualitative change in the nature of classical economy. In one field alone were there notable technical achievements—in that of building and engineering, where the Hellenistic age had already given a lead, under the stimulus of interstate warfare; but even here the Romans were concerned with the amplifying and application of old processes rather than with the creation of new. Thus, behind the rosy hues of Gibbon's picture of a prosperous Antonine world, we are now in a position to detect at least one fatal weakness—the complete stagnation of technique. . . .

The contraction of the population and the shrinkage of resources were not, unfortunately, accompanied by a decline in the cost of imperial administration. An empire stretching from Northumberland to the Euphrates, from the Carpathians to the Sahara, could not reduce its expenses below a certain minimum. Governors had to be sent out, taxes collected, frontiers garrisoned; the empire had to be policed, its waters swept clear of pirates, roads kept in order, the imperial post maintained. Of the vast network of cities which were the guardians of ancient culture, each had its own local problems of municipal administration, its council of *decuriones,* with a certain prestige to maintain in the provision of appropriate buildings, festivals, and benefactions; and the upholding of the Roman standard of culture demanded throughout this wide area an adequate supply of the amenities of civilized life—baths, gymnasia, theaters, amphitheaters, wrestling schools, aqueducts, town halls, ceremonial arches, elaborate tombs, triumphal columns, marketplaces, colonnades, and temples—all of them considered essential to the full life of a Roman citizen. Finally the costs of the court, with its luxuries and its grants of "bread and circuses" to the pampered metropolis, were by no means a negligible item of the imperial budget.

The empire possessed no larger resources to meet this heavy bill in a time of contraction. Indeed, private indebtedness was so widespread as to be a damper on economic enterprise, and in AD 118 Hadrian agreed to wipe off a bad debt to the treasury of some £7 million sterling, and subsequently remitted many sums outstanding for rent. But when the citizens of the empire could not pay, remission of debts was clearly no permanent solution! The problem was quite simply to make sixpence do the work of a shilling; and the whole question of finance became cardinal from the second century onward. Sooner or later taxpayers must be compelled to find what the state demanded, which, in turn, implied that the state must be strengthened, since it must, in its new role of extortioner, become increasingly the enemy of the ordinary man. Hence the growth of the bureaucracy and of those features of administration which we regard today as characteristic of the "police-state." It is a melancholy reflection that the emperors were led to extract by force from their subjects the revenues that in the hardier days of the republic had been provided by the plunder of foreign war; and that the counterpart of the *pax Romana* was legalized extortion.

Both Trajan and Hadrian are reckoned among the "five good emperors." Personally their characters left little ground for criticism; they had the good of the empire at heart and they labored unceasingly on its behalf. To Pausanias, who lived under his two successors, Hadrian was the ruler "who gave the utmost to all for the happiness of the world." Yet it is under precisely these two emperors that the first ugly signs of bureaucratic tyranny appear:

> Self-government was restricted by Trajan (anticipated to some extent by Nerva) so that the control of city finances might give the state greater opportunities of making inroads on their funds. Compulsory state leases, and compulsory recruiting for the lower and middle grades of local officials, reached an advanced stage during his reign.[2]

In the correspondence between Trajan and Pliny, his deputy in Bithynia, we have the first reference (in AD 113) to those *qui inviti fiunt decuriones* —those who serve on the town councils under compulsion (Pliny, *Epist.* X. 113).

It is under Hadrian, however, that a more odious phenomenon appears—the secret police and informers, who evolved out of the commissariat officials known as *frumentarii*. From Hadrian's time onward, this ancient Gestapo functioned uninterruptedly until its modification by Diocletian; and the fact that it was an emperor so enlightened as Hadrian who introduced it shows the inevitability of the development.

The financial crisis, which Hadrian's swift reversal of Trajan's policy of expansion succeeded temporarily in staving off, continued to develop beneath the surface; and naturally it was reflected in the currency. We have already mentioned the excellent gold *aurei* which were minted

[2] F. Oertel in *Cambridge Ancient History*, XII, p. 259.

from Caesar's time onward. Augustus stabilized the relationship between the gold *aureus* and the older silver *denarius* at 25:1, which represented a gold:silver ratio of about 12:1. But under the strain of the foreign demand, and the constant flow of currency eastward in consequence of the unfavorable trade balance, Nero (AD 54-68) was driven to contaminate the *denarius* with base metal and to reduce both coins by clipping. As a result of this measure, the *denarius* now ceased to circulate in India, and the whole of the debt to this area had to be paid in gold; and though the *denarius* continued to be accepted in Germany, its weight and quality both fell constantly until the time of Commodus (AD 180-193), when, as we shall see, the inflation became catastrophic. Meanwhile, immense damage was done to the credit system, and so directly to any trading ventures relying upon it. A document of AD 260 from Egypt records a local bank strike when, at a predetermined moment, all the banks in Oxyrhyncus refused pointblank to accept the bad money issued by the imperial government. It is hard to imagine a more damning indictment of a financial system which still professed to support an internationally based economy.

The crisis in the financial structure was accompanied by increased pressure upon the bourgeoisie throughout the empire. Municipal office, which it had once been an honor to undertake, was transformed into an overwhelming burden imposed by force upon the richer families in the towns. An Egyptian papyrus of AD 250 tells of a certain Aurelius Hermophilus of Hermopolis who, after holding the municipal office of *Kosmetes* at great personal expense, is now trying to obtain his son's release from a similar "honor" by offering the authorities the whole of his property; he is arrested by the town council for his pains. From the time of Diocletian (AD 284-305) and Constantine (AD 306-337) municipal office is the duty of a hereditary caste of *curiales*, who have lost most of their old functions to imperial officials, but are held jointly responsible for the collection of taxes and for provisioning the town. In these conditions there could be no civic sense: but equally there was no escape. Severe penalties were laid down for *curiales* who sought to abandon their property, take holy orders, enter the army, fly to join the anchorites in the desert, or in any other way avoid their prescribed duties. Under Maxentius (AD 306-312) we read of Christians, and under Honorius (AD 393-423) of apostate Christians being punished by compulsory enrollment in the *curiales*. Under Justinian (AD 527-565) the same penalty is invoked against Jews, heretics, and clerics repeatedly convicted of dicing!

It is hardly strange that these conditions led to a decline in both the quality and the extent of urban civilization. Alongside the growth of the large estates went the shrinkage of the towns. After AD 275 Autun had shrunk from nearly five hundred to less than twenty-five acres; indeed hardly any city in France after AD 300 exceeded sixty acres. Bordeaux was down from one hundred seventy-five acres to fifty-six, Nantes, Rouen, and Troyes to thirty-nine. Britain tells the same story; at Verulamium (St. Alban's) the town walls fell into ruin and the theater ceased to be used; and much of Wroxeter was burnt and never rebuilt. Nor was the picture very different in other parts of the empire. The raids of barbarians into the Balkan peninsula during the third century AD reduced its towns to a plight even worse than those of Gaul; and in the safe province of Egypt it is estimated that by AD 260 Alexandria had lost some 60 per cent of her former population.

The most typical institution of ancient civilization, the city, was in decay. The middle class of the towns, who had carried Greek and Roman culture to the Tyne and the Indus, to the Tagus and the Dnieper; who had peopled the steppes of Bactria and the river valleys of France with a constellation of cities, each a replica of the older cities of Greece and Italy, each, let us in fairness admit, a hive of industry and useful activity as well as a center exploiting the lower classes and the peasants of the surrounding countryside; the urban middle class who, for all their faults (and they were many), had been the instrument of nearly everything that we value most today in classical civilization—the Attic drama, the histories of Herodotus, Thucydides, and Polybius, the sculptures and the temples of Greece, the first eager groping after scientific concepts, the speculations (magnificent even when most perverse) of Plato, Aristotle, and Epicurus, the verse of Catullus and Virgil, the noble crusade of Lucretius, the satire of Tacitus and Juvenal, the triumphs of Roman architecture, and the majestic structure of Roman Law—were now in precipitate retreat before the demands of their own creature, the imperial state.

## 13 / THE BYZANTINE ADMINISTRATION / C. DIEHL

### Central Government

Rarely has any administration been more strongly centralized or more ably run than that of Byzantium. In the capital, grouped about the head of the state, ministers and heads of departments directed the government and transmitted the emperor's decrees throughout the empire. The *Logothete* of the *Dromus* (this word, which basically means "running," here signifies transport and communications) was a most important figure, as he combined the offices of high chancellor of the empire, min-

Reprinted with permission from C. Diehl, *Byzantium: Greatness and Decline* (New Brunswick, N.J.: Rutgers University Press, 1957), pp. 66-68.

ister of police and the interior, and secretary of state for foreign affairs. He was later known simply as the Grand *Logothete*. There was the *Logothete* of the Treasury, or finance minister; the *Logothete* of the Military Chest, or army paymaster, and the *Logothete* of Flocks and Herds, who administered the emperor's studs and crown estates. There was the *Sacellarius*, a kind of comptroller-general; the *Quaestor*, or minister of justice; the Grand *Domestic*, commander-in-chief of the army; and the Great *Drungarius*, minister of the navy. In addition to these there was the *Eparch*, the prefect of Constantinople, a great personage whose task was to maintain order in the capital.

The majority of these dignitaries had seats in the senate: a sort of council of state which assisted the emperor. It was small and had nothing in common with the senate of ancient Rome, though it retained certain traditional constitutional privileges—perhaps more theoretical than real —and might, under a weak sovereign or one still a minor, invoke its former rights. The συγκλητος βουλή, as it was called, could intervene in political and religious matters; but the officials of which it was composed were meek servants and rarely ventured to oppose their master's will.

On a lower level were countless offices, known in the sixth century as *scrinia,* and later as *logothesia* or *secreta.* Just as Rome in the old days had ruled the world by the strength of its bureaucracy, so Byzantium owed its firm and integrated government to this crowd of obscure σεκσετικοί who formed the staff of the imperial chancellery and the ministries. Theirs was the task of examining matters of detail, formulating decrees and making them universally known. At certain periods this bureaucracy was powerful enough to direct the general policy of the empire.

### Provincial Government

Each province was ruled by a governor or *Strategus,* nominated by the emperor and in direct communication with him. This high officer had authority over both local troops and local government; he also administered justice and controlled finance. Within his own district he was vice-emperor, and more than one *Strategus* was tempted—at least in earlier times, when *themes* were fewer and larger—to abuse his power. For this reason the central government placed beside him, though in a subordinate capacity, a representative of the civil interest: the *Protonotary* and judge of the *theme.* He, too, had the right to correspond directly with the emperor, and was concerned chiefly with justice and finance. Nevertheless it was the military leader who was in command, and it is a fact worth noting that at every level of the administration, soldiers took precedence over civilians and exercised more real power. It was by virtue of this principle that Byzantium, for all its Roman descent, developed into a medieval state.

## Administrative Centralization

The staff, from top to bottom of the administrative ladder, was directly dependent on the emperor. It was he who nominated, promoted, and dismissed the highest officials in government employ, and conferred upon them the emblems of office. Their titles (*Magister, Proconsul, Patrician, Protospatharius, Spatherocandidatus, Spatharius,* and so on) formed the various grades of a kind of administrative aristocracy by which the hierarchy of Byzantine society was rigidly fixed. In Byzantium, every official bore two titles, one honorary, marking his rank in the administrative nobility, the other indicating the actual office with which he had been invested; and between office and rank there was a fixed relationship. (In this, as in many other respects, Imperial Russia based its administrative and social order on that of Byzantium.)

It was usually from among the great families, those known as the συγκλητικοί, that the empire recruited its highest functionaries. Moreover, in order to insure the supply of competent, experienced men for the public service, the imperial government provided special institutions where they might be trained. Such were the law schools founded by Justinian in Constantinople, Rome, and Beirut, and the law school reorganized in the capital in the middle of the eleventh century. These produced a corps of well-trained, disciplined, and devoted civil servants whose zeal was fanned throughout their careers by the hope of greater rewards and of promotion to a higher rung of the administrative and social ladder. Such promotions were entirely at the discretion of the emperor; and though too often this made for intrigue and favoritism (there are instances of scandalously rapid advancement), more often it was an encouragement to efficient service. Moreover the central power kept a close watch on the activities of executive officers. The emperor left them in no doubt of the dire consequences of failure or neglect of duty; he also encouraged his subjects to lay complaints against those in authority before the imperial tribunal; he urged bishops to watch the conduct of officials and denounce their faults; and he despatched special investigators to tour the provinces, examine accounts, invite petitions, and impose sanctions. No other administration, it seems, was more completely under the control of one master.

## 14 / SOCIAL STRUCTURE AND ECONOMIC POLICIES IN THE BYZANTINE EMPIRE / *PETER CHARANIS*

From the very beginning of its history, the large estate had been a feature of Byzantine society. The complicated and burdensome fiscal administration affected by the reorganization of the empire following the political and economic crisis of the third century worked in such a way as to give impetus to the growth of the large estates. The society revealed by the papyri and the great legislative monuments of the fifth and the sixth centuries is a society dominated by these estates. *Coloni,* reduced to serfs, composed the vast majority of the agrarian population, although the free peasant proprietors did not disappear completely. The development of the soldiery-peasantry in the seventh century lessened the extent of the large estates, but did not eliminate them. By the end of the ninth century they had become larger and more numerous. Those who possessed them occupied important positions in the administration and used these positions to increase their holdings. This they did by absorbing, often through dubious means, the properties of the small peasants. Thus the small, free peasant proprietors began to disappear.[1]

The great emperors of the tenth century realized the dangerous social and political implications of this development and tried to check it. Every major emperor from Romanus Lecapenus to and including Basil II, with the exception of John Tzimeskes, issued more than one novel for this purpose. These emperors sought to preserve the free peasantry because they considered it an essential element for the health of the state. As Romanus Lecapenus put it in one of his novels:

> It is not through hatred and envy of the rich that we take these measures, but for the protection of the small and the safety of the empire as a whole. . . . The extention of the power of the strong . . . will bring about the irreparable loss of the public good, if the present law does not bring a check

Reprinted with permission from Peter Charanis, "Economic Factors in the Decline of the Byzantine Empire," *Journal of Economic History,* 13 (1953), 415-23.

[1] For the essential bibliography see Charanis, "On the Social Structure and Economic Organization of the Byzantine Empire in the Thirteenth Century and Later," *Byzantinoslavica,* Vol. XII (1951), 94, n. 2. To the works listed there the following should be added: D. A. Zakythinos, "Crise monétaire et crise économique à Byzance du XIIIᵉ au XVᵉ siècle," *L'Hellénisme contemporain* (1948), pp. 50 f.; E. E. Lipsic, *Byzanz und die Slaven. Beiträge zur byzantinischen Geschichte des 6-9. Jahrhunderts,* trans. from the Russian by E. Langer (Weimar: Hermann Böhlaus Nachfolger, 1951), pp. 5-105; Zakythinos, "La Société dans le despotat de Morée," *L'Hellénisme contemporain* (1951), pp. 7-28; Zakythinos, "Étatisme byzantine et expérience hellénistique," *Annuaire de L'Institut de Philologie et d'Histoire Orientale et Slave. Tome X: Mélanges Henri Grégoire,* II (1950), 667-80.

to it. For it is the many, settled on the land, who provide for the general needs, who pay the taxes and furnish the army with its recruits. Everything falls when the many are wanting.[2]

The strictest among the measures taken for the protection of the free peasantry was that issued by Basil II concerning the *allelengyon,* a measure which required the landed aristocracy to pay the tax arrears of peasants too poor to meet their own obligations. But, with the death of Basil (1025), the effort to stop the growth of the large estates came to an end. His law concerning the *allelengyon* was repealed and the other measures, although kept in the books, were not enforced. The fate of the free peasantry was definitely decided.

Meanwhile, a similar fate befell the class of the enrolled soldiers, holders of the military estates. For the aristocracy, which, by one means or another, absorbed the estates of the small peasants, absorbed also those of the soldiers. The protection of the interests of these soldiers had been one of the deepest concerns of the emperors of the tenth century. Wrote Constantine Porphyrogenitus in the novel that he issued for the protection of the estates of the soldiers:

> The army is to the state what the head is to the body. . . . He who neglects it neglects the safety of the state. . . . Therefore in promulgating our constitution [on the military estates], we feel we are working for the welfare of all.[3]

But in this, as in the case of the small peasants, the measures taken by the emperors of the tenth century were of no avail. It proved impossible to stop the aristocracy from absorbing the properties of the small, whether the latter were soldiers or not.

What consummated the depression of the enrolled soldiers, however, was the antimilitary policy which some of the emperors of the eleventh century followed in order to reduce the power of the military magnates in the administration of the empire. Those who occupied the high military posts in the empire were also great landholders. Their wealth, plus the powers which they exercised as military commanders, made them extremely dangerous to the central government. This danger, indeed, was one of the principal reasons why Basil II issued the novel concerning the *allelengyon* to which reference has already been made. He had faced two formidable revolts, both headed by members of the powerful aristocracy, and it was only with difficulty that he survived. When, after 987, Basil

---

[2] Zachariae von Lingenthal (ed.), *Jus-Graeco-Romanum,* Vol. III (Leipzig, 1857), pp. 246-47. On the efforts of the emperor to check the growth of ecclesiastical properties see Charanis, "The Monastic Properties and the State in the Byzantine Empire," *Dumbarton Oaks Papers,* Vol. IV (1948), pp. 53-64.

[3] von Lingenthal, *op. cit.,* Vol. III, pp. 262 ff.

was reconciled with Bardas Skleros, one of the powerful rebels, the latter advised him that, if he wished to preserve the imperial authority, he should permit no one of the aristocracy to prosper and should exhaust their means by heavy taxes.[4] Hence, the various measures he took, including that of the *allelengyon,* were designed not only to protect the poor peasants but also to crush the aristocracy. But on both the question of land and that of taxation the aristocracy triumphed.

One of the important reasons for the triumph of the aristocracy was the very strong hold that it had upon the military organization of the empire. If it could be shaken from this hold, it would lose in power and influence and would become more amenable to the wishes of the imperial government. And this is precisely what certain emperors of the eleventh century, notably Constantine IX Monomachos (1042-1055), Michael VI (1056-1057), and Constantine X Dukas (1059-1067), tried to do. The means of attack which they employed was to weaken the military organization by reducing the size of the army, thus depriving the aristocracy of its military commands. The great military triumphs of the tenth century, the crushing of the Saracens and the Bulgarians and the pushing of the frontiers to the Euphrates and the Tigris in the east and to the Danube in the Balkans, created a sense of security and the feeling that the maintenance of a powerful army was no longer necessary. With Constantine IX, peace became the keynote of the imperial foreign policy, and there began a systematic elimination of the aristocracy from the army while at the same time the development of a civil bureaucracy was promoted. But the aristocracy fought back, and a new struggle ensued, this time between the aristocracy as a military class and a new party of civil officials who came to dominate the imperial court.

The struggle plunged the empire into a series of civil wars that squandered its resources and manpower at a time when new and formidable enemies were making their appearance, both in the East and in the West. But the most serious result of the imperial policy was the deterioration of the army and the depression of the enrolled soldiers. By the time of Constantine X Dukas, the profession of the soldier had lost much of its attraction and so, as a Byzantine historian puts it, "the soldiers put aside their arms and became lawyers or jurists." [5] The same author, writing of the army that took the field in one of the expeditions against the Seljuks, states:

[4] M. Psellus, *Chronographie,* ed. and trans. into French by E. Renauld (Paris: "Les Belles Lettres," 1926), pp. 1-17. English trans. E. R. A. Sewter, *The Chronographia of Michael Psellus* (London: Routledge & Kegan Paul, 1953), p. 23.

[5] Cedrenus, *Historiarum Compendium,* Vol. II (Bonn, 1839), p. 652.

The army was composed of Macedonians and Bulgarians and Varangians and other barbarians who happened to be about. There were gathered also those who were in Phrygia [the *theme* Anatolikon]. And what one saw in them [the enrolled soldiers of the *theme* Anatolikon] was something incredible. The renowned champions of the Romans who had reduced into subjection all of the East and the West now numbered only a few and these were bowed down by poverty and ill treatment. They lacked in weapons, swords, and other arms, such as javelins and scythes. . . . They lacked also in cavalry and other equipment, for the emperor had not taken the field for a long time. For this reason they were regarded as useless and unnecessary and their wages and maintenance were reduced.[6]

The enrolled soldiers, depressed and forgotten, became more and more a minor element in the Byzantine army. The bulk of this army, in the eleventh century and later, came to be composed almost entirely of foreign mercenaries—Russians, Turks, Alans, English, Normans, Germans, Patzinaks, Bulgarians, and others. These mercenaries were swayed more by their own interests than by those of the empire.

Meanwhile, the development of two institutions, the *pronoia* and the *exkuseia,* added further to the wealth and power of the landed aristocracy, both lay and ecclesiastic. The *pronoia*[7] was the principal means that the emperors of the second half of the eleventh century, but especially later, adopted to recuperate much of the deserted land, to reconstitute the class of soldiers with landed interests, and to reward many of their partisans. A *pronoia* was granted to an individual for a specific period of years, usually his lifetime, in return for military or other services rendered or to be rendered. It was never hereditary, unless it was specifically declared so by a special measure. It consisted usually of land, but it could be a river or a fishery. Some of the *pronoiae* were very extensive, others less so, but the general effect of all was to increase the power and influence of the aristocracy and to lessen the hold of the central government over the agrarian population. For the holder of a *pronoia* exercised over those who inhabited it important financial and judicial powers which were granted to him along with the land. He was expected

[6] *Ibid.,* Vol. II, p. 668.

[7] For the essential bibliography on the Byzantine *pronoia* see Charanis, "On the Social Structure and Economic Organization of the Byzantine Empire in the Thirteenth Century and Later," *Byzantino-slavica, op. cit.,* p. 97, n. 11. To the works listed there should be added the important work by G. Ostrogorsky, *Pronoia, A Contribution to the History of Feudalism in Byzantium and in South-Slavic Lands,* Vol. I (Belgrade: Serbian Academy of Science, Special Editions, CLXXVI, Byzantine Institute, 1951). Unfortunately Ostrogorsky chose to write this book in Serbian. However we have now a lengthy summary of it in English: Ihor Ševčenko, "An Important Contribution to the Social History of Late Byzantium," *The Annals of the Ukrainian Academy of Arts and Sciences in the United States,* Vol. II (1952), 448-59.

to serve in the army and also to furnish troops according to the size of his *pronoia*. But when we first meet with the *pronoia* in the second half of the eleventh century, it was not primarily a military grant; it became so during the reign of Alexius Comnenus and those of his successors. The *pronoia* differed from the old military estate in that it was held by persons high in the social order, whereas the recipients of the latter were peasant soldiers. In a study which I devoted to the aristocracy of Byzantium in the thirteenth century, I showed that many of the holders of *pronoiae* belonged to the great families of the empire, families that were related to each other and to the ruling dynasty.[8] The extensive use of the *pronoia* contributed not only to the increase, relatively speaking, of the power and wealth of the aristocracy, but also to the development of the appanage system and thus weakened the central administration.

The central administration was weakened also by the development of the *exkuseia*.[9] The term, which derives no doubt from the Latin *excusatio* (*excusare*), refers to the fiscal and judicial immunities that the imperial government often granted, especially to monasteries. It was formerly thought that the *exkuseia* first appeared in the eleventh century, but it is now known to be older than that,[10] and may have developed out of the various privileges granted to the Christian clergy in the fourth century. Its use on a wide scale, however, is associated with the eleventh century and later. As the monastic properties during this period were very extensive, the revenue that the imperial government lost by the grant of *exkuseiae* must have been considerable. At the same time, the *exkuseia* contributed to increasing the wealth of members of the lay aristocracy, for the emperors of the second half of the eleventh century and later often rewarded their partisans by granting to them the revenues of monasteries, such grants being then known as *kharistikia*. And monasteries whose revenues were thus granted often enjoyed the privilege of *exkuseia*.

Thus the failure to enforce the measures that had been issued for the protection of the soldiery-peasantry and the various grants of privileges made to the aristocracy had made the large estates, by the eleventh century, the dominant features of the agrarian landscape of Byzantium. These estates were worked by tenant peasants, the *paroikoi* of the Byzan-

[8] Charanis, "The Aristocracy of Byzantium in the Thirteenth Century," P. R. Coleman-Norton (ed.), *Studies in Roman Economic and Social History in Honor of Allan Chester Johnson* (Princeton, N.J.: Princeton University Press, 1951), pp. 336-55.

[9] For the essential bibliography on the *exkuseia* see Charanis, "The Monastic Properties and the State in the Byzantine Empire," *op. cit.*, p. 65, n. 31.

[10] *Ibid.*, pp. 64-67. For a reference to *exkuseia* in the tenth century, 995, see F. Dölger, *Aus den Schatzkammern des Heiligen Berges. Textband* (Munich: Münchner Verlag [Bisher F. Bruckmann], 1948), p. 155, l. 3.

tine texts, people who were personally free, but who were tied to certain obligations and *corvées* that curtailed their movement. Some free peasant proprietors continued to exist, but they had become hardly distinguishable from the *paroikoi*. Besides working for the lord, the *paroikoi* had allotments of their own for which they paid rent and performed various obligations and from which, after the passage of a number of years, they could not be evicted. These allotments were transmissible from father to son. These tenant peasants, weighed down by the heavy burden of taxation and numerous *corvées*, lost all feeling for the welfare of the state as a whole. It is well known that the peasantry of the interior of Asia Minor offered no resistance to the Seljuk Turks, whose establishment in Asia Minor after Manzikert started the empire on the road to general decline. In the twelfth century the Comneni, by utilizing every resource at their disposal, succeeded in bringing about a partial recovery of the political power of the state, but neither they nor their successors tried to check the economic decay of the agrarian population. In the fourteenth century the deplorable economic conditions of the population were a big factor in the social and political strife that shook the empire and opened the way for the rise of the Ottoman Turks.[11] In the tenth century, as we have pointed out above, Romanus Lecapenus had declared in one of his novels designed to protect the free peasantry that the extension of the power of the strong and the depression of the many would "bring about the irreparable loss of the public good." His prediction had come true. The disappearance of the free peasantry, the increase in the wealth, privileges, and power of the aristocracy, and the consequent depression of the agrarian population constitute, I think, some of the principal factors in the decline of the Byzantine Empire.

But the society of the Byzantine Empire was not purely agrarian. Included in the empire were a number of cities—Constantinople and Thessalonica immediately come to mind—whose role in the economic life of the empire was by no means insignificant. The penury of the sources makes impossible a detailed analysis of the urban economy of Byzantium, but that it was comparatively highly developed there can be no doubt.[12]

[11] On the social upheavals in Byzantium in the fourteenth century see Charanis, "Internal Strife in Byzantium in the Fourteenth Century," *Byzantion*, Vol. XV (1940-41), 203-30.

[12] There is really no systematic and exhaustive study on the commerce and industry of Byzantium. The latest general survey is that by S. Runciman, "Byzantine Trade and Industry," *The Cambridge Economic History of Europe*, Vol. II (Cambridge: Cambridge University Press, 1952). The chapter by R. S. Lopez in the same publication, entitled "The Trade of Medieval Europe: the South," also bears upon the commerce of

What characterized the urban economy of Byzantium during the great days of the empire was its strict regulation by the state. This regulation consisted of two elements: the strict control over foreign commerce[13] and the organization of the domestic trades and professions into private and public guilds supervised by the government.[14] The object of this regulation was both political and economic: political in that the government sought to assure for itself arms and an ample supply of manufactured goods—in the main, luxuries—not only for the imperial household but also for the use of its diplomacy in the form of presents to barbarian chieftains and other princes; economic in that the government sought to keep the great cities well provisioned with the necessities of life, assure the quality of goods, and prevent exorbitant prices. The urban economy was also an important source of revenue. All imports and exports were subject to a 10 per cent duty, and the professions and trades, besides being liable for certain taxes, also performed various liturgies.[15] The precise amount of this revenue, because of the fragmentary nature of the sources, cannot be determined, but it must have been considerable.[16]

The regulation of urban economy was relaxed beginning with the last quarter of the eleventh century. The significant step in this development was taken in 1082 when Alexius Comnenus granted to the Venetians,

---

Byzantium. For the industry and commerce of the Peloponnesus there is now the book by A. Bon, *Le Péloponnèse byzantin jusqu'en 1204* (Paris: Presses Universitaires de France, 1951), pp. 119-53. On the silk industry the important study is by Lopez, "Silk Industry in the Byzantine Empire," *Speculum*, Vol. XX (1945), 1-43.

[13] As an illustration of this one may consult the commercial treaty which the Byzantines concluded in the tenth century with the Russian Prince Igor: S. H. Cross, "The Russian Primary Chronicle," *Harvard Studies and Notes in Philology and Literature*, Vol. XII (1930), 159 ff. A new edition of Cross's translation of this chronicle will soon be published by the Medieval Academy of America.

[14] The fundamental source for the guild organization in Byzantium remains the *Book of the Prefect* of which there is an English translation, A. E. R. Boak, "The Book of the Prefect," *Journal of Economic and Business History*, Vol. I (1929), 600 ff. For the essential bibliography see Charanis, "On the Social Structure and Economic Organization of The Byzantine Empire in the Thirteenth Century and Later," *Byzantino-slavica*, Vol. XII (1951), 149, n. 247.

[15] G. Rouillard, "Les Taxes maritimes et commerciales d'après des actes de Patmos et de Lavra," *Mélanges Charles Diehl*, Vol. I (Paris: Librarie Ernest Leroux, 1930), pp. 277-89; John Danstrup, "Indirect taxation at Byzantium," *Classica et Mediaevalia*, Vol. VIII (1946), 139-67.

[16] For the twelfth century, we are told by the traveler Benjamin of Tudella, the daily revenues of Constantinople amounted to 20,000 nomismata. For the essential bibliography concerning the meaning of this figure and in general about the revenues of Byzantium see Charanis, "Internal Strife in Byzantium during the Fourteenth Century," *op. cit.*, p. 224, n. 62. The nomisma was a gold piece which weighed about 4.50 gr.

in return for their alliance against the Normans of Sicily, various privileges among which the most important was that of trading freely, without the payment of any duty, in virtually all the cities of the empire, including the capital. These privileges, renewed by the emperors of the twelfth century, although not without reluctance,[17] rendered the Venetians virtual masters of the commercial life of the empire. In the thirteenth century, in an effort to lessen the influence of the Venetians, similar privileges were granted to the Genoese (the treaty of Nymphaeum, 1261), but that was the substitution of one exploiter for another. The Italian merchants, whether Genoese or Venetians, became so entrenched in Constantinople that they controlled the economy of that city and determined the price of even the daily necessities. According to the patriarch Athanasius (end of the thirteenth century), the fate of the Romans had completely passed into the hands of the Latins, "who," he complained bitterly to Emperor Andronicus II, "make fun of us and scorn us to the point that, full of overweening conceit, they take the wives of our compatriots as security for the wheat which they deliver to us."[18]

Meanwhile, the guild organization which was such a strong feature of the urban organization of the tenth century had virtually ceased to exist by the end of the thirteenth century. This at least is the impression created by the letters of the patriarch Athanasius which, although not yet published, have been analyzed by two different scholars.[19] The patriarch complained to the emperor that false weights were used, that the wheat was hoarded, was often mixed with chaff or wheat that had rotted, and was sold at exorbitant prices. He urged the emperor to appoint a commissioner to supervise everything that concerned the provisioning of the capital. The emperor (Andronicus II) took cognizance of the complaints and ordered an investigation. He was especially anxious to determine who were those who exercised the trade of baker, how many of them there were, and under what conditions were the ships, which brought the food supplies to Constantinople, sold and bought. Thus, at the end of the thirteenth century it was not officially known who were the bakers in Constantinople and how many of them there were. Nor were they supervised with the view of assuring the quality of and a fair

[17] John Danstrup, "Manuel I's Coup against Genoa and Venice in the Light of Byzantine Commercial Policy," *Classica et Mediaevalia*, Vol. X (1948), 195-219.

[18] See n. 19.

[19] R. Guilland, "La Correspondence inédite d'Athanase, patriarch de Constantinople (1289-1293; 1304-1310)," *Mélanges Charles Diehl*, Vol. I (1930), 121-40; N. Bănescu, "Le Patriarch Athanase I et Andronic II Paléologue. État religieux, politique et social de l'Empire," *Académie Roumaine: Bulletin de la Section Historique*, Vol. I (1942), 35 ff.

price for their produce. Contrast this with what the *Book of the Prefect* says about the bakers as they functioned in the tenth century:

> The bakers shall make their profits according to the amount of grain purchased at the order of the Prefect. They shall purchase the proper amount of grain by the *nomisma* from their assessor. When they have ground it and leavened it, they shall calculate their profit at a *keration* and two *miliarisia* on the *nomisma*.[20] The *keration* will be pure profit, while the two *miliarisia* will go for the support of their workmen, the food of their mill animals, the fuel for the ovens, and the lighting. . . .
>
> Whenever there is an increase or decrease in the supply of grain, the bakers shall go to the Prefect to have the weights of their loaves fixed by the assessor in accordance with the purchase price of grain.[21]

Obviously by the end of the thirteenth century the bakers' guild had completely broken down; there was not even a semblance of governmental control over the baker's trade. And what was true of this trade was probably also true of the others. The only indication of a trade organization in the fourteenth century was that of the mariners of Thessalonica. It has been suggested that this guild was organized by the mariners themselves in order to protect their interests, but more probably it was a continuation of an older organization which became more or less autonomous as the power of the central government declined in the fourteenth century. The guild of the mariners took the leadership in the terrible social upheaval that shook Thessalonica in 1345 and resulted in the slaughter of about one hundred members of the aristocracy.[22]

## 15 / THE TRADITIONAL CHINESE CENSORATE AND THE NEW PEKING REGIME

*CHARLES O. HUCKER*

The "People's Government" at Peking, which has been functioning since October 1949, under the sponsorship of the Chinese Communist Party,

[20] Subdivision of Byzantine money was as follows:

    1 pound of gold = 72 nomismata
    1 nomisma = 12 miliarisia = 24 keratia = 288 folleis

See further G. Ostrogorsky, "Die ländliche Steurgemeinde des byzantinischen Reiches im X Jahrhundert," *Vierteljahrschrift für Sozial-und-Wirtschaftsgeschichte,* Vol. XX (1927), 63.

[21] I have used Boak's translation, pp. 616-17.

[22] On this see Charanis, "Internal Strife in Byzantium in the Fourteenth Century," *op. cit.,* pp. 211 ff.

Reprinted with permission from Charles O. Hucker, "The Traditional Chinese Censorate and the New Peking Regime," *American Political Science Review,* 45: No. 4 (1951), 1042-52.

includes a system of disciplinary surveillance over government personnel that in several aspects is reminiscent of one of the world's most remarkable institutions. This is the Chinese Censorate, traditionally a highly systematized organ of administrative and political control that was an integral, and usually a prominent, part of China's governmental structure for more than two thousand years.

The new control system in China bears only a partial resemblance to the old. It is even possible that China's censorial heritage may not have had any part in shaping its development. However, since that heritage may conceivably channel its future development in directions that would be unforeseeable and unexplainable in any other context, it would appear to be desirable to take a fresh look at this long-lived institution. Aside from prospects of future influence, the Censorate, as a unique and, in its setting, a durable solution to the universal and ever-present problem of control in government, has intrinsic significance for students of political science.

What is happening now may prove to be the greatest change yet to occur in China's censorial history, but it is by no means the first. Through its long and almost uninterrupted existence,[1] the Censorate underwent successive developments in organization and prescribed functions, as well as numerous fluctuations in the scope and influence of its actual activities. Since it can be said of no period that the Censorate had then arrived at a typical status, it is difficult, if not impossible, to make accurate generalizations about its true nature, its power, its effectiveness, or its importance. Yet it is possible to point out in general that the Censorate provided a service in Chinese government that has no institutionalized counterpart in any modern Western nation. This service was not censorship, as of the press or the theater, like that exercised by many other governments. It was not primarily control of thought among the people of the state. Rather, it was usually and characteristically surveillance over governmental activities and exposure of violations of law and derelictions of duty by government personnel, with the intent both to purge the administration of incompetence, arbitrariness, and malfeasance and to stimulate the implementation of prevailing political doctrine. Many familiar aspects of government in the West have elements in common with this system, but the West has never developed the specialization and institutionalization of control techniques that are the preeminent characteristics of the Chinese Censorate.

[1] Brief summaries of the history of the Censorate appear in Hans Wist, *Das Chinesische Zensorat* (Hamburg, 1932), and in Richard L. Walker, "The Control System of the Chinese Government," *Far Eastern Quarterly*, Vol. 7 (November 1947), 2-21. A most useful short history in Chinese is Kao I-han, *Chung-kuo yü-shih chih-tu ti yen-ko* [*Evolution of the Chinese Censorial System*] (Shanghai, 1934).

The traditional Chinese government, developing under the influence of Confucian philosophy, became what might be described, at least in principle, as a government *of* hereditary emperors removable by revolution, *by* nonhereditary officials selected on the basis of individual merit, and *for* the people.[2] Censors served a twofold purpose in this system. In the beginning they seem to have been created only as investigators to satisfy the emperors' natural desire for a check on policy at the level of execution. But eventually they took over the additional function, as remonstrators, of checking on policy at the level of formulation. For this they had unchallengeable justification in those precepts of China's revered ancient sages, Confucius and Mencius, which made it a part of every official's moral duty to criticize the ruler fearlessly and forthrightly if he deviated from the true aim of government, the happiness of the people.[3]

The general idea of censorship was translated into functional reality in different forms at different times, and, as has been noted above, none can be considered typical. In addition, since no adequate general history of the Censorate in action has been written, no period can yet be confidently represented as either the high point or the low point of censorial effectiveness. Typical or not, especially significant or not, however, a sampling must be taken within some narrowly delimited period if valid answers are to be obtained to specific questions about the institution. For this paper, the Ming Dynasty will be the period under review.

## I The Censorate of the Ming Dynasty[4]

The Ming Dynasty governed China from 1368 to 1644, after bringing a century of Mongol rule to an end. It was the last native dynasty in

[2] A discussion of the theoretical basis of government in imperial China can be found in Hsieh Pao Chao, *The Government of China, 1644-1911* (Baltimore, 1925), pp. 1-23. Also see Kenneth Scott Latourette, *The Chinese, Their History and Culture* (New York, 1946), pp. 513-51.

[3] See H. G. Creel, *Confucius, The Man and the Myth* (New York, 1949), pp. 142-72; and James Legge, *The Chinese Classics* (Oxford, 1893-1895), Vol. I, pp. 245, 269, 285 [Analects of Confucius, Chap. 11, Sec. 23; Ch. 13, Sec. 15; Ch. 14, Sec. 23], Vol. II, pp. 161, 219, 319 [Mencius Bk. 1, Pt. 2, Chap. 4, Sec. 10; Bk. 2, Pt. 2, Chap. 5; Bk. 4, Pt. 2, Chap. 3].

[4] The following discussion of censorial practices under the Ming Dynasty is derived essentially from the present writer's *The Chinese Censorate of the Ming Dynasty, Including an Analysis of Its Activities during the Decade 1424-1434* (unpublished ms., 1950), which is obtainable on microfilm from The University of Chicago Library. This work is based primarily on standard Chinese historical sources: *Ming-shih* [*History of the Ming Dynasty*], Chaps. 72-76; *Ta Ming hui-tien* [*Collected Institutes of the Ming Dynasty*], Chaps. 209-11; and the sections of the *Ming shih-lu* [*True Records of the Ming Dynasty*] that pertain to the reigns of the Emperors Jen Tsung (1424-1425) and Hsüan Tsung (1426-1435).

China, for it was succeeded by new, Manchu conquerors, who occupied the imperial throne until the republican revolution of 1911. Thus it represents the end point in the native development of imperial governmental institutions, free of the special considerations deriving from conquest situations.

The Ming emperors wielded theoretically absolute power, and the early ones actively and personally directed the work of the government. The later ones frequently permitted an informally organized grand secretariat (*Nei-ko*), consisting of a few eminent and trusted officials, to manage affairs for them. At the worst, they slothfully turned over their prerogatives to ambitious eunuchs, who nominally were concerned only with household tasks in the palace. In any case, routine governmental chores were attended to by a hierarchy of civil service career men, at this time recruited primarily through large-scale public examinations based on mastery of the Confucian classics.

The Censorate was one of three agencies in the top level of the governmental structure, supplementing a disunited civil administration consisting of six ministries (*Pu*) and a similarly disunited military administration consisting of five chief military commands (*Tu-tu fu*). This perpetuated, in outline, the central government of the preceding Mongol period, which Kublai Khan once described as a civil administration serving as his left hand, a military administration serving as his right hand, and a Censorate serving as his means of keeping both hands healthy.[5]

Known by a designation that literally means "chief investigating bureau" (*Tu ch'a-yüan*), the Ming Censorate had a prescribed staff of two censors-in-chief (*Tu yü-shih*), two vice-censors-in-chief (*Fu Tu yü-shih*), four assistant censors-in-chief (*Ch'ien Tu yü-shih*), 110 investigating censors (*Chien-ch'a yü-shih*), and an assortment of administrative and clerical personnel. Investigating censors were the backbone of the censorial service, and in some degree they were considered to be independent of the censors-in-chief.[6]

Though the Censorate specialized in supervisory-critical functions, it did not monopolize them. In Confucian theory, as has been observed above, every official had the right and obligation to criticize the government; and the early Ming emperors particularly prided themselves on maintaining freedom of criticism even for the humblest citizens. They installed outside the palace a "complaint drum," which, when struck,

---

[5] Kao I-han, *op. cit.*, p. 43.

[6] After Nanking was made auxiliary capital in 1420, a second Censorate was set up there. It had a smaller staff than the Peking Censorate, nominally including thirty investigating censors, and had jurisdiction only over the city and its immediate environs.

summoned an attendant to transmit to the emperor any citizen's complaint.[7] Moreover, the Censorate was not even the only agency that specialized in censorial functions. Independently there existed six offices of scrutiny (*K'o*), normally stalled by sixty supervising secretaries (*Chi-shih-chung*), who were expected to attend the emperor at state functions, to remonstrate against unwise policies, and especially to maintain systematic surveillance over the six ministries by editing incoming memorials and outgoing orders. They and the censors shared the unofficial designation of *speaking officials*.[8] Also, there existed in each province, alongside a provincial administration office (*Pu-cheng ssŭ*) and a provincial military command (*Tu ssŭ*), a provincial investigation office (*An-ch'a ssŭ*) which, though not directly subordinate to the Censorate, exercised functions on a local scale similar to those exercised throughout the empire by the censors. They specially watched over the administration of justice and served as courts of judicial appeal.[9]

The Censorate proper, nevertheless, was the control organ par excellence. On the establishment of his government, the founder of the Ming Dynasty pointed out that, of its three great organs, the civil administration was to be in general charge of governmental matters; the military administration was to be in charge of the armies; and the Censorate was to be in charge of "investigations." "The dynastic principles," he said, "are all suspended upon these, and the investigatory duties of the Censorate are of especial importance."[10] This was the general mandate under which the censors functioned. In time it was particularized and clarified in a constantly increasing number of specific and detailed directives that called upon the Censorate to provide the kind of disciplinary surveillance that has been described above. Based on these directives, also, were two perhaps separable but related functions, which were supervisory in part and substantive in part: participation in judicial processes and participation in the formulation and execution of government policies.

Though not all of the questions that come to mind in relation to an institution so organized and so directed can be answered with complete satisfaction, the more significant ones may at least be discussed in some detail.

1. *Who were the censors?* At the outset it must be emphasized that

[7] *Ming-shih*, Chap. 94, pp. 10b ff.

[8] *Ibid.*, Chap. 74, pp. 11a-13a.

[9] *Ibid.*, Chap. 75, pp. 13b-15b.

[10] *Ibid.*, Chap. 73, p. 4b.

censors were civil servants who in general shared the conditions of service to which all civil servants were subject. That is, although in organization and functions the Censorate stood somewhat apart from the central administration, the censors did not consitute an élite corps with personnel rules distinct from those of the bureaucracy. Before even becoming censors, they had to be admitted to the civil service. While admission could be arranged in several ways, primary emphasis under the Ming Dynasty was given to recruitment through periodic written examinations of students who had been approved and recommended by appropriate government authorities. The cream of the recruits were not necessarily earmarked for the Censorate; but constant efforts were made to obtain for the Censorate men who had entered the service in at least the second-best category of recruits, and few officials could expect an appointment there unless they held the doctorate (conferred at triennial palace examinations) or the lesser degree of licentiate (conferred at preliminary provincial examinations) or had graduated from the National Academy, the highest educational institution in the empire. Even licentiates and National Academy graduates were intermittently ineligible for censorial appointments.

It should also be noted that censors generally cannot be considered to have been the men who in the West are called *elder statesmen*. The prescribed rank for investigating censors, who carried on the bulk of the Censorate's work, was only 7a in a scale of civil-service ranks running from 1a at the top to 9b at the bottom, indicating that their previous experience in government service could not have been great. Indeed, a sample analysis of censorial appointments made in the decade 1424-1434 reveals that 215 of 319 appointments went to men who presumably were entirely new to the service. Subsequent rules restricted eligibility to men who had at least three years' prior experience and, furthermore, required that new investigating censors serve probationary periods of six months or one year before being confirmed in substantive appointments. Even so, it is clear that appointment as investigating censor was not the climax of a civil service career.

Aside from these formalistic regulations regarding experience qualifications and the avenues of original recruitment, there was repeated insistence on the need to obtain for the Censorate men who were thoroughly indoctrinated in the principles of government and were just, honest, intelligent, and upright. The Emperor Ch'eng Tsu (1402-1424), for example, once proclaimed:

> As censors it is necessary to employ incorrupt, cautious, resolute, and upright men. If incorrupt, they will lack selfishness. If cautious, they will lack indiffer-

ence. If resolute and upright, they will dare to speak out. Those who are not capable of this should forthwith be demoted.[11]

In fact, selection of relatively young and inexperienced men for the Censorate may reflect a conscious, though unstated, policy directed toward obtaining men before their idealism and ardor had waned through long acquaintance with official corruption or through the forming of political ties.

2. *What were their techniques and powers?* The techniques of the Censorate were adapted to the three large categories of its prescribed functions. The first of these was disciplinary surveillance over the government as a whole. This surveillance was maintained primarily through a system of "commissioning" individual investigating censors to specific supervisory chores, a system which made it possible for almost all types and areas of government operations, both in and outside the capital, to be subject to thorough routine inspections. Of the commissions, those of provincial inspectors (*Hsün-an Chien-ch'a yü-shih*) seem to have been most significant. Provincial inspectors, as general field representatives of the Censorate, probably most nearly deserved the traditional censorial appellation, "the ears and eyes of the emperor." In theory at least, "they honored what was good and exterminated tyranny and corruption so as to rectify public morale and activate the governmental principles." [12] For these purposes, they served one-year tours of duty on which they were expected to make visits of inspection to all localities within their respective jurisdictions and to investigate the conduct of all government personnel. Specifically, wherever they went, they were expected first to conduct judicial reviews of local prisoners, checking their case records for evidence of injustice. Then they inspected the condition of installations and equipment at local ceremonial areas. They also inquired after, and provided for, the relief of orphans and the aged; inspected public granaries and storehouses, checking their funds and contents; and visited schools in order to observe the progress of students. These and similar commissions permitted the censors to gain information about government personnel and practices by direct personal observation and investigation. They also were able to gain information by accepting criticisms and complaints from other officials or from the public, and by receiving routine reports from various other agencies.

A primary aim of this surveillance, of course, was to ferret out cases that required disciplinary action. Thus, on the basis of the information they received, censors were individually empowered to submit impeach-

[11] Sun Ch'eng Tsu, *Ch'un-ming meng-yü lu* (blockprint pocket ed., n.d.), Chap. 48, pp. 6a-7a.

[12] *Ming-shih*, Chap. 73, p. 2b.

ments directly to the throne. For lesser offenses, they might warn the responsible officials. In the case of low-ranking civil service personnel on duty outside the capital, they could even seize and try offenders on their own authority. Also, they participated in the Ministry of Civil Service's (*Li pu*) periodic formulations of merit ratings for administrative officials, which served as grounds for routine promotions and demotions. Beyond this, they could, if so inclined, remonstrate with the emperor, in person or in memorials, about his own part in the conduct of affairs. Some emperors urged them to do so, taking an attitude shared by the Mongol Kublai Khan, who once said:

> The duties of the Censorate's officials lie in speaking out straightforwardly. If I perchance commit improprieties, let them speak out to the extreme without concealment and without fearing others.[13]

As their second major responsibility, censors engaged in various kinds of judicial functions. After inspecting reports of legal cases submitted from provincial investigation offices, they participated with the Ministry of Justice (*Hsing pu*) and an autonomous agency known as the Grand Court of Revision (*Ta-li ssŭ*) in the ratification of important sentences. They investigated complaints about official injustice. Moreover, they took part in judging major offenders who were tried at the capital, and they themselves conducted special trials and judicial investigations when so ordered by the emperor. Provincial inspectors, and on occasion other censors, paid particular attention to persons detained in local prisons, ordering suitable adjustments on their own initiative when case records indicated that prescribed punishments were disproportionate to the crimes. Also, on their own authority and without recourse to the impeachment process, censors were capable of inflicting punishments on government personnel of certain categories. Altogether, they exercised more than supervisory powers of criticism. They exercised substantive judicial powers and were, in effect, what might be called *judges at large*.

Thirdly, censors participated actively in many ways in the formulation, and even the administrative implementation, of government policies. Holding a wide general mandate to speak out forthrightly about the advantageousness or disadvantageousness of government policies, they could individually submit recommendations for the emperor's consideration if they saw the need for action of any kind. The censors on duty in the capital attended and participated in policy deliberations that were convoked irregularly by the emperors. While they were on commissions in the provinces, they even had considerable opportunity to participate actively and directly in administration. A provincial inspector, for exam-

[13] *Yüan-shih* [*History of the Yüan Dynasty*], Chap. 6, p. 15b.

ple, was more than a mere inspector: he and the high provincial authorities jointly deliberated about important problems and approved plans offered by lesser officials. Wherever he went, if he noted things that ought to be done, he could order the local authorities to undertake them. Sometimes censors were specially deputed to direct such undertakings as the capture of bandits and the extermination of locusts. And at times it seems that some went so far as to authorize expensive relief measures in disaster areas without obtaining specific imperial sanction.

The censors' power to intervene directly in administration and to take punitive and corrective action on their own authority seems to have been an innovation of the Mongol period that was carried over to the Ming Dynasty. It perhaps diluted their proper censorial function, criticism, by robbing them of the objectivity that is every critic's best claim to a hearing. What is more, it undoubtedly subjected them to temptations toward arbitrariness that only the most exceptional men could resist with complete success.

3. *What was their freedom to act?* The fact that censors were members of the regular civil service had significant implications regarding their freedom to act. Primarily, it meant that they were appointed officials whose tenure in office was by no means guaranteed. Normal tenure in any one administrative office was nine years. Except in the highest-ranking posts, to exceed this limit was apparently a rarity. There was no such thing, therefore, as life tenure for a censor; and to fall short of even a nine-year tenure in any office was quite common. An official might be specially promoted, transferred, demoted, or dismissed entirely from the service at any time. The Ministry of Civil Service had over-all charge of promotions, transfers, demotions, and dismissals; and censors were subject to its dispositions on an equal basis with all other officials, except for one important consideration—that is, no censor could be removed from his office without the express consent of the emperor. This in some degree protected censors from the enmity of their superiors in the Censorate and of personnel in the Ministry of Civil Service. However, it left them entirely defenseless against the whims of the emperor or of whoever might have the emperor's confidence.

Neither did censors enjoy immunity of person; for the Ming emperors, when aroused, took full advantage of their absolute authority and imposed flogging, exile, imprisonment, and sometimes death on whoever displeased them or their favorites.

It is even questionable that investigating censors in practice were significantly independent of their immediate nominal superiors, the various censors-in-chief. According to law, individual censors had the right to make proposals and impeachments in sealed memorials submitted directly to the throne. They were also assigned to major commissions by choice of the emperor, and on returning from commissions were required to report to the throne before filing reports with the Censorate itself. However, their superiors periodically gave them merit ratings which determined their future careers, unless the emperor vigilantly intervened, and this fact cannot have failed to influence relations among members of the Censorate staff. One censor-in-chief, as a matter of fact, so dominated the investigating censors that they took orders from his civilian son, altered records to conceal his own misdemeanors, unanimously impeached at least one official at his insistence, and submissively paid him fees for the privilege of going out on and returning from commissions.[14]

The independence of Ming censors was also restricted by the fact that they were individually accountable for the accuracy of their memorials. In submitting impeachments, they were specifically required clearly to set forth the evidence, and were enjoined from incorporating careless accusations, slanderous gossip, or trifles. The founder of the dynasty once demoted a censor for impeaching an official on the basis of what he had overheard "in the streets." Under the earlier T'ang (618-907) and Sung (960-1279) native dynasties, censors had the right to impeach on the basis of hearsay, using the phrase *I have heard a rumor that;*[15] but this practice was apparently discontinued. The lack of protection for informants that derived from the custom of using only open evidence must have reduced the censors' sources of information in some degree.

All these factors make it clear that the position of a censor was a somewhat precarious one. If he offended the emperor, he could lose his life. If he offended his superiors within the Censorate, he risked getting an unfavorable merit rating, which could result in his demotion or dismissal from the service. And, in dealing with other censors and officials in general, he was aware that he, too, could be impeached and that the victim of his action today might be his superior or an imperial favorite next year. These considerations might seem to have constituted, in actual practice, a tight restriction indeed. On the other hand, however, there were compensations. In the first place, censors were expected and urged to act, and emperors repeatedly assured them that it was needless to be afraid. Moreover, there was some consolation in the fact that they could be disciplined only with the emperor's consent. But the greatest shield of all was the tremendous prestige that custom gave the censor's status. This status was realistically derived from the fact that effective control of the

[14] This was Liu Kuan, who held office from 1415 to 1428. See his biography in *Ming-shih*, Chap. 151, pp. 11a-12b.

[15] Hung Mai, *Jung-chai sui-pi (Ssŭ-pu ts'ung-k'an* ed.; Shanghai, 1935), Pt. 4, Chap. 11, p. 8a.

empire depended upon the emperor's knowledge of actual conditions. Of necessity restricted in his own movements and observations, no wise emperor could allow himself to become dependent for information upon only one minister or only one element in the government. As the Chinese put it, the "avenues of expression" had to be kept open. What could better serve this need than an active and unintimidated Censorate? And what could sooner deprive the emperor of trustworthy information than the determined silence and noncooperation of a whole officialdom sullenly resentful of autocratic maltreatment of censors who, from its point of view, were its champions? At least one Ming emperor, victimized by such a campaign of passive resistance, came to terms in the end, crying, in substance, "Nobody tells me anything any more!" [16] Thus, when emperors did punish censors, they usually tried to convince the public at large that the punishments were deserved, not because of excess zeal in line of duty, but because of heinous offenses that made the censors unworthy of their exalted and responsible offices.

4. *What were their motivations?* The problem of censors' independence is related closely to the problem of motivation. In actual practice, what impelled censors to act or not to act? No conclusive and generally valid answer can be given, of course; but a detailed analysis of the recorded activities of Ming censors during the decade 1424-1434 suggests some observations that appear to be valid at least for this one brief period. It indicates that many censors were undoubtedly motivated by greed. Succumbing to the lure of bribes was probably their most common failing. Whereas 128 investigating censors were promoted out of the Censorate during this period, 135 lost their offices through disciplinary action, and 22 others were disciplined without losing their offices. Venality, occurring in 45 instances, was the most frequent charge against them. Several cases, reported in detail in the historical records, show that some censors, for example, were willing to reduce judicial sentences in return for bribes.

Objectivity among censors was, of course, the ideal, and many provisions were made to guard censors against irrelevant personal or political pressures. It was generally the rule that no relative of a high official in the central administration might be appointed to the Censorate. While traveling on commissions, censors were not allowed to be accompanied by relatives, to receive private letters, to attend banquets, to accept presents or loans, or to work in areas of which they were natives or in which they had previously resided or served in office. Yet personal enmity

[16] *Ming-shih*, Chap. 164, pp. 4a-5b; *Ming shih-lu*, Jen Tsung, Chap .7B, p. 2a, Ch. 8A, pp. 4b-5b.

was clearly evident in some of their acts, and the influence of friendship can be inferred without much difficulty in others. (Broad political alignments were not apparent at this time, although they became of great historical significance late in the Ming era.)

One emperor of this ten-year period complained that censors were the easy dupes of flattery because of youthful desires to exaggerate their importance, and the charge is plausible. The investigating censors were usually in their early years of government service and relatively young. Thrust into positions of great traditional prestige, glorified as the "ears and eyes of the emperor," given precedence over much higher-ranking officials (as in the relations between a provincial inspector and the regular provincial authorities), and empowered to punish, or at least to impeach, all whom they encountered, censors understandably might have been carried away by a sense of their own importance. Abuse of authority was specifically cited as the ground for seven disciplinary actions against censors during the decade analyzed.

On the other hand, it is not surprising to find evidence that censors were to some extent inhibited by fear. The Chinese social order was such that his status as an official was among the most prized possessions of every civil servant. The fact that investigating censors were subjected to disciplinary action at an average rate of fifteen per year during this decade, even though such disciplinary action was intended to stimulate and encourage the censorial staff as a whole, served in fact as a reminder that censors had no guaranteed tenure and no immunity of person. This reminder probably induced many weaker censors to adhere closely to the seemingly safe policy of caution and irresolution, except insofar as greed, friendship, or the desire to seem important overcame their fears.

It would be misleading, however, to suggest that censors' acts and omissions were always based on such motives. The recruitment of men for the Ming civil service was based primarily on educational qualifications, with the education of a would-be civil servant beginning at a very early age. The Confucian classics served as the content of his education, and the method was predominantly memorization. By the time he entered the service—especially if he did so through the examination process —he had necessarily become saturated with the language of these works. At the very least, he could reproduce passages of the Analects of Confucius from memory, and it would appear improbable indeed that the ethical ideals of Confucianism could have escaped him entirely. Among other things, the classics laid upon ministers the obligation fearlessly and resolutely to criticize the government. Men so indoctrinated, when appointed to an office of which the prescribed function was criticism, can hardly be supposed to have renounced without qualms the ideals that had virtually been bred into them. And Ming censors did at times act vigorously on their principles.[17]

5. *What did they accomplish?* Evaluations of censors' accomplishments and effectiveness can properly be made only on the basis of their actual activities during a given period, insofar as they are recorded in historical sources. What, then, can be discovered from the decade 1424-1434, to take this one sampling again? It is clear that relatively good government prevailed during this time, but one must inquire about the extent to which the prevailing good government was attributable to the censors.

The policies of the two emperors whose reigns are considered here, Jen Tsung and Hsüan Tsung, do not appear to have been instigated or notably altered by the censors. The historical records reveal that censors did, however, submit 169 proposals that seem on the whole to have been sincere attempts to make implementation of the policies more successful. 143, or approximately four fifths of them, were approved by the emperors. It appears reasonable, then, to assert that censors assisted and encouraged the emperors to follow their desirable inclinations. Nevertheless, they did not reprove some injudicious aberrations on the part of Jen Tsung, and they apparently made no attempt to alter the less desirable policies of the emperors, which included at least one—the increasing employment of eunuchs in positions of trust and authority —that had clearly ominous implications. Thus this period, undoubtedly because these emperors were on the whole conscientious and "constitutional" in the Confucian sense, does not show censors at their legendary and dramatic best in fearlessly challenging the autocratic and arbitrary powers of tyrannous rulers. But the fact remains that many later Ming censors rose to such heights when conditions prompted them to do so.[18]

Censors were also active in seeking to discipline or remove unworthy officials and so to improve the quality of the personnel charged with administering the emperors' policies. How many persons were punished by censors on their own authority is not revealed by analysis of the records; but 13,814+ persons were denounced during these ten years in recorded impeachments by censors. Even disregarding two almost incredible mass impeachments that resulted in investigations, trials, or finings of 13,259 government employees, there were 555+ individual denunciations, of which only 122 were ignored by the emperors. Forty-nine, or 8.8 per cent, of the persons denounced were promptly demoted,

---

[17] For numerous examples, see Lin Yutang, *A History of the Press and Public Opinion in China* (Chicago, 1936), pp. 58-73.

[18] *Idem.*

dismissed, or disgraced by the emperors, apparently without benefit of trial or any further hearing; 353+, or 63.6 per cent, were fined, reprimanded, imprisoned, or otherwise punished, sometimes summarily and sometimes after investigations; nineteen, or 3.4 per cent, were subjected to further investigations the results of which do not appear in the records; and twelve, or 2.2 per cent, were subjected to trials the results of which are similarly not indicated. Thus, although the emperors sometimes complained that the censors were not diligent and just in making impeachments, they nevertheless took positive action on approximately four fifths of the censors' denunciations. Moreover, merit ratings by censors brought about the demotion of at least 264+ other civil and military officials. Many persons, therefore, were affected by the surveillance of censors.

The analysis reveals that censors of this period did accomplish much that seems to have been good. But it also suggests that they neglected other things that they might, and perhaps should, have accomplished. The types of activities for which many censors were disciplined, together with those for which censors generally were criticized, make it evident that the venality and petty vanity of some censors must have reduced general confidence in the integrity of the censorial force, and thereby in the government service as a whole. The power of censors to discipline certain categories of persons on their own authority may also have tended to stifle initiative by restraining such persons from action not clearly sanctioned by orders and regulations.

Perhaps the most significant effect of the Censorate's work was an indirect one. Such an organization, specially devoted to criticism and supporting a widespread net of surveillance, must have had considerable influence of a cautionary nature. Emperors as well as officials and citizens probably were not so concerned about what censors did as about what they could do, and such considerations may well have served as restraints in ways both detrimental and beneficial. As was said at an earlier time: "The Censorate is like a sleeping tiger. Even if it does not bite men, men still dread its tigerishness." [19]

## 16 / THE BIRTH OF CAPITALISM IN CHINA / E. BALAZS

The relations between the officials and the merchant class were stamped by the fact that the officials, in their capacity as the ruling class—en-

[19] Yüan-shih, Chap. 148, p. 8b.

Reprinted with permission from E. Balazs, "The Birth of Capitalism in China," *Chinese Civilization and Bureaucracy* (New Haven: Yale University Press, 1964), pp. 41-45, 49-54.

dowed with learning that enabled them to supervise and coordinate the activities of an agrarian society, and thus to acquire their dominant position in the state—enjoyed an all-pervading power and prestige. In these relations, . . . every means of keeping the merchant class down and holding it in subjection seemed permissible. Compromises, exceptions, favors, pardons—all were allowed so long as they were retracted at the earliest opportunity. Claims, titles, privileges, immunities, deeds, charters were never granted. Any sign of initiative in the other camp was usually strangled at birth, or if it had reached a stage when it could no longer be suppressed, the state laid hands on it, took it under control, and appropriated the resultant profits. As seen from below, there was, in these relations, no legal way of obtaining an immunity, a franchise, since the state and its representatives, the officials, were almighty. There remained only an indirect way of obtaining one's due: bribery.

The outstanding feature in these relations is the absence of pluck, the complete lack of a fighting spirit, on the part of the middle class. On the one hand, they felt impotent in the face of a competitor who seemed to hold all the advantages. On the other, they had no real desire to be different, to oppose their own way of life to that of the ruling class —and this inhibited them even more. Their ambition was limited: to find a position, if only a modest one, inside the ruling class, reflecting the social prestige attached to officialdom. Their consuming desire was that they, or their children, should become scholar-officials.

This is one of the secret springs accounting for China's particular course of development. The other is corruption. Corruption was, in fact, the main point of contact between the opposing classes. The merchants could not have operated their policy of bribery if it had not been for the practices of embezzlement and "squeeze" on the part of the officials. This kind of division of labor, while it may have been advantageous for a few individuals, not only was eventually to spell ruin for officialdom, but also was lethal so far as improvement of the status of the bourgeoisie is concerned. It prevented the middle classes from consolidating and extending momentary advantages, and prevented the bourgeoisie from achieving consciousness as a separate, autonomous body with its own interests.

Let me illustrate what has so far been said with a few examples chosen at random.

Private initiative was responsible for the invention of the first instruments of credit. In the eighth century AD, under the T'ang Dynasty, when commercial activities were expanding rapidly, merchants found that large-scale transfer of cash was cumbersome, laborious, and perilous. They invented "flying money," by means of which merchants, on depositing cash at certain specified offices, received a written receipt guaranteeing reimbursement in other provinces. In 811 the government prohibited the use of flying money by private citizens and adopted the system for its own credit transfers. Merchants were allowed to deposit cash at government finance offices in the capital against payments to be received in the provinces. A 10 per cent fee was charged on the drafts.

During roughly the same period, the Buddhists invented printing for the purpose of religious propaganda. The state took over this invention and used it for the contrary purpose of diffusing the Confucian doctrine, and then proceeded to persecute the Buddhist church—not, it is true, because of this, but for several other reasons.

The first protobanks to issue promissory notes, which soon became a kind of paper currency, were founded by rich merchants in Szechwan, which was one of the trading centers during the eleventh century. To begin with, the government recognized sixteen of the larger merchants, and granted them a monopoly in the issue of these "exchange media" (*chiao-tzu*), which brought in a fee of 3 per cent. But a few years later in AD 1023, a government monopoly replaced the private monopoly.[1]

Another example is afforded by the practice of lending money. In the Chinese economy, usury played perhaps an even greater role than it did in Europe during the Middle Ages. The crucial point, however, is that lending at exorbitant interest was not only not prohibited by law, but actually practiced by the state. During early T'ang times, the highest legally permitted rates of interest were 6 per cent per month on private loans, and 7 per cent on government funds. During the Sung Dynasty, the corresponding ceiling rates were 4 and 5 per cent.[2]

In the Sung period merchants' guilds were obliged to supply government needs on demand. This obligation was the cause for many grievances, because the price paid by the government was lower than the market price, and the merchant whose turn it was to supply the goods had himself to pay the transport costs. At the petition of the butchers' guild in the capital, the government granted, in AD 1073, a kind of "privilege," according to which members of the corporations were to pay a monthly fee for exemption from this obligation and the government was to pay the market price for the goods. Twelve years later, however, the state returned to the former system. One of the reasons for this setback is quite typical. The guilds forced petty merchants to join the corporation if they had not yet done so in order that they would share the burden of paying the exemption fee.[3]

[1] L. S. Yang, *Money and Credit in China* (Cambridge, Mass., 1952), pp. 51-53.

[2] Yang, *op. cit.*, p. 95.

[3] S. Katō, "On the Hang or the Associations of Merchants in China," *Memoirs of the Tōyō Bunkō*, Vol. VIII (1936), 62.

Yet another example, which is an excellent illustration of the different pattern of urban development in China and in the West, is provided by the ownership of house property in the cities. In the big cities that grew up during Sung times, many houses were built for letting purposes. Most of the houses, shops, and building lots were government owned, and a special state agency was established for their administration, rent being collected on a daily basis from the poor people in the cities lest the arrears should be too great.[4]

It is not fortuitous that these examples I have chosen should all come from late T'ang or Sung times, for this was the period during which urban development went hand in hand with intense commercial activity. We are therefore compelled to look for the germs of capitalism as early as the latter half of the eighth century. But, in doing so, we must never forget the essential difference between Chinese and Western towns—of which my last example is a case in point. The difference is this: while the Western town was the seedbed and later the bulwark of the bourgeoisie, the Chinese town was primarily the seat of government, the residence of officials who were permanently hostile to the bourgeoisie, and thus always under the domination of the state.

Nor is it a matter of chance that the first great thrust of the Chinese bourgeoisie happened during a period—late T'ang and more especially Sung times—when national sovereignty was divided. It is my firm belief that, whenever national sovereignty was divided and the power of the state and the ruling scholar-officials was consequently weakened, the middle class flourished as a result. Other instances, apart from the Sung period, are provided by the lively, brilliant epoch of the Warring States in ancient times and, during the Middle Ages, the period of the Three Kingdoms and of the division of China between the northern barbarian and the southern national dynasties. But even in times which favored the merchants, the state and the state monopolies were a heavy drag on commercial activities.

This can be illustrated in greater detail by mining and the salt industry, which afford typical examples of how the workings of early capitalism in China were hampered by bureaucratic regulations. Both were outstandingly thriving enterprises, in which the largest fortunes were acquired. Yet both, together with the tea trade, foreign trade, and military supplies, were more or less equally prosperous whether they operated under state license, state control, or state monopoly.

Mining had always been under state control, particularly the copper and silver mines, which provided metal for the mints, and the iron workings, which provided the raw material for tools and weapons. From

[4] S. Katō, *Shina keizaishi kōshō* (Tokyo, 1953), pp. 2, 239-46.

Sung times onward, the use of coal became more and more widespread, replacing charcoal in foundries and for cooking. We have detailed descriptions of mines dating from around AD 1600, from which we learn that the galleries went to a depth of one hundred feet, and that equipment included bamboo pipes for drainage, pumping fresh air into the tunnels, and evacuating the gases.

Since theoretically all the soil belonged to the state, state ownership of metal ores was an established principle. But this did not hinder private enterprise. At the beginning of the Ming Dynasty (1368-1644), the state produced for its own needs. There was no market, and the mines were closed down if metal reserves were considered to be sufficient. The state-owned mines employed large numbers of miners and foundry workers who were exempt from *corvée* and military service but had to pay the ordinary tax. Usually they provided the tools and the fuel. The labor force was assessed not on an individual basis but per household, these households or families being regarded as tax units, corresponding to the peasant households. In the iron works of Tsun-hua near Peking, founded by the famous Yung-lo Emperor (1403-1424), at the beginning of the fifteenth century there were about 3000 workers, including professional metal workers, artisans on duty, civil and military unskilled helpers, and convicts. The output of this particular iron works was about 500,000 catties (or pounds), and the production figure for all iron works combined was somewhere between 10 and 20 million catties (that is, between 6000 and 12,000 tons). Miners and smelters worked only during the six winter months, when there was no agricultural work to be done. The workers received as wages one pint (about 0.028 bushels) of grain a day.

But during the late sixteenth century a great change took place. Taxes on mines ceased to be a previously fixed amount and became a percentage of actual output. This stimulated the growth of private enterprise and brought about the decline of state-owned mines. There were now prosperous entrepreneurs, and among the workmen there were foremen and specialized professional miners, both of whom were paid according to output, the foremen receiving in addition a refund for moneys spent on tools, fuel, and wages. . . .

Once the government had received its share and had bought up the quantity of copper it required, it had no further interest in the production or the profit margin of the entrepreneurs. But until then supervision was arbitrary and tyrannical. In order to prevent smuggling, the furnaces were kept under strict control, and the copper was immediately checked, weighed, and taxed as it came out of the furnace. According to a contemporary account, the tax varied arbitrarily between 9 and 20 per cent. In addition, there were the exactions, the inevitable "squeeze," extorted by corrupt officials. The whole administration was more concerned with policing activities than with promoting production. The response on the workers' side was to organize in secret societies.

The contractors were rich merchants from the neighboring provinces of Kiangsu, Hupei, Szechwan, and Kuangtung. They provided the capital and hired the manager, the technicians (for dealing with props, ventilation, pumping, and so on), the foremen, and the workers. The latter were recruited from among the poor people of the same provinces, and they usually sought work in the mines when the harvest was over, but came swarming in crowds at any season as soon as word went around that a new and prosperous mine had been opened.

There were two forms of remuneration for the workers: monthly wages, not related to output and profits, and the share system, known as *rice and shares (mi-fen),* or *association of brothers (ch'in-shen ti-hsiung).* Under this partnership system the workers received their food and 30 per cent of the profit; 10 per cent of the profit went to the manager, the technicians, and the foremen; the share of the entrepreneur—the lion's share—was 60 per cent.[5]

I should like to lay special emphasis on this system, because a similar system was a feature of early Western capitalism, especially in the silver mines from the fourteenth century. Found mostly in German silver mines, it is known by the German name *Verlag.* Another point that deserves attention is that both partners in the entrepreneurial system of the Yunnan copper mines, entrepreneurs and wage workers alike, came from other provinces and so were in fact strangers. This was a noteworthy feature, involving among other things a certain lack of submissiveness.

The salt monopoly had always been a major source of revenue for the Chinese state. Taxes on consumer goods are attested as early as the sixth century BC. From T'ang times on, the *gabelle* produced a large proportion of the state revenue. In order to enforce the monopoly against smugglers and make the salt industry a going concern, the government had recourse to merchants to distribute salt, as this was too cumbersome an undertaking for the state agencies to carry out, particularly with a growing increase in population.

Under the last dynasty, the salt tax amounted yearly to about 5 million taels. Originally half the amount of the salt tax—and, after the

---

[5] On the mines of Yunnan, see Wang Ming-lun, "Ya-p'ien chan-cheng ch'ien Yün-nan t'ung-k'uang-yeh ti tzu-pen chu-i meng-ya," in the symposium Chung-Kuo-tzu-ten chui-weng-ya wen-t'i t'ao-lun chi (Peking, 1957), pp. 2, 673-84.

middle of the eighteenth century, 40 per cent of it—was collected in the largest and richest of the eleven salt administration areas of middle and southeast China, called Liang-Huai. Thanks to the existence of a large number of documents, it is possible to calculate that the Liang-Huai traders—those "unchallenged merchant princes of China"—distributed annually to 75 million people (a quarter of the total population in the eighteenth century) more than 600 million pounds of salt, with an average annual profit of about 7 million taels. Let us see how this trade worked and what became of the money earned by the merchants.

The salt masters were originally small independent manufacturers who had a small but quick return and no risk; but during the eighteenth century they came more and more under the sway of the wholesale dealers. By 1800, only half of them remained owners of salterns, and even when they were the legal owners of their small manufacturing works, they were in fact wage-earners under the control of the capitalists. The wholesale dealers at first only bought salt from the owner-manufacturers and sold it to the salt distributors, but later they became large-scale producers. As such, they ran a considerable risk because of the perishable nature of salt. Salt was stored for a year before being sold to the transport merchants. The factory merchants bought up the property of bankrupt salt masters, or shared profits with them as joint owners. These factory merchants owed their position to government recognition. Only thirty of them were recognized, and, in a jump from the *Verlag* system to full-fledged capitalism, they were able to keep tight control not only over the manufacturers, but also over the small-scale merchants, who were often their agents. The producers made an annual profit of about 1.5 to 2 million taels, of which they pocketed 60 per cent, leaving the remaining 40 per cent to be divided half-and-half between the depot merchants and the salt makers.

Profits were even higher on the distribution side of the trade. The transport merchants made about 5 million taels annually. Since Sung times a grain-salt exchange system had operated. The merchants transported grain to the frontier for military supplies, and received in exchange salt tickets, issued by the government, which authorized the receipt of government-monopoly salt in the interior. During late Ming times (sixteenth and seventeenth centuries), salt tickets could be bought for cash, and the frontier merchants became salt merchants of the interior. The established practice, typical of the whole organization, which remained in operation until the middle of the nineteenth century, was as follows: the inalienable right to sell salt was farmed out to rich merchants who could pay the *gabelle* in advance; the names of these licensed monopoly merchants were entered in an official register, called the *shipment register* (*kang-ts'e*), because the annual quota of salt distributed in the Liang-Tuai area was divided into so many shipments.

The organization of these transport merchants, of whom there were only 230 in Liang-Huai, is a revelation for anyone interested in Chinese capitalism. There were, in fact, only thirty head merchants, half of them owners of the monopoly license, the other half only leaseholders. They were responsible for arrears in tax payment and for the conduct of the whole merchant body, that is, for the 200 retailers—"small" men compared with the head merchants, but mostly men of substantial means, usually required to trade under the name of one of the head merchants. They were milked by the head merchants by two main devices: the high rate of interest on loaned capital, and the practice of shifting the burden of "squeeze" to the entire group of transport merchants; meanwhile, the head merchants appropriated a large share of the "treasury fee" (*hsia*). The treasury fee was money for expenses incurred in entertaining officials and for contributions to local administration; it was paid out of the common treasury of the entire merchant body, but handled exclusively by a few merchant treasurers. This practice was of course encouraged by high officials in the salt administration, who shared the fat bonus with these few merchants. There was a powerful clique of four or five merchant chiefs selected by the salt administration, but this arrangement became a public scandal and had to be abolished in 1724. Even so, the hierarchy, with all its tensions of give and take, stands out clearly enough: high officials → local administration → merchant chiefs → head merchants → small merchants. And below them, of course, were the consumers—the peasants who bore the burden of the tax.

We come now at long last to the crucial question of accumulation: What did the salt merchants do with the enormous profits gained during the years of high prosperity, profits estimated at 250 million taels for the second half of the eighteenth century? Let us first answer another question: Where did the merchants come from and how did they live?

Most of the Liang-Huai merchants were either emigrants from Shansi who had formerly been frontier merchants, or men from Hui-chou in Anhui province who became famous as the Hsin-an merchants, so called after the ancient name of their home town. By late Ming times both groups were notorious. For those who recall the connection established by Max Weber between the austere Puritan tradition of thrift and early capitalism, the following passage from a description of China about AD 1600 will have a familiar ring:

> The rich men of the empire in the regions south of the Yangtze are from Hsin-an [ancient name of Hui-chou], in the regions north of that river, from Shansi. The great merchants of Hui-chou have made fisheries and salt their

occupation and have amassed fortunes amounting to one million taels of silver. Others with a fortune of 200,000 or 300,000 can only rank as middle merchants. The Shansi merchants are engaged in salt, silk, reselling of grain. Their wealth even exceeds that of the former. This is because the Hui-chou merchants are extravagant, but those of *Shansi are frugal.* In fact, *people of Hui-chou are also extremely miserly as to food and clothing,* . . . but with regard to concubines, prostitutes, and lawsuits, they squander gold like dust.[6]

The descendants of these hard-working and frugal men, in the second or third generation after the original fortune had been made, acquired very different habits. They became status-seekers, spending fabulous sums in an endless quest for social prestige. Their response to the ruling-class principle of "keeping tradesmen in their place" was to compensate for lack of social prestige by ostentatious living. They indulged in eccentricities and expensive hobbies, "dogs, horses, music, and women"; they owned beautiful pleasure gardens; they became bibliophiles, collectors, and art connoisseurs; they patronized and subsidized scholars on a lavish scale and held veritable literary salons. Dozens of famous literati—poets like Yüan Mei (1716-1798), philosophers like Tai Chen (1724-1777), historians like Ch'ien Ta-hsin (1728-1804)—were their guests and protégés. And it is certainly a fact that, even allowing for the not entirely voluntary contribution of 41 million taels to the imperial treasury (for the emperor's personal expenses) during the second half of the eighteenth century, their mode of life, clan solidarity, and expenses for education diverted most of the accumulated capital to noneconomic uses.

Another impediment to the development of capitalism was the traditionally preferred investment in land. Although the rent from land probably amounted to no more than 30 to 40 per cent of the return from businesses such as pawnbroking, moneylending, and shopkeeping, we find that the laws of the Peking club of the townsmen from Hui-chou —the famous Hsin-an merchants—decreed that any unused public funds of the club "should be invested only in the purchase of real estate for receipt of rent, and should not be lent for interest, *in order to avoid risks.*" "Small risk and high prestige were two major factors which had made investment in land attractive."[7]

The history of the development of Chinese capitalism has an intermittent character and is full of leaps and bounds, regressions and relapses. I should like to give one last example to illustrate this discontinu-

---

[6] *Wu-tsa-tsu* 4.25b, trans. and quoted by Ho Ping-ti in his excellent article, on which I have leaned heavily here, "The Salt Merchants of Yang-chou: A Study of Commercial Capitalism in Eighteenth Century China," *Harvard Journal of Asiatic Studies,* Vol. XVII (1954), 130-68; see pp. 143-44 Cf. Saeki Tomi, *Shindai ensei no kenkyū* (Kyoto, 1956).

[7] Yang, *op. cit.,* pp. 102-03.

ity. With the decline of the salt trade, the capital of the salt merchants was transferred to the more profitable business of pawnbroking. The chain of pawnshops founded as a state institution at the beginning of the eighteenth century was taken over by them, and the capital invested was called public funds "entrusted to merchants to produce interest." [8]

The following points may serve as a summary of the arguments presented above.

First: I can give no exact date for the birth of capitalism in China. All I know is that the tendency will be to set this date further and further back, from the nineteenth to the eighteenth to the seventeenth century and so on, finally arriving at the Sung dynasty (tenth to thirteenth centuries), which in my opinion marks the beginning of modern times in China. Still, the discontinuity just mentioned distorts the steady, simple, ascending line so much favored by school textbooks.

Second: with regard to industrial capitalism, we must never forget that the purpose of machines is to economize labor or time. In China there was never any dearth of labor; on the contrary, China always had plenty of it. The superabundance of cheap labor certainly hampered the search for time-saving devices. Nevertheless, what was chiefly lacking in China for the further development of capitalism was not mechanical skill or scientific aptitude, nor a sufficient accumulation of wealth, but scope for individual enterprise. There was no individual freedom and no security for private enterprise, no legal foundation for rights other than those of the state, no alternative investment other than landed property, no guarantee against being penalized by arbitrary exactions from officials or against intervention by the state. But perhaps the supreme inhibiting factor was the overwhelming prestige of the state bureaucracy, which maimed from the start any attempt of the bourgeoisie to be different, to become aware of themselves as a class and fight for an autonomous position in society. Free enterprise, ready and proud to take risks, is therefore quite exceptional and abnormal in Chinese economic history.

Third: if capitalism is interpreted as meaning only competitive capitalism, or free enterprise (which has nearly disappeared in our world), then there never has been capitalism in China. But if state capitalism is admitted as forming an integral and important part of the phenomenon we call capitalism, then it appears to us in China as a hoary old man who has left to his sturdy and reckless great grandson a stock of highly valuable experiences.

---

[8] Cf. Abe Takeo, "Pawnbroking in the Ch'ing Period," in *Haneda Tōyōshi ronsō* (Kyoto, 1950), pp. 1-36. The total number of pawnshops went up from 7,685 in 1685 to 23,139 in 1812.

And just because we live in the epoch of state capitalism, both in the old capitalist countries of the West and in the new "People's Democracies" of the East, the matter is one of great relevance to us today.

# 17 / EVOLUTION OF LANDOWNERSHIP IN FOURTH- AND FIFTH-CENTURY CHINA* / E. BALAZS

During the course of Chinese history, the free peasant was frequently reduced to servitude as a result of the formation of large estates, and whenever this threatened to occur, voices were raised warning the government against the fatal consequences of the latifundia, and demanding a return to the *ching-t'ien* system.

The *ching-t'ien* system was traditionally regarded as an ancient system of communal ownership, in which the land was supposed to have been divided in the form of the Chinese character *ching* ("water well"), with a central field, belonging to the lord and worked in common, surrounded by eight square fields (*t'ien*) of equal area, each measuring one hundred *mou* (one *mou* is about six acres). Whether the tradition was actually based on historical fact has been, and will long continue to be, a topic of debate.[1] But however difficult it may be to sift out the *Dichtung und Wahrheit* of the matter, there is no doubt that the poetry became more important than the truth; for, whatever significance the *ching-t'ien* system may have had in the past, the demand to return to it was a way of expressing a utopian demand for greater social justice through equal distribution of land, and this utopian ideal became much more significant than the vague memories that had been handed down of how the system had actually operated.

This is a paradox that can be more readily understood if two points are taken into consideration. First, the Chinese literati, traditionalists by inclination as well as necessity, were unable to formulate any program of social reform without cloaking it in a reference to the golden age of antiquity. Chinese reformers, unlike their Western counterparts, never projected their ideals into the future. They would have found it not

Reprinted with permission from E. Balazs, "Evolution of Landownership in Fourth- and Fifth-Century China," *Chinese Civilization and Bureaucracy* (New Haven: Yale University Press, 1964), pp. 101-103.

* This article originally appeared under the title "Transformation du régime de la propriété dans la Chine tartare et dans la Chine chinoise aux IV<sup>e</sup>-V<sup>e</sup> siècles," *Cahiers d'Histoire Mondiale*, Vol. I (1953), 417-26.

[1] On communal ownership of land, see Henri Maspero, *La Chine antique*, pp. 109-10, and *Études historiques* (Paris, 1950), pp. 124, 199; Swann, *Food and Money in Ancient China*, pp. 116-20. For current discussion of the question, see L. S. Yang, "Notes on Dr. Swann's *Food and Money in Ancient China*," *Harvard Journal of Asiatic Studies*, Vol. XIII (1950), 531-42.

only meaningless and frightening to do so, but impractical as well; for since public opinion was formed by scholar-officials like themselves, equally steeped in tradition, their only hope of finding support for their programs was to give them a halo of historicity, and thus lend to their demands the prestige of the past. They did this in all good faith, themselves believing in the ideal society vouched for by scholastic reconstructions of a bygone age. Second, the same habit of referring to the past is found in imperial decrees, which were designed to express ethical postulates rather than to lay down rules for administrative practice. Imperial edicts, couched in the most florid style and packed with classical allusions, were often no more than exhortations to the officials pointing out what they *ought* to do. Thus, whether the magic words *ching-t'ien* were used to formulate a utopian demand or to express an ethical postulate, their real meaning can faithfully be interpreted as "equal distribution of land," and over the centuries their connotation was quite simply "agrarian reform."

This becomes clear when it is realized that the question of re-establishing the ancient system agitated the leading spirits and became a hotly debated topic in government circles (the only circles whose opinion is known to us) at certain particular moments—namely, when an economic crisis was brewing. The essential features of such economic crises were as follows: as a result of increases in population and in the number of large estates swallowed up by the rich and powerful at the peasants' expense, peasant landholdings became so small that the peasants could no longer maintain their independence and were forced to become tenant farmers, agricultural laborers, or serfs attached to a large landowner. The situation was usually further aggravated by famine or floods, by the precarious state of public finance (the large landowners being exempt from tax), and by profound social unrest—in short, a crisis that made it imperative for the ruling classes to consent to a reform that would include limitation or breakup of the large estates, under the threat of seeing their land seized, and perhaps even their rule brought to an end, by the forces unleashed in the eruptive violence of a peasant revolt.

Crises of this kind were part of a recurring social and economic cycle, the stages of which are clearly mirrored in the agrarian policies of the Former Han (206 BC–AD 9). Toward the end of the second century BC, a celebrated Confucian scholar-official took the ancient system of land distribution as his authority when putting forward a proposal for "limiting private estates" (*hsien ming-t'ien*). His proposal was never carried out, but it dominated agrarian policy until the end of the dynasty. In 7 BC, a similar proposal was adopted, aiming to limit private estates to 3000 *mou,* but came up against the opposition of the influential large landowners and could not be put into effect. When the usurper Wang Mang, imbued with ideas of the past, attempted to carry out a more equitable distribution of land under the guise of a theoretical nationalization, it was already too late. The reform, promulgated in AD 9 and abolished three years later as inefficacious and impossible to carry out, was stillborn, and the revolt of the "Red Eyebrows" not only put an end to Wang Mang's clumsy attempts, but also brought to a close both his reign and the reign of the Former Han Dynasty.[2] The bloodletting of this tremendous peasant rising having to some extent re-established a balance between available land and population, the Later Han (25-AD 220) followed a moderate policy aimed at restricting the size of large estates. This continued until the next large-scale crisis arose, when the revolt of the "Yellow Turbans" made a holocaust of China, burying in its ruins city and countryside, great landowner and expropriated peasant, rulers and ruled.[3]

# 18 / LANDOWNERSHIP IN CHINA FROM THE FOURTH TO THE FOURTEENTH CENTURY * / E. BALAZS

The agrarian problem, of primary importance in any agricultural society, has always been China's major problem. Its solution determined the well-being of the peasant masses and of the ruling minority, the fate of governments, and, in the last analysis, the rise and fall of dynasties.

The Han (206 BC-AD 220), who ruled over the whole of China, never succeeded in restricting the size of large landed estates, and the attempts of the Chin (265-420), which were interrupted by the barbarian invasions, were not likely to meet with any greater success. The national catastrophe that divided China into North and South for three centuries had profound repercussions on agrarian questions. The incessant wars leading up to it resulted in widespread destruction and a fall in population which, even if it has often been exaggerated, did nevertheless greatly ease population pressure. Agrarian problems were somewhat different under the barbarian dynasties of the North from those in the South, where national

[2] The economic treatise of the *Han-shu,* Chap. 24 A, trans. Swann, pp. 183, 200-204, 210-11.

[3] See Chapter 13 [of *Chinese Civilization and Bureaucracy*], "Political Philosophy and Social Crisis at the End of the Han Dynasty."

Reprinted with permission from E. Balazs, "Landownership in China from the Fourth to the Fourteenth Century," *Chinese Civilization and Bureaucracy* (New Haven: Yale University Press, 1964), pp. 113-15, 117-21.

* This article originally appeared under the title "Le Régime de la propriété en Chine du IV⁰ au XIV⁰ siècles. État de la question," *Cahiers d'Histoire Mondiale,* Vol. I (1954), 669-78.

dynasties continued to rule. The South was a vast territory not yet fully colonized, with any amount of uncultivated land, where small nuclei of Chinese settlers lived amidst a scattered population of indigenous peoples; whereas in the North the Yellow River basin had a dense population of Chinese farmers under the yoke of the barbarian nomads, who were warriors and herdsmen. The contrast between the North and the South was not, of course, so clear-cut as this might suggest, but I have purposely emphasized those aspects that help to explain why it was a Northern dynasty that inaugurated the era of agrarian reform.

The celebrated agrarian reform of the Later Wei (the dynasty of the house of T'o-pa, 386-534), known as the "equalization of land," was part of a whole series of reforms carried out by Emperor Hsiao-wen (471-499) with the purpose of placing his state upon a definitively Chinese basis. It was proclaimed in 485-486, its main object being to protect the peasants against encroachment by landowners who had begun acquiring large estates as soon as the T'o-pa conquerors had consolidated their position. It was accompanied by a reorganization of the tax system, necessitated by the fiscal requirement of providing a broader basis for taxation. With the assimilation of the tribal aristocracy at the end of the wars of expansion, the old Chinese gentry exerted a growing influence, and the ancient ideal of "equal distribution of land" (chün-t'ien) once more came to the fore. The land reform allotted to each family a certain amount of land in perpetuity, and to each individual a quota of arable land that had to be handed back when the owner reached the age limit. The reform was sufficiently flexible to allow for regional variations; it distinguished between owners who did and owners who did not possess cattle; and it granted a special status to the privileged classes (nobles and officials). Because of these variations in its application, the law may be regarded as primarily normative in character. In fact, legislators at the end of the fifth century were not so much haunted by utopian visions of equality as concerned with counteracting existing inequalities, and the fame acquired by Emperor Hsiao-wen's decree was due less to its intrinsic merits than to the fact that its clauses served as model for all later enactments, the expression "equalization of land" winning a prestige that still clings to it today.

The Ch'i (534-577) and Chou (534-581) Dynasties that succeeded the Wei as rulers of the northern part of the still partitioned empire maintained a policy of allotting land, but it is evident from the few surviving contemporary documents that hereditary holdings, supposed to be inalienable, did nevertheless change hands; soon, even land allotted to individuals was sometimes exchanged, mortgaged, or sold. The amount of land available for allocation was correspondingly diminished by such transactions, a process that probably began even in its earliest stages to undermine the land regulations of the Middle Ages. Before discussing the nature and causes of the process, let us note the significant fact that when the Sui (581-617) came to power, even though the empire was once again unified, an adult peasant had difficulty in obtaining a holding as small as twenty *mou* (about two and a half acres), at least in the "restricted districts," where the available land was inadequate for the density of the population.[1] . . .

More important, however, than the status enjoyed by the privileged were the actual social and economic developments reflected in these significant figures. The situation that was typical of the Middle Ages is repeated: the small peasant, so deep in debt that he cannot meet his obligations, seeks the protection of "the powerful," and becomes the tenant farmer or serf of a large landowner. Whether he does so voluntarily or involuntarily, the cause always lies in the overheavy burden of the government taxes, of official and unofficial *corvées*, of legal and illegal exactions, of pressure from the tax collector and demands from the usurer. From the end of the seventh century, incessant complaints were made that the independent peasant had disappeared. Tax evasion and the flight and vagabondage of peasants who should have supplied *corvée* labor and taxes had a cumulative effect, because those liable for tax who remained in the villages found their burden augmented by the amounts due from those who had taken flight. The administrative and military machine was burdensome and costly enough in times of peace, but when the government was faced with the necessity for extra expenditure in times of war or rebellion, the situation became critical, and the difficulty of maintaining legal fictions became insurmountable.

This difficulty was particularly acute during the eventful period between the middle and the end of the eighth century. Two contemporary texts will throw more light on the state of affairs than could the subtlest of analyses. A decree of 752 contains the following statement:

> Officials and rich families vie with each other in founding villas [on this term, see p. 122]; they silently compete with each other as to who will swallow up the most land. They have no fear of the regulations; they all pretend to own waste land, and their fields are all cultivated. . . . As for lots for distribution, they buy and sell them against the rights of inheritance and against the law; or they change the titles in the registration lists; or they take the lots as pledge for debts. The result is that the common people no longer have any land of their own. Further, they get hold of men from other parts and hire them as agricultural laborers, and take possession of land belonging to local inhabitants.[2]

[1] See Balazs, *Le Traité économique du Souei-chou.*

[2] Maspero, *Les Régimes fanciers en Chine*, p. 175.

Forty years later, after the celebrated fiscal reform of 780 had confirmed the breakdown and exposed the fictitious nature of the principle of equality of rights and obligations, a great writer gives the following description of the plight of the tenant farmers:

When the peasant is ruined, he has to sell his field and his hut. If it happens to be a good year, he may just be able to pay his debts. But no sooner has the harvest been brought in than the grain bins are empty again, and, contract in hand and sack on back, he has to go off and start borrowing again. He has heavier and heavier interest to pay, and soon has not got enough to eat. If there is a famine, he falls into utter ruin. Families disperse, parents separate, they seek to become slaves, and no one will buy them. . . . The rich seize several times ten thousand *mou* of land, the poor have no land left, and attach themselves to the big powerful families and become their private retainers. They borrow seed and food, and lease land as tenants. All the year round they work themselves to death without a day's rest, and when they have paid all their debts they live in constant anxiety whether they will be able to make both ends meet. The large landowners, however, live on the rents from their land, and are trouble-free and carefree. Wealth and poverty are clearly separated; this is why the stage has been reached where rents [on privately owned land] are much higher, and collected in a more pitiless way, than the government tax. In the regions surrounding the capital, each *mou* of land pays at present [i.e., 794] a tax of five *sheng*, while the landowner receives a rent of up to one *shih* [or one hundred *sheng*] per *mou:* that is to say, twenty times the amount of the government tax. If one goes down the scale to land of medium category, the rent may be half as much, but is still ten times the amount of the government tax.[5]

The civil war that followed upon the rebellion of An Lu-shan put the finishing touch to the breakdown of the land regulations. From the end of the eighth century, we witness the spread of a different system of land-ownership.

The new system was a manorial system of "villas." It appeared at first sporadically, and was tacitly tolerated. But by the end of T'ang times and throughout the reign of the Sung dynasty (960-1279) it had become the predominant system of landownership.

The first "private villas" were in the nature of a gentleman's country seat with garden, and were known as "separate" land or country (*pie-shu, pie-yeh*). Later these developed into proper farming estates which consisted of the owner's country house, outbuildings called *guest quarters* (*k'o-fang*) for housing the farm hands, and fields and gardens (*t'ien-yüan*) worked either by the "guests" or, as they were also called, the *villa families* (*chuang-k'o, chuang-hu*), or possibly by tenant farmers (*tien-k'o,*

[5] Lu Chih (754-824), "Criticism of the Large Landowners," trans. Balazs, *op. cit.,* pp. 204-205.

*tien-hue*). The owners, usually officials and hence exempt from tax, were often absent, and so employed a bailiff (*chuang-li, chien-chuang*) to manage the farming of their estate, at any rate on the larger estates. The bailiff supervised the farm workers, and also the tenant farmers if the fields were much dispersed and the land let out in small parcels. He was in charge of all the farming operations, of getting in the harvest and selling it, of seeing to the upkeep of the estate, and probably also of recruiting the "people of the villa" from among those "wandering guests," the strangers in the village who, not being on the census list and owning no land, had no tax to pay, no *corvée* to perform, no military service to fulfill. These estates bore the name of the owner's family or office, or were sometimes known by the name of the place where the villa was situated. They were usually regarded as a unit, and passed, along with animals, equipment, and farm workers, into the hands of the new owner in the event of sale or inheritance. Many a village or small town of Sung times had its origin in a villa.

It is difficult to say whether the security gained by the tenant farmers and agricultural laborers at the expense of their independence was any real compensation for their lost liberty, or, to put it another way, whether their lot was any more enviable than that of a peasant vegetating on his own little plot of land. The ground rent or farm rent (*chuang tsu*) paid to the owner was usually 50 per cent of the harvest, and on an average came to 1.2 *shih* (about 1.7 bushels) of grain per *mou*. This was many times more than the government land tax, and there were other prestations that had to be made. S. Katō, the chief expert on the manorial system of landownership, admits that the comparative productivity of free and serf labor depended on the treatment meted out by the public authorities on the one hand and the private owners on the other; nevertheless, he maintains that the continuous increase in both population and area cultivated from the tenth century onward proves the superiority of the system of large estates.[6] This may be true insofar as the total amount of agricultural production and national revenue was greater in Sung times than in T'ang times. But the picture changes if one inquires into the price paid for the progress achieved.

If the testimony of contemporary accounts is to be believed, in Sung times both serfs and peasants lived under equally appalling conditions. Here is a description of the former by a well-known writer of the eleventh century:

> Those who till the fields do not own them, and those who own the fields do not till them. . . . The men at work are urged on with whip and cudgel,

[6] Katō Shigeshi, "Organization of the Chuang-yüan or Manors during T'ang and Sung and Their Development into Communities," *Mélanges Kano* (Kyoto, 1928), pp. 244-45 and 256 ff.

and the master treats them like slaves. He, on the other hand, sits at his ease and sees that his orders are carried out. . . . Of the produce of the fields, he takes half, although there is but one owner and ten laborers. Hence the owner, his half daily accumulating, attains wealth and power, while the laborer, his half merely providing his daily fare, falls into poverty and starvation.[7]

Ssu-ma Kuang (1019-1086), the famous historian and conservative minister, speaks of the peasant in these terms:

He is exposed to periodic catastrophes such as floods, droughts, frost, hail, locusts and other insects. If the harvest happens to be good, public and private debts [to the tax collector and the usurers] use it up between them. Grain and silk have ceased to belong to him before they have even left the threshing floor or been removed from the loom. He eats the husk, wears coarse cloth, and remains neither nourished nor clothed.[8]

## 19 / THE STATE AND RELIGION: AN EXPLORATORY COMPARISON IN DIFFERENT CULTURES / JOSEPH R. STRAYER

### Greece and Rome, the West, Islam

This paper is intended merely to frame certain hypotheses and present some comparisons and contrasts which may stimulate discussion.

Our basic problem is one which has been important and persistent in the history of all societies which have risen above the primitive level. Both the optimists and the pessimists about human nature have over-estimated the significance of self-interest in creating advanced societies. Enlightened self-interest is one of the rarest of human qualities—at least as rare as altruism—and it is difficult to imagine any large group of men voluntarily renouncing immediate advantages or making radical changes in their way of life just because they were promised great material gains in return for decades of struggle and self-repression. Unenlightened self-interest—pure selfishness—is an even less promising basis for organizing a society. As St. Augustine said, a state without justice—that is, without ideals—would be no state at all, but merely a great assembly of robbers.

It is probably true that man is by nature a social animal and that the small groupings of primitive peoples are formed spontaneously without

[7] Su Hsün (1009-1066), *Chia-yu chi* 5.7b, trans. Maspero, *op. cit.*, p. 178.

[8] *Sung-shih* (Official History of the Sung Dynasty) (*T'u-shu chi-ch'eng* edition of 1888), 179.3a-b.

Reprinted with permission from Joseph R. Strayer, "The State and Religion: Greece and Rome, the West, Islam," *Comparative Studies in Society and History*, I, No. 1 (1958), 38-43.

any organizing force or principle. But it is hard to see how any larger grouping—anything embodying the intensive and extensive cooperation which makes a civilization—could be formed as the result of mere natural instincts. Any really complicated social grouping must have required both a vision and a conscious effort at organization, that is, both the persuasive force of an ideal and the coercive force of a government.

In the early stages of any society, the ideal is almost always some form of religion and the government some form of monarchy. The two are so closely associated that it is sometimes difficult to separate them. The king who is high priest of his people, the high priest who wields the ultimate political authority are common and familiar figures. Often it seems that the state exists primarily to honor the golds and the gods exist primarily to protect the state.

But the close connection between religion and government, which must have been typical of many early states, was easily troubled by the flow of events. As we all know, institutions and ideas have a life of their own; they often outlive the society which created them. Nothing is more common than for a religion to survive the state which it helped to create. The gods of Asia Minor and of Syria were worshipped—many of them more widely—long after the city-states where they had originated had been swallowed up in great empires. It is perhaps a little less usual for a state to survive the religion on which it formerly based its authority, but the example of Rome shows that this is by no means impossible. Short of these catastrophes, it is still true that the ideals (religious or otherwise) of a society are apt to become fixed in an early stage of its development, and that as the society becomes more complicated it finds increasing difficulty in keeping a close relationship between its ideals and its political behavior. What was once an easy and natural symbiosis becomes a difficult and artificial process of reconciling conflicting interests and demands.

Western Europe inherited one of the most complicated and difficult of all these problems of religion and the state. The Roman Empire had outlived its old religion; it had then officially adopted a new religion which, in the West, outlived the empire. The new religion had not been universally accepted within the limits of the old empire, yet while the empire was falling the religion began to spread to people who had never accepted the authority of Rome. Thus it was at the same time both an official, established religion, and a voluntary, missionary religion. Christian ideals were fully developed and widely held before any real states rose in the West to replace the empire. Then, as Western rulers gained power, these ideals had to be reconciled with new forms of political authority. There are parallels to each of these stages in the history of other religions, but I know of no other religion which had to go through quite such a long and complicated process of defining its relations with political authority.

Moreover, one of the longest and most significant stages of defining religious-political relations in the West was the stage for which it is hardest to find a parallel elsewhere—the stage in which the church not only survived the Roman Empire, but took over much of its political machinery and law. The medieval church—as Maitland pointed out long ago—had many of the aspects of a state: involuntary membership, coercive power through laws and courts and taxation, even at times an army. For centuries during which political authority was weak and divided, it was more of a state than most of its secular rivals. During the feudal period the church alone had a centralized government, the church alone had a bureaucracy, the church alone kept records and followed legal precedents. And yet the church, at the height of its power, never took over all the functions of the state; secular rulers were always necessary. This made it possible for real states to rise again in Europe, but when they appeared, clashes with the church were almost inevitable. This was not merely because religious ideals and political commands conflicted; much more often it was because the boundaries between the state-like activities of the church and those of secular rulers had never been clearly drawn, or because they had been drawn at a point which seemed intolerable to the ruler of a real state. Thus what we call struggles between state and church were often purely political conflicts between two states, an old clerical state and a new secular state.

This unusual institutional situation was reflected in an unusual political theory—the theory of the two coordinate powers first clearly stated by Pope Gelasius (492-496). According to this theory the world is ruled by two powers, the priestly and the royal, both deriving authority directly from God. Each power must obey the other in its proper sphere—the bishops are bound by civil law in worldly matters, but secular rulers must submit to the judgment of prelates in religious affairs. And while the two powers are coordinate, they are not equal. Even Gelasius, at the very beginning of the Middle Ages, suggests that the responsibility of the clergy is great—later writers compare the church to the sun and the empire to the moon. Thus the interests of religion, as determined by the clergy, should always prevail over the interests of secular rulers, if there is a conflict between them.

This is a very difficult theory to apply in any specific situation; even in the Middle Ages extremists on both sides sought to modify it. It was easy to push it into theocracy, as many ardent supporters of the papacy did. It was somewhat more difficult to explain it away as giving the church mere moral authority, with no coercive power, yet this feat also was accomplished. But these extreme positions never gained many adherents, and Western peoples continued to believe in the two coordinate powers. Men were subject to both, they had to obey both, and if there was a conflict there was no logical, often no honorable way out. One loyalty had to be sacrificed to another, and while the balance of loyalties might shift, the conflict of consciences remained.

Now, as I suggested earlier, this seems to me an extreme case, far at the end of the spectrum of possible relations between religion and government, by no means typical of the experience of other peoples. Even if we try to eliminate the unique historical conditions in which the Christian church came to maturity, we still have throughout the Middle Ages a religion which demanded, and indeed required, special treatment by secular authorities. It was a religion which claimed exclusive possession of the truth and was unwilling to admit that other faiths might teach the same truth in a different guise. It therefore demanded the cooperation of the state in supporting the truth and in suppressing error. It was a religion in which salvation was based on sacraments, which could be administered only by a self-perpetuating, specially consecrated body of priests. It demanded obedience to these priests in matters of faith and morals, and it could enforce its demands by withholding the sacraments from any layman. It was a religion which insisted that salvation was incomparably more important than worldly comfort, and which therefore could reject proposals based on political expediency. In short, it was the right and duty of the church to be independent of lay authority, and it was therefore very easy for it to come into conflict with lay authority.

These are truisms, but their full force can be felt only if we compare Christianity with religions which had none of these characteristics, religions which were not exclusive, not sacramental, not greatly concerned with the future life. On the whole, the official religions of the Greek city-states and of the Roman Republic and early Empire conform to this definition. They were quite ready to admit that the same god might have many names and many forms, and that new divinities might be added to their pantheons. Many local gods had to be combined to form a Jupiter, and a Roman of the early Republic would not have recognized all the divinities worshipped under Augustus. Neither governments nor their religious experts were greatly concerned with the private religious practices of individual citizens; they made little effort to organize and regulate them. The only salvation with which they were concerned was the salvation of the state—its continuous existence on this earth. The only future life they foresaw for their citizens was uninteresting and unimportant—as far as there was any concern about life after death, that again was a private matter. Thus, instead of setting up goals and standards which might conflict with those of the state, Greek and Roman religion lived only through and for the state, and almost by necessity had the same objectives.

It has been said, loosely, that the ancients deified the city-state. This is not quite accurate, but they certainly came very close to it. Monarchy, after all, had had many religious aspects; in the absence of monarchy it was necessary to give the state the same religious aura. In Greece the city was identified with its protecting god or goddess; in Rome not only the protecting gods but the ideals and ideas of the republic were worshipped. These beliefs certainly made it easier to reverse the earlier process and to go back to the idea of a deified ruler when the city-state was swallowed up in great empires and monarchy had replaced democracy. The new rulers embodied the state, which had had sacred characteristics; it is not surprising that they themselves became sacred. Thus, obedience to the ruler was obedience to the gods, and a real conflict of loyalties was rare, if not impossible.

I have been speaking, of course, of official religions. It is true that this type of religion became increasingly unatisfactory to both Greeks and Romans, as they moved from the city-state to the imperial phase of their political development. New religions sprang up which stressed the future life and the idea of salvation, which had sacraments and organized priesthoods. But none of these religions had the exclusive character of Christianity; they recognized the existence of other gods and other rites. Even more important, they remained almost entirely in the sphere of private life. They were substitutes, not only for the old religion, but also for the old political system in which the citizen had rights and responsibilities. They enabled the individual to endure a society in which he no longer had influence; they did not set goals and standards for that society. The best proof of this is that every attempt to associate these new religions with the state, to use them to revivify political loyalty and political interest, was a failure. They remained cults; they could not clash with the government because they took little interest in public affairs.

Thus, if the Western experience in the Middle Ages stands at one end of the spectrum of possible relationships between religion and the state, the Greek and Roman experience stands at the other end. Official religion existed chiefly to serve the state; private religion had little influence on politics.

Islam, it seems to me, occupies a middle ground between these two extremes. It had a more typical history than Christianity in that it developed steadily along with its society; it did not have to face, early in its history, the problem of surviving the collapse of the civilization in which it had originated. It was more closely associated with the state than medieval Christianity was with any government. During its formative period, the caliph was more like the Roman combination of emperor and pontifex maximus than he was like the Christian pope. And when the power of the caliph declined, it was lost to new political leaders and not to religious authorities. On the other hand, Islam was as exclusive as Christianity and just as insistent on the importance of the future life. It lacked, however, both the sacramental system and the organized priesthood which were so important in the history of the Christian church.

These characteristics explain, to a large extent, the nature of the relation between state and religion in Mohammedan countries. Obviously, it was possible to have a conflict of interest between the demands of the state, centered on worldly prosperity and survival, and the demands of religion, centered on right behavior in this life, and salvation in the future. Religious dissidence in Islam could easily lead to political dissidence, even if the religious dissidence was more a matter of the strict application of moral principles than a dispute over doctrine. Witness the Almoravides of the eleventh century, or the Wahabis of the nineteenth and twentieth. But while there could be conflicts between religious principles and political expediency it was much harder—in fact, almost impossible—to have conflicts between religious *institutions* and political institutions. There was nothing like the church in Islam, no separate organization devoted to the preservation of the faith and the salvation of the individual. There were preachers and teachers, there were doctors of law and theology who headed rival schools of interpretation of the Koran and the Sunna. These men might have great influence and moral authority, but they had almost no power of their own. They did not control the "divine mysteries"; they did not stand between the individual and God. They were not even presiding officers of congregations of the faithful; they could not inflict penalties like the Christian excommunication. Without the support of the secular power, their decisions could not harm a private citizen. Much less could they contradict the authority of the state, short of joining a political revolution. They did not have the independence, the authority, the organization or the autonomy which enabled the Christian church to stand in open opposition to secular rulers for decades at a time. If a ruler's name were omitted from the Friday prayer in the great mosques—the most solemn politicoreligious ceremony in Islam—it simply meant that he had lost political control of that area, not that he had erred in faith or in morals.

On the other hand, the secular ruler was responsible for the religious welfare of his people—he was a defender of the faith, both against the infidel on the outside and the atheist or idolater within. The state had to be a Mohammedan state; neutrality or hostility to the established religion was unthinkable. Law was supposed to derive from the Koran and the Sunna, and in many respects it did lean very heavily on religion, though purely secular additions could be and were made. But the law, religious or otherwise, could be enforced only by the ruler, even when decisions were made by semireligious judges such as the cadis. And, after the early caliphate, purely secular courts and the even more purely secular police power made all important decisions. Even more significant was the fact that the permissible limits of religious speculation and divergence were determined by the ruler. For example, the rationalistic Mutazilah movement flourished under al-Mamur (813-833), but was abandoned in favor of a rigid orthodoxy by al-Mutawakkil in 848. In short, a religious leader who felt strongly about some problem of doctrine or morals could gain his point only by converting or dethroning the ruler.

Thus, the general rule in Mohammedan countries—stemming back to the Prophet himself—was that political power was necessary to achieve religious ends. The list of religious leaders who have headed rebellions is a long one, from the martyr Husain down to the Mahdi of our own age. If it seemed politically impossible to gain control of a large state, then the minority might secede and found a new and smaller state, as the Ismailites did. Short of this, the reformers could stir up public opinion, put pressure on the ruler, use the threat of disobedience or rebellion to make him change his conduct. But in a showdown, when there was a real conflict between the will of the ruler and the desires of the religious leader, the latter had to back down, or risk rebellion.

This really amounted to the primacy of the state in matters of religion, tempered by the fear of revolution. As long as the ruler remained officially Mohammedan, as long as the government adhered to the few essential tenets of Islam, religious opposition was difficult. And, as I said earlier, this strikes me as being, over-all, the most common pattern in history, certainly in recent history. The autonomous state-like medieval church, the political religions of Greece and Rome are both extremes. Much more common is the religion which is neither state-controlled nor yet a state in itself, which harmonizes with its society without being entirely dominated by it, which is a moral force, an influence on public opinion, but which becomes a political force only in exceptional circumstances.

## 20 / THE PLACE OF CONFUCIANISM IN THE CHINESE EMPIRE / *RUSHTON COULBORN*

The case of China is far simpler and better known than those of Iran and India. It is one of a peculiar importance of its own for reaching an understanding of the division of church and state.

Our earliest knowledge about China which is useful for this purpose is of a period about 1000 BC at the transition from Shang rule to Chou rule. It is quite clear that at that time religion and government were so closely united as to be, in effect, one. Political authority brought with it leadership in religion in almost mathematically exact correspondence.[1] As a feudal polity—or something very much like a feudal polity—arose in the century or two after the Chou conquest, religious leadership as well as political authority was feudalized. It is positively astonishing how closely the Chou polity, as it developed, resembles the polity of medieval Western Europe minus the church and the clergy, with the nobility, however, doubling in the character of clergy. This, of course, is to put the matter the wrong way round; correctly, we should say that medieval Western Europe resembles Chou China, but for the addition of a dichotomous church and its clergy. We reach our understanding of the resemblance, however, by seeing in the Chou *wang* pope and Holy Roman Emperor rolled into one; in the *chun tzu*, dignitaries who were at once barons and prelates; in the whole class of *shih*, men who were both knights and clerks.

In the religion of feudal Chou China there were ancestors to be cared for in their needs in the next existence and to care for their descendants yet remaining in their earthly existence, and there was an array of more or less animistic deities of which soil and sky were the chief. It was Hou T'u, god of the soil, who became mostly clearly feudalized, for every magnate had his altar to the Hou T'u of his own fief, and the monarch had his alter to Hou T'u for all humanity. From about the seventh century BC nations began to emerge in China,[2] as they did in Europe about the fourteenth century AD. That age in China was also the age of the great classical philosophy, which corresponds for Europe with the thought of the schoolmen and of the Reformation, of the Renaissance and of early modern philosophy. The Chinese classical philosophy pro-

Reprinted with permission from R. Coulborn, "The State and Religion: Iran, India and China," *Comparative Studies in Society and History,* 1, No. 1 (1958), 52-54.

[1] A good recent account of the phenomenon is H. Maspero, *Mélanges posthumes sur les religions et l'histoire de la Chine,* I. *Les religions chinoises* (Paris, 1950), p. 1947.

[2] Cf. Owen Lattimore, *Inner Asian Frontiers of China* (London and New York, 1940), pp. 392-93.

foundly changed religion, but left its relation to the state virtually unaffected. No church arose, and only the specialized politicians and philosophers who emerged from the *shih* class look slightly clerical in the European sense.

Toward the end of the second century BC, about the middle of the rule of the Prior Han Dynasty, Chinese civilization began to undergo one of those declines, soon overtaken by a revival, which we have met in the history of India and Iran. The decline involved a great upsurge in superstition, the revival a regrowth of religion and the intrusion of alien religions, most notably of Mahayanian Buddhism from India via eastern Iran. There thus arose in China rival cults—not that rivalry began with the appearance of alien cults; it first arose between native Confucianism and Taoism, as those two formerly severe philosophies became transformed into religions.

As they developed, the new religions came to have certain institutions which might be considered as incipient churches. The Confucianists indeed never developed a distinct institution, but, as theologians in the service of the state, they early sought to impress upon the state their views of doctrinal orthodoxy and to guide state policy by divination.[3] The Taoists, during and after the Han Empire, produced an organization which may have amounted to an actual theocracy. At any rate, it had some sort of a polity in Szechuan and Shensi and was headed by a personality called the "T'ien Shih," whose title Europeans have translated overfreely as "Taoist Pope." In the fifth century AD, Taoism was influential in Wei, a state in northern China, but no Taoist church ever came to be the leading institution.

From the third to the sixth centuries AD, there was no unitary empire in China. The Han Empire broke into three states, and later there were many states. It was in this period that Buddhism built up considerable political influence which continued long after the re-establishment of the united empire. Yet the Buddhists never organized themselves even as the Confucianist had done. They remained monks, living in convents, depending for their influence upon laymen, especially upon emperors, who accepted their teachings and governed in the light of Buddhist morals. There can be no doubt—though there is still argument—about the profound and far-reaching influence of Buddhism upon the Chinese mind from top to bottom of the society, but the cult produced no institutions other than monasteries.

[3] Yao Shen-yu, "The Cosmological and Anthropological Philosophy of Tung Chung-shu," *Journal of the North China Branch of the Royal Asiatic Society*, LXXIII (1948), 40-68; Hu Shih, "The Establishment of Confucianism as a State Religion during the Han Dynasty," *ibid.*, LX (1929), 20-41; W. K. Shryock, *The Origin and Development of the State Cult of Confucius* (New York, 1932).

Nor did it by any means wholly dominate the official mind in China at any time. The T'ang Dynasty, not long after its establishment at the beginning of the seventh century, reorganized the governing bureaucracy and regularized, probably for the first time, the system of examinations by which the bureaucracy was recruited.[4] While it is unlikely that the examinations at the time were only in the Confucianist classics, the bureaucracy as an institution and the idea of recruiting it by examination are Confucianist. At its origin the practice may have been Legalist rather than Confucianist, but by T'ang times there was no Legalist school of thought, and Confucianism had ingested certain Legalist ideas. There can, in fact, be no doubt that the form of the state, as understood by T'ang rulers was Confucianist even though T'ang rulers were personally more of Taoist than of Buddhist views. It is clear, therefore, that Confucianist views had survived, at least in some Chinese states, during the period of division between the third and sixth centuries.

The Confucianist bureaucracy was not a church in T'ang times. In fact, there was really no institution then or later which could be so called. Neither was Confucianism a state religion then; it was simply one among several religions. In the ninth century, when the T'ang government was in full decline, the influence of Buddhism in politics was also declining. The Sung Dynasty, which reestablished the empire in the later tenth century, came under the influence of the great Confucianist revival of the eleventh and twelfth centuries. The neo-Confucianism of Sung times became official, but as a religion it was quite peculiar. It was an effective and vigorous philosophy, one of the world's greatest. With it was associated a kind of vestigial cult. There were temples in which Confucius and his chief followers were revered, yet not, after the revival of the philosophy, worshipped. If this was a church, it was the slightest and most discreet such institution which ever existed.

## 21 / REVENUE FARMING / W. LOTZ

Revenue farming is the practice of assigning public revenue to private individuals or institutions in return for the payment of a lump sum to

---

[4] R. des Rotours, "Les grands fonctionnaires des provinces en Chine sous la dynastie des T'ang," *T'oung Pao*, XXV (1927), 219-332; des Rotours, *Le traité des examens traduit de la nouvelle histoire des T'ang* (Paris, 1932); des Rotours, *Traité des fonctionnaires et traité de l'armée traduits de la nouvelle histoire des T'ang*, 2 vols. (Leyden, 1947-48).

the public treasury. The difference between the amount paid and that actually collected constitutes the profit of the revenue farmer. The practice may be applied to revenue derived from public property or from taxation. While the farmer of revenue from public property may derive his return from the application of improved methods in the utilization of the specific property, thereby creating the source of his profit, the tax farmer as a rule secures his profit by increasing the collections at the expense of the taxpayer. Fiscal opinion generally regards tax farming as a wasteful form of revenue administration which has no place in a modern system of fiscal organization. A method intermediate between direct collection of taxes by government organs and revenue farming is the device, employed in several countries, of entrusting the collection of revenue, particularly of taxes, to private individuals who act on account of the fisc and receive a definite percentage of the receipts as commission.

Tax farming is an ancient practice. It arose whenever the growth of public revenues was not accompanied by the development of a permanent and salaried body of government officials equipped for the complex task of assessing and collecting taxes. This was the case in Greece and in the early period of the Roman Republic, where government offices were positions of honor assigned by rotation to all free men. As the officials were not trained in financial matters, they inevitably assigned the collection of customs duties and other fiscal levies to wealthy citizens who advanced the funds to the treasury and employed commercially trained slaves to collect the taxes.

In the Greek cities and in the early period of the Roman Republic, the results were not unsatisfactory; the amounts involved were not large and the compactness of the state made possible effective public control which prevented the tax farmers from reaping huge profits at the expense of the taxpaying citizenry. But with Rome's territorial expansion the fiscal administration became increasingly complicated. Farming of taxes and of the rents and taxes to be paid by tenants of the *ager publicus* in the provinces involved large funds of capital and serious financial risks. Pledges had to be given to the treasury for the sums due to the state. In order to raise the necessary capital, tax farmers united into companies (*societates publicanorum*), which secured profitable contracts to supply the materials for public works and also engaged in usurious lending to provincial municipalities. The increasing size of administrative areas and the growing economic and political power of the tax farmers prevented an impartial control of the provincial magistrates in checking the manifold abuses of the tax farmers.

With the inauguration of the empire, certain reforms were initiated: the farming of direct taxes was abolished and an impartial administration by permanent and well-trained officials was attempted, although never fully realized. The emperors continued to farm indirect taxes, especially customs duties, but provided some measure of supervision to counteract the high profit and other abuses of the tax farmers. After the first century of prosperity, when taxes were relatively low, the position of the taxpayer in the Roman Empire became progressively worse and, from the time of Diocletian, Roman subjects were no better off than under the *publicani*. Collection of direct taxes in the provinces was more and more entrusted to the municipal authorities. The municipalities, however, were in such bad financial shape that they were unable to guarantee the public revenue as the tax farmers had done during the republican period. In order to protect the treasury against financial losses, the Roman government finally adopted a system in which the wealthier citizens were made to answer for the taxes owed by all inhabitants; the ten or twenty wealthiest members of the local communities were forced to make up any deficit in the amount assessed to their district. This system could have no other effect than to deter people from saving and investing.

Difficulties also multiplied in the administration of indirect taxes. As the government tightened the control over the activities of the farmers of customs duties and other indirect taxes, the profits tended to decline and there was no incentive for private capitalists to bid for tax farming. Consequently the government resorted to compulsory methods; the person designated was obliged to assume the task of tax farming and was personally responsible for the delivery of the assessed amount. Nominally farmers of taxes, these persons became in reality unpaid or badly paid state officials. A general system of despotic compulsion prevailed first in the oriental provinces and, from the third century AD, in the other parts of the empire. The position of the tax receiver, whether or not he was a tax farmer, was universally dreaded. That of the taxpayer was still worse, for nonpayment of taxes involved not only confiscation of property but also corporal punishment. The emperor endeavored to check the harsh methods employed in the collection of taxes by appointing *procuratores* to supervise the activities of the tax collectors; but from the third century abuses continued to multiply.

In the later period of the empire, the big landlords offered to deliver in a lump sum to the treasury the taxes due from their possessions in return for their right to collect taxes from their tenants. This system was still more pernicious than tax farming, since it favored the spread of feudalism. In the cities the corporations of artisans and of small traders were held responsible for the sums imposed upon them and individuals were not allowed to leave their trade or to relinquish their membership in the corporation. The failure of the Roman Empire to develop an effective and impartial tax administration undoubtedly contributed greatly to the ruin not only of private households but finally also of the public finances.

Another instance in which long retention of the system of tax farming ended in abuse and financial disorder is to be observed in the history of the French kingdom. The early resort of the French kings to revenue farming was probably due to the general absence of a permanent body of government officials in the early Middle Ages. The practice may have been further suggested by the custom whereby the *prévôtés* collected the rents and taxes from the king's domain. The farming of special forms of revenues, such as fees, was resorted to as early as the thirteenth and the fourteenth century. Whatever the origin of the different forms of revenue farming in France, there is general agreement that the retention of tax farming long after the development of a permanent bureaucracy as an instrument of public administration was due to bribery of prominent members of the court and to the chronic financial difficulties of the treasury, which came to depend largely upon the advances of the wealthy tax farmers. Even such honest and able financial administrators as Sully and Turgot could not abolish tax farming, because the government was never able to repay the advances of the farmers when they became due. As late as 1706 out of 150,277,864 livres of public revenue farmed revenue amounted to not less than 59,520,000 livres.

Similar conditions and abuses existed in medieval and postmedieval Spain and Portugal. For a short time, tax farming was tried in the Netherlands, in England, in Germany, and in the Italian cities. It was resorted to at Baghdad during the decay of the Arabian Empire and continued into the modern period in Turkey. In Russia taxation of alcoholic drinks was farmed out from the time of Peter the Great until 1861. Two features characterized many of these tax farming experiments: foreigners figured prominently among the revenue farmers, and the accumulation of vast fortunes by the tax farmers provided a stimulus to the development of modern capitalism.

While tax farming assures the government a fixed income and thus enables it to plan the budget, the abuses attendant upon the device of farming and the dangers inhering in the existence of a wealthy group of tax farmers, whose interests frequently conflict with those of the taxpaying citizenry and of the state, outweigh the possible benefits of the system. Fiscal doctrine and practice in modern times regard the collection and administration of taxes as a direct function of public authorities. Turkey, for instance, abolished tax farming as soon as modernization of its political and fiscal system permitted. The collection of indirect taxes of municipal bodies by farmers against payment of a lump sum is not generally held as dangerous but is uncommon at the present time. Special forms of collection by private individuals on government account, against the payment of a commission, are in use in Italy; and a somewhat similar measure (the "tax ferrets" system) whereby percentage rewards are given to private persons instrumental in tracking down tax delinquencies has been used in the state of Ohio in the United States.

In the administration of public revenue other than taxation the tendency is likewise toward direct state management. With the exception of public farmlands, which are generally let to tenants for private utilization in return for fixed rental, other forms of public property, such as utilities, mines, forests and mints, are administered in most countries directly by public authorities. Frequently such enterprises adopt the form of joint stock companies, whose shares are owned by public authorities. In recent years some countries in search of credit have resorted to a form of revenue farming; for example, the revenue from the match monopoly was assigned to the Swedish match concern of Ivar Kreuger in return for a loan secured by the latter. Considerations of state prestige probably account for the retention of the practice of farming revenues from gambling establishments.

## INTRODUCTION

*We may now proceed to the last—and also, in a way, the major —part of our analysis: an examination of the process of the decline of these empires.*

*The crux of the process was the interplay between the goals and policies of the rulers, on the one hand, and the political orientations and activities of the major social groups, on the other. These conflicts became especially serious when the rulers emphasized very "expensive" goals which exhausted the available economic and manpower resources, or when the different social groups developed strong, autonomous political orientations. Such situations aggravated the special sensitivities of these political systems, and gave rise to forces that helped to undermine the delicate balance between political participation and apathy on which the continuity of these systems depended. In such situations, the rulers tended to maintain active control over different strata of the society, thus increasing the power of the more conservative traditional elements and weakening or alienating the more flexible, differentiated groups.*

*The process of imperial decline was also usually closely connected with the "aristocratization" or ossification of the bureaucracy and with its growing parasitic exploitation of the economy, and consequently with the depletion of the more active political leadership identified with the regime. With this depletion of leadership, there often developed a continuous flow of foreign elements into the centers of the realms, mainly into the military. These foreign military groups initially were mere mercenaries—the hirelings and personal helpers of the rulers. Gradually, they succeeded in infiltrating some of the most important political posts (becoming eunuchs, military commandants, and viziers), and finally totally usurped the highest political power. In similar fashion, foreign merchants (as in Byzantium or in the Ottoman Empire), sometimes succeeded in monopolizing all the tradeposts vacated by the depleted indigenous merchant groups. In Europe, where these economically and socially more active elements were not weakened, they became alienated from the rulers and from the political institutions of the society, and became sources of political revolt and social change.*

*The general process of decline was rooted in the basic characteristics of the social and political structures of all these empires, and it was common to all. However, the exact ways in which this process developed in the different empires varied according to the specific structural characteristics of that empire and the various external processes to which it was subject. For example, the existence of cultural and political bonds between the major groups in the society and the rulers (as in the case of the Confucian order in China) facilitated the absorption of change and made possible the continuity of the social system. However, in those empires where the various social and cultural groups did not entirely identify with the rulers and the polity, the process of disintegration was accelerated. Among the more "accidental" or "external" reasons of such decline the most important are: external pressures of different intensity, major movements of population, conquests of nomads, international economic fluctuations, and the degree to which there existed from the beginning ethnic heterogeneity in a given society.*

*The various essays presented in this section indicate some of the causes and processes of change common to all the empires, but they also emphasize some differences. Thus we see that, in the Roman and Byzantine Empires, for instance, the alienation of major groups within the society, accompanied by foreign invasions, brought about the decline of the whole imperial system. In others, especially in China, the process of Change usually gave rise only to the replacement of one dynasty by another. It is in this context that Kracke's exposition of Sung society as "Change Within Tradition" is especially important. The analysis of these differences is of special interest from our point of view.*

*Among the excerpts presented here, those by Parsons on China and by Diehl on Byzantium treat specific historical incidents, while the others— those by Jones on Rome and by Kracke on China—emphasize the "deeper" processes of change. Although Kracke's essay deals with the possibility of change within an existing framework and others, especially Jones' essay, deal with the downfall of a whole system, some common strands run through all.*

*The last excerpt attempts to weave these strands together, nevertheless stressing the differences among empires and attempting to analyze them systematically.*

## 22 / SUNG SOCIETY: CHANGE WITHIN TRADITION

### *E. A. KRACKE, JR.*

When we speak of social change in China, we most often have in mind one or the other of two pictures.[1] The first is the change that we see today, when radically new ideas, techniques, and forces from foreign countries have shaken the traditional social order, altering the old patterns rapidly and sometimes violently. The second picture is that of the dynastic cycle, a concept that we have inherited from the traditional Chinese historian, sometimes adding a few embellishments of our own. The political fortunes of a ruling house are often reflected (and perhaps affected) by a characteristic cycle in the whole political and economic order of the nation: from successful adjustment and control to maladjustment and chaos. The end of each cycle, if we focus our attention only on these factors, leaves Chinese society much as it was at the end of the cycle before. But this perspective tends to omit qualitative changes that occur in Chinese society on a different plane.

The kind of social change to be considered now differs from both of these. It is the long and continuous process of social development that in China as in our own civilization has accompanied the interplay between the traditional ideas and ways of life and the new concepts, techniques, and patterns of activity that evolve at home or enter from abroad. While at times this process of development moved slowly, and at times even retrogressed in some respects, the Chinese way of life nevertheless underwent through the centuries a cumulative alteration that was essentially irreversible. At times the forces of change so interacted that their gathered momentum was almost revolutionary in its social impact. An outstanding example of such rapid and far-reaching change is supplied by the Sung period, from the tenth century to the thirteenth.

The beginnings of the movement that attained so dramatic a tempo in the Sung period can be traced back, in some respects, through several centuries. Perhaps the first clearly perceptible aspect of the movement is the striking shift in the mass of China's population, from the northern plain country to the valleys of the mountainous south and the southeast coast. This migration had begun in the early centuries of our era, impelled both by economic difficulties and by foreign invaders of the old homeland; but as late as the middle of the eighth century the Yangtse

Reprinted with permission from E. A. Kracke, Jr., "Sung Society: Change Within Tradition," *Far Eastern Quarterly,* 14 (1955), 479-89.

[1] This article follows in outline and general content a paper presented at the symposium on traditional Chinese society during the Far Eastern Association sessions at New York, April 1954.

valley and the areas further south still held only some 40-45 per cent of China's people. By the end of the thirteenth century, this area reported no less than 85-90 per cent of the nation's population, and no less than 20 per cent were established in the valleys of Fukien and eastern Chekiang along the southeast coast.[2]

The rich new delta lands of the south became the chief suppliers of China's granaries. Some of the economic consequences of this are already well known, and need only be recapitulated here. To feed the armies guarding the northern border, and to provision the capital in the north, the central administration undertook to expand the canal system and subsidiary land communications from the south on a mammoth scale. Aided by the new facilities, private commerce grew rapidly. The Chinese now living along the remote southern coast no doubt found it necessary to import tools and other goods from the older settlements, and exchanged for these the new products native to the semitropical land in which they found themselves, as well as products from the South Seas and the countries of the Indian Ocean.[3] Easier contacts by sea with Persia and Arabia encouraged the growth of foreign commerce, soon bringing to the growing coastal cities settlements of Hindu and Arab merchants. The Chinese also . . . turned to the sea and assumed a leading place among maritime peoples. Internal commerce among the regions of China, at first confined for the most part to luxury items for the few, now expanded in variety and in its significance for larger groups of the nation. With the growth of interregional trade, money came into its own, for

[2] See census for mid-eighth century in Stefan [Etienne] Balazs, "Beiträge zur wirtschaftsgeschichte der T'ang-Zeit, I," *Mitteilungen des Seminars für Orientalische Sprachen*, 34 (1931), 19-20; and Hans Bielenstein, "The census of China during the period 2-742 A.D.," *BMFEA* 19 (1947), 125-63. For 1290 census see Herbert Franke, *Geld und wirtschaft in China unter der Mongolen-herrschaft* (Leipzig, 1949), 127-31; for southeastern provinces at this time see *Yüan-shih* (*Po-na pen* ed.), ch. 62, passim. The growth of population in south China was from about 4 million households around 750 to a little under 12 million in 1290. The highest recorded south Chinese population (before the seventeenth century) was that of about 1220 which exceeded 12.5 million households (*Wen-hsien t'ung-k'ao*, 11: 18b-20a; *Sung-shih*, 85: 4a). The small number of individuals per household reported in Sung census data has led to much discussion. A rough average of around five persons per household seems most probable, but differing local methods of tabulation caused variations inversely proportionate to the size of the local unit in question. See Katō Shigeru (Shigeshi) . . . , *Shina keizaishi kōshō* (Tokyo: Toyo Bunko Publications, Series A, No. 34, 1952-1953). The reported fall of the north Chinese population from some 10.5 million households about 1110 to under a million in 1235 is staggering to the imagination though reasonably well supported by the records of the Mongol period (H. Franke).

[3] For the place of local and imported products from the Canton area in the trade of Central and North China as early as the Latter Han, see E. H. Schafer, "The Pearl Fisheries of Ho-p'u," *JAOS*, 72 (1952), 155-68. The area was even to some extent reliant on cereal imports from more settled parts of China.

many purposes rapidly superseding the old transactions in kind. By the eleventh century, a system of regulated paper currency was in operation, and the coinage of copper money reached proportions never again approached in Chinese dynastic history. Facilities for the transfer of funds and the provision of credit also developed. The various regions of China were no longer self-sufficient economically, but increasingly specialized in their produce—foods or goods or services—and therefore interdependent. These developments brought into being, by the eleventh century, a Chinese economy apparently far more complex than any of earlier times.[4]

Of the social change that accompanied this economic development, we have as yet only a very incomplete picture. But certain of its aspects stand out strikingly in the records. One aspect—perhaps of key significance—is the changing role of the great city. In earlier periods the few outstanding cities had achieved their greatness and economic importance only after designation as national capitals. Their symmetrical and regular plan, centered on the principal imperial palace, gave visible evidence of their origin and purpose. From the tenth century to the thirteenth this was not so. In this later period the cities chosen as capitals had already achieved importance as trade centers at strategic points on the lines of communication.

K'ai-feng, the first Sung capital, exemplified this particularly well. Originally a regional administrative seat at a main transfer point on the arterial canal from the south, its access to southern rice supplies recommended it during the troubled years succeeding the T'ang [period]. The city had grown with its commercial importance, as successive new walls enclosed the suburbs that grew spontaneously beyond the older city gates. Within the sixteen-mile circuit of the outer walls, space was at a premium. The second Sung emperor renounced the planned expansion of his palace because it would have forced the demolition of private dwelling quarters. As a result of this history, although the city lay in the level valley of the Yellow River, it lacked the symmetry that had marked earlier national capitals and would later distinguish Peking (also primarily political in its character).[5]

The later Sung capital of Hang-chou was also an important trade center at the time of its political elevation in 1135. Its population was huge: the numbers within its walls during the later years of the dynasty

---

[4] On currency and credit facilities, see L. S. Yang, *Money and Credit in China* (Cambridge, Mass., 1952) esp. pp. 38, 51-61, 71-80; and his "Buddhist Monasteries and Four Money-raising Institutions in Chinese History," *HJAS*, 13 (June 1950), 174-79. For a general description of economic developments in the Sung and further references see E. A. Kracke, Jr., *Civil Service in Early Sung China* (Cambridge, Mass., 1953), pp. 11-18.

[5] See E. O. Reischauer, *HJAS* 2 (March 1937), 29 (résumé of article by Miyazaki Ichisada); Kracke, *op. cit.*, pp. 13, 25; *Sung-shih*, 85: 4b-9a.

have been estimated as 900,000, and those in its suburbs as some 600,000 more.[6]

While the capitals of the eleventh to thirteenth centuries had thus grown strongly commercial in character, their supremacy among Chinese cities was challenged by other urban centers still more reliant on business activity. By the year 1100, at least four urban areas far surpassed the capital area in population. We have no exact data on the numbers living within the walls of these cities or in their immediate suburbs, but census reports suggest that each of the urban areas held a million or more people within the borders of its prefecture—a space very roughly comparable to the greater metropolitan areas of London or New York. Such population concentrations would seem to outdistance by far the largest urban agglomerations of that time in Europe, even by the largest estimates of the latter.

During the next two centuries the urban growth continued, and in several instances the prefectural populations apparently doubled, tripled, or quadrupled by 1290. Among the most dramatic increases, three were on the southeast coast (Hang-chou, Su-chou, and Fu-chou), and one (Jao-chou) near the inland trade route from the Yangste to Canton. The prefecture of Fu-chou in 1290 reported approximately 3.875 million people, suggesting an urban concentration of impressive proportions.[7]

It was just around this time, soon after the Sung downfall, that Marco Polo visited these places as an agent of the Mongol conqueror Kublai. His descriptions of the magnificence of Hang-chou, the capital, and of the trade metropolis Ch'üan-chou, are well known. But he also observed

[6] Katō Shigeru, *Shina keizaishi kōshō*, 2: 417-418. This estimate is based on numbers of households and rice-consumption data. Others have placed the total both higher and lower.

[7] The rough area of a prefecture varied in different circuits from around 1200 square miles to around 6000. The largest prefectures were K'ai-feng and those in Fu-chien, Ching-hu-pei, and Ching-hu-nan. Those in the south of course included large wild and mountainous portions, and the populations were actually concentrated in much more restricted areas. Compare the 1725 square miles of metropolitan London, with some 9.835 million population, or 3550 square miles of New York, with 13.175 million. London and Paris did not exceed some 500,000 persons until about 1700. See W. S. and E. S. Woytinsky, *World Population and Production: Trends and Outlook* (New York, 1953), p. 113. In general the larger estimates for ancient Rome and medieval Constantinople do not exceed this figure, and conservative opinion seems to favor much smaller figures for these. The two subprefectures of Fu-chou with seats within the city walls counted some 60,000 families, probably around 300,000 individuals, accepting Katō Shigeru's interpretation of the Sung data (*Tōhō gakuhō* (Tokyo), 11: 1-15.) Other large subprefectures were clustered close by. See also E. H. Schafer, *The Empire of Min* (Rutland, Vt., and Tokyo, 1954), p. 79. For other cities about 1075 see Kracke, *op. cit.*, p. 13. By 1290 the prefectures of Su-chou, Jao-chou, and Hang-chou were reported to have respectively around 2.434 million, 4.037 million, and 1,835 million (*Yüan-shih*, Chap. 62, passim).

another phenomenon that is suggested by contemporary census figures —the growth and multiplication of smaller cities and towns. In describing the journey from Hang-chou to Fu-chou (less than three hundred miles as the crow flies), he tells of no less than six "large, noble, and beautiful" or "noble and great" cities, and in the stages of his journey between these he notes no less than seven times "always finding cities and villages enough, very beautiful and very great"; on one two-day ride he remarks that these are "so frequent and continuous that you seem as you ride to go through the middle of a single city." [8] Allowing for the colorful exaggerations we must permit to this oldest of China-hands, the regions that Polo saw along the southeast coast must certainly have been advanced in urban development compared with his native Italy—the most urbanized part of Europe in that day. While most of the terrain was mountainous and poorly adapted to farming, the few lands available had been fully exploited. A Sung writer notes that intensive cultivation had transformed once worthless acres to the most fertile in the empire, and while Marco Polo refers occasionally to the livestock he saw (oxen, buffalo, cows, goats, swine, and fowl) and to certain special plant products, he speaks not of fields but of "fine gardens."

But rich as the fields were, they were still too few. The coastal regions still depended for their prosperity on the income from their mines, commerce, manufactures, tea, and sea produce, and beyond the narrow valley floors must have preserved some of the air of an unsettled borderland. On four stages of his journey Polo mentions the "hunting and chase enough of beasts and birds" and refers as many times to the great and fierce "lions" (tigers?) that molest travelers, to such an extent that in one part of the route at least "it is very dangerous to pass through those regions unless people go in great numbers." [9] In an area seeming thus sparsely settled over much of its extent, and developing rapidly in industry and trade, typifying the new trend, it is difficult not to suspect analogies with the frontier of opportunity that played a vital role in the development of our own civilization.

Who were the people that lived in the growing cities of this area? We have no clear picture of them, but there are at least some clues to their character. As in earlier times, there must have been a considerable number of civil and military officials, stationed there for limited terms by the central government, along with a more or less permanent corps of clerks and official underlings. There were the army garrisons usually stationed in all large places. There were no doubt well-to-do scholars

---

[8] A. C. Moule and Paul Pelliot, *Marco Polo, the description of the world,* 1 (London, 1938), pp. 343-47.

[9] Moule and Pelliot, *op. cit.*

without official employment, and poorer scholars who lived on their earnings as teachers, or from such miscellaneous employments as public letter-writing or storytelling. And there were the merchants and artisans, great and small, blending at the lowest economic level with the unskilled laborers. Considering the indicated sizes of the cities, the last three occupations must have constituted the preponderant group of inhabitants in most cases. The composition of the Sung populations cannot have differed too greatly from that observed by Marco Polo only around a decade after the dynasty's fall: in all his comments on the six larger cities he saw between Hang-chou and Fu-chou, and in four of his comments on the places between, he notes that the inhabitants "live by trade and by crafts," and implies mercantile activities indirectly by repeated references to the "abundance of all things for life," which he notes were very cheap. (To other activities he makes very little reference.) [10]

What was true of this area was probably true also, to a more limited degree, of the great cities more widely scattered in other parts of China at this time. All were joined by the same commercial links, and often frequented by the same far-traveling merchants.

Surviving records tell us of the merchants' activities and mode of life chiefly at the capitals, but in these respects too different regions may have presented a rather similar picture.

The merchants, artisans, and providers of services were organized in guilds, which had powers of discipline over their own members, although these organizations had no apparent role in the general administration of the cities. The guild members had to some extent emancipated themselves from the close official supervision that existed during the T'ang [period]. Their business activities were no longer confined within the great walled markets, or limited to the hours in which the government permitted the opening of the market portals. Commerce and manufacture were now carried on in shops scattered throughout the city or beyond the city gates, though establishments of the same trade tended to group together.[11]

Long and persistent governmental efforts to regulate trade and control prices were matched by equally persistent and largely successful evasion on the part of the merchants. Attempts of the state to monopolize certain profitable industries had been costly and only partly successful. But in the Sung [period] the state had learned to apply its taxes more

[10] Moule and Pelliot; Etienne Balazs, "Les villes Chinoises,' in *Recueils de la Société Jean Bodin, 6; La ville* (Brussels, 1954), p. 236.

[11] Katō Shigeru, "On the Hang or the Associations of Merchants in China," *Memoirs of the Research Department of the Toyo Bunko,* Vol. VIII (1936) 53-71; Ch'in Kuan . . . (1049-1100), *Huai-hai chi* . . . (*Ssu-pu ts'ung-k'än* ed.), 15: 6b.

flexibly and to restrict its monopolies to certain key operations of an industry; through such policies the state diverted what was perhaps the lion's share of the profits to its treasuries.[12]

Such state controls may well have retarded significantly the growth of commercial activity and power. At the time, however, there must have been little evidence of this. The more successful merchants accumulated great wealth, and their style of living vied with that of the imperial princes. Sumptuary laws had always, before this, restricted the colors that should be used by each class of society. By 995, however, sumptuary laws were unenforceable, and all were repealed but the ban on a certain shade of deep purple reserved for the imperial house and the highest officials. There is evidence that even this color was taken over by commoners within a few years.[13] We read that the families of great merchants wore pearls and jade. Their carriages thronged the roads, and in the words of a contemporary "rubbed hubs with those of distinguished families." In the T'ang [period], we are told, even a servant who had served in an aristocratic family scorned a master who haggled in person with a merchant. By the eleventh century, even important officials had discovered the attractions of commerce, and many augmented their income by combining business operations with their official journeys. Merchants were socially accepted in élite circles. Through such connections, or through their wealth, some of them secured government office, and served in positions of some importance.[14]

But the professional trader still found certain barriers to his social advancement. He still lacked the approval of more conservative scholars. His indulgence in luxuries elicited complaints very much like those that had been evoked by a more modest commercial expansion a millennium earlier. His pursuit of money was felt to be unworthy. The officials criticized his disposition to make profits by cornering the market; because this was at the expense of the poor—and no doubt because the official preferred that the state monopolies should garner such profits. The grumbling of the conservatives, however, may have been in itself another indication that [the] power of commerce was recognized as a

[12] Chao Ching . . . , "Sung-tai chih chuan-mai chuh-tu" . . . , Yen-ching she-hui k'o-hsüeh, 2 (October 1949), 59-94.

[13] See Sung hui-yao chi-kao . . . , "Yü-fu" . . . , 4: 5a.

[14] See Hsia Sung . . . (984-1050), Wen-chuang chi . . . (Ssu-k'u ch'üan-shu chen-pen ed.) 13: 15b-16b; Li Kou . . . (1009-1059), Chih-chiang Li hsien-sheng wen-chi . . . (Ssu-pu ts'ung-k'an ed.) 18: 7a-8b; Ch'in Kuan, Huai-hai chi 15: 4a-6a; Ch'üan Han-sheng . . . "Sung-tai kuan-li chih ssu-ying shang-yeh" . . . , Bulletin of the Institute of History and Philology, Academia Sinica, 7.2 (1936), 205-206. An interesting example is Ma Chi-liang . . . , of a family of tea-merchants, who married into the imperial circle and had reached high office when his instinct for profit brought misfortune (Sung-shih, 463: 18b).

potential threat to the supremacy of the bureaucrat; in fact, specific complaints of the growing influence that merchants exercised over officials are not lacking.[15]

The new social environment created by the cities surely had its impact on the evolution of Chinese culture. The operation of any but the simplest business naturally required at least a certain minimum of literacy, and the city environment gave better opportunities for even the poorest to gain a smattering of the written character. The successful and ambitious tradesman would naturally hope that education would win for his sons an entrée into the bureaucracy. When the new urban reader competed with the older scholar for written texts, a new demand for books was created. In the century after 950 the technique of wood-engraving, long used to multiply Buddhist charms and texts, suddenly found new users, and in a short time the art of printing was applied to practically all the existing varieties of literature.

For the relatively unlettered, a multiplicity of entertainments was also devised, ranging from troops of acrobats and displays of fireworks to puppet shows, shadow plays, and simple theatrical presentations. Through the stories that served as themes for such public performances, some parts of the sophisticated culture could reach the illiterate, and facilitate a sharing of the great tradition with larger groups. Particularly important in this respect was the role of the storyteller: unemployed scholars frequently made their living by recounting some of the dramatic episodes of history to audiences in the market place. Through the prompting-books some of them wrote to aid their confreres, they created the proto-types of the later great fictional themes. At the same time the old themes were presented in the language of the people and transmuted to appeal to a more popular audience, until the content itself reflected their viewpoint and their tastes. It could scarcely be accidental that the Chinese popular novel traces back to this period.[16]

The influence of the new city life also had its impact on society beyond the city walls. The growing importance of a money economy must surely have contributed a significant share to the increasing complications of the farm problem. The crops of different regions were becoming more specialized, leaving the farmer often less self-sufficient, and more vulnerable in years of crop failure. While the farmer probably relied little on the cities for his basic necessities, it seems that traveling mer-

[15] Li Kou and Hsia Sung, *op. cit.*

[16] Yoshikawa Kōjirō, *Gen zatsugeki kenkyū* (Tokyo, 1954), 72-73; R. G. Irwin, *The Evolution of a Chinese novel, Shui-hu-chuan* (Cambridge, Mass., 1953), 23-24; J. I. Crump, Jr., "P'ing-hua and the early history of the San-kuo chih," *JAOS*, 71.4 (1951) 249-58; Balazs, "Les villes Chinoises," 231-33; Wang Ling, "On the invention and use of gunpowder in China," *Isis*, 37, Pts. 3-4 (July 1947), 163.

chants from the cities already came to the country fairs to sell such things as salt, and buy for the city market. The glamor of the city had its weakening effect on the old rural patterns of life in other ways. The wealthy peasant, we are told, tended to emulate the merchant's style of living, and we hear repeatedly that the rewards of commerce tempted the poor farmer to abandon the hard and often unrewarding work on his lands, sell his farm implements, and engage in trade.[17]

Finally, we must note the change that came about in the bureaucratic class itself. It was also in this period that new recruitment procedures opened a governmental career to far wider numbers than before. Competitive recruitment examinations were regularly used from the beginning of the eleventh century on a scale far greater than ever before. Improved through the development of elaborate techniques to make the examinations more objective, the new system helped to break the power monopoly once held by a small group of northern aristocratic families. The social origin of the newcomers who replaced them is not entirely clear. The broader distribution of opportunity was certainly made possible by the increase in literacy and the wider availability of books that we have already noted. Several hundred candidates commonly passed the final stage of the triennial examinations, and we are told that for each of these some hundred candidates had attempted the local preliminary tests. The competition was wide indeed. But the fiercest rivalry and the most numerous successful candidates during most of the dynasty came from the southeast coast, where we have seen the rapid pace of urbanization at this time.

How many of these men came from the great cities? How many traced their educational opportunity to families of ultimately mercantile origin? It is still impossible to say. But data from two lists of graduates that have come down to us from the twelfth and thirteenth centuries show that the regions with more and larger urban concentrations tended to supply not only more graduates in proportion to their area, but also more graduates per family, so that they clearly dominated the field. Moreover the largest proportion of apparently new blood tended to appear in the circuits of most rapid population growth, if we may judge from the numbers of graduates counting no officials among their direct paternal forebears. Conspicuous among these regions of growing population were again those containing the great coastal cities and those on the main inland trade routes. We have here, then, a seeming link between the broadening social base of the bureaucracy and the social mobility that probably

[17] Ch'üan Han-sheng, "Sung-tai nan-fang ti hsü-shih" . . . , *Bulletin of the Institute of History and Philology, Academia Sinica,* 9 (1947), 265-74; Hsia Sung and Ch'in Kuan.

characterized the great cities in their period of most rapid expansion.[18]

The political importance of this changing character of the bureaucracy is obvious. Its cultural effect, while less tangible and less calculable, was perhaps nonetheless real. For while the Sung [period] was a time of beginnings for the more popular literary forms, it was also a time of great vigor, and in some ways a time of culmination, in the intellectual activities practiced or patronized by the bureaucrat: the fine arts, the more sophisticated literary forms, and critical scholarship. In government, it was a time of imaginative reform schemes and experiments. It saw great advances in several fields of technology. In all of these realms the contribution made by men of the southeast was outstanding.

Thus we have evidence that a genuine alteration of Chinese social patterns accompanied the rise of the great city. The influence of the city extended beyond the bourgeois to the farmer and the bureaucrat. Despite the inhibiting pressures of official conservatism, and at times in disregard of laws and decrees, the merchant had expanded his influence and breached many of the barriers that surrounded him when the period of change began.

The limits of his rise are also apparent. If he achieved a place in government, it was by transforming himself into a bureaucrat; as a merchant he still enjoyed no active political role. The professional official remained supreme, and steadfastly unsympathetic toward the development of private economic interest.

The history of Chinese urbanization after the thirteenth century, and the reasons why the movement failed to go further than it did, are beyond the scope of the present topic. As we contemplate the situation of the thirteenth-century bourgeois, however, it is difficult to discern any single insuperable barrier to his further social rise. Most of his disadvantages were also faced by some at least of his European confreres during the later Middle Ages or the Renaissance. In the thirteenth century, the Chinese bourgeois had demonstrated by his will and his resourcefulness that under favorable conditions, the traditional Chinese social patterns could be significantly modified through the operation of internal forces.

[18] Kracke, *op. cit.*, pp. 68-69; data on regional distribution of examination graduates are drawn from Hsü Nai-ch'ang . . . (ed.), *Sung Yüan k'o-chü san lu* (1923), passim.

## 23 / THE CULMINATION OF A CHINESE PEASANT REBELLION: CHANG HSIEN-CHUNG IN SZECHWAN, 1644-46 / JAMES B. PARSONS

### Introduction

Studies of peasant rebellions in China are significant because of the key role such disturbances have played in Chinese history. Merely from the point of view of numbers, one is impressed by the many references to agrarian violence in the historical records of the various dynasties. To be sure, usually these outbreaks were short-lived, but at times they reached such serious proportions as to become one of the major causes for the fall of a dynasty. Furthermore, as is well known, two major dynasties, the Han and the Ming, were founded by peasant rebels.

The present article is concerned with the culminating phase of the rebellion of Chang Hsien-chung, who shares with Li Tzu-ch'eng[1] the distinction of being a major figure in the late Ming rebel movement. It

Reprinted with permission from J. B. Parsons, "The Culmination of a Chinese Peasant Rebellion," *Journal of Asian Studies*, 16 (1957), 387-89, 391-95, 398-9.

[1] Li Tzu-ch'eng was the most important of the Ming rebels and a contemporary of Chang Hsien-chung. It was he who captured Peking in the spring of 1644, and had it not been for the Manchus, might well have established an enduring dynasty. For a translation of his biography in the *Ming shih*, see Erich Hauer, "Li Tzu-ch'eng und Chang Hsien-chung: Ein Beitrag zum Ende de Mingdynastie," *Asia Major*, Vol. II (1925), 437-498. Throughout the footnotes the following abbreviations will be used:

> *HLLK* for Tai Li and Wu Shu, *Huai-ling liu-k'ou shih-chung lu* (in *Hsüan-lan-t'ang ts'ung-shu* [Nanking, 1947]);
> *HS* for Fei Mi, *Huang shu* (Chengtu: I-lan-t'ang, probably 1860);
> *KTS* for *K'o T'ien shu* (anonymous, in *T'ung shih* [Shanghai: Commercial Press, 1912]);
> *MCNL* for Chi Liu-ch'i, *Ming-chi nan lüeh* (Peking: Liu-li-ch'ang, undated);
> *MCPL* for Chi Liu-ch'i, *Ming-chi pei lüeh* (Peking: Liu-li-ch'ang, undated);
> *MS* for *Ming shih* (Wu-chou t'ung-wen ed.);
> *MSCSPM* for Ku Ying-t'ai, *Ming shih chi-shih pen-mo* (Shanghai, 1934);
> *PKC* for P'eng Sun-i, *P'ing k'ou chih* (Peking, 1931);
> *SC* for *Shu chi* (anonymous, in *T'ung shih* [Shanghai: Commercial Press, 1912]);
> *SKCL* for Wu Wei-yeh, *Sui k'ou chi lüeh* (Chao-k'uang-ko ed., K'ang-hsi period);
> *SP* for P'eng Tsun-ch'iu, *Shu pi* (probably late Ch'ing).

cannot be claimed, however, that Chang is even remotely comparable in importance to such a figure as Chu Yüan-chang, the illustrious peasant founder of the Ming. Chang's rebellion failed, and he is now all but forgotten. Even where memory of him has survived, as in Szechwan folk tales, he is usually depicted as a veritable ogre. However, a proper understanding of peasant rebellions requires the study of even unsuccessful ones, and it was with this belief in mind that the present article was written.

Chang Hsien-chung was born about 1606, and, like his fellow rebel, Li Tzu-ch'eng was a native of northern Shensi. In the late 1620s, his native area became the scene of widespread disorders, the most immediate cause of which was a series of natural calamities whose effects were aggravated by governmental corruption and inefficiency. Numerous bands plundered the countryside, and about 1630 Chang joined the disorders after he had been dismissed from the army apparently as a result of having participated in a mutiny.

The first phase of Chang's rebellion lasted until roughly 1643, and was characterized by disorganized raiding. During this period his primary objective was plunder, and he had only the vaguest notion of overthrowing the Ming Dynasty and establishing one of his own. His forces rarely numbered more than a few thousand at most, and he conducted guerrilla-type warfare with no attempt to hold fixed positions. His area of activity was extremely widespread and extended all the way from Shensi to Kiangsu.[2] He was capable of incredibly swift movement, and it was a rare year that did not see him appear in at least four provinces. His fortunes fluctuated wildly, and several times he was on the verge of being eliminated by the Ming forces. However, he always managed to save the situation usually either by temporarily surrendering to the government or by fleeing to remote mountain areas. The ease of his surrenders in the face of his obvious lack of sincerity demonstrates the weakness of the government forces and the desperate situation faced by many local officials who were willing to make almost any compromise in order to maintain peace. Furthermore, the fact that he was always capable of making a comeback even after the most crushing defeat is but another indication of the general instability of the late Ming period.

The second phase of his rebellion can be dated from 1643, for in that year he began to have more serious objectives. He declared himself "King of the West" (*hsi wang*) and attempted to set up a government

[2] During the Ming period modern Kiangsu and Anhwei were one province with the name *Nan-chih-li*.

first at Wuchang and later at Changsha.[3] This change from mere raiding to dynastic ambitions primarily resulted from an enhanced military potential, which was made possible by the progressing collapse of the Ming administration and the concentration of rebel leadership in the hands of Chang and Li Tzu-ch'eng.

Chang's attempts to establish a base of power in Hupeh-Hunan[4] did not meet with any great success. Ming forces led by his arch-foe, Tso Liang-yü, recaptured Wuchang in September 1643,[5] a little over two months after it had fallen to Chang.[6] However, from a center at Changsha, Chang did retain control over most of Hunan and a portion of central Kiangsi. Furthermore, the Ming generals did not dare risk pressing the fight against him to a decisive point, and a kind of stalemate between the two forces was reached.

Apparently this stalemate in the military situation was one reason why Chang decided to abandon the Hunan area and invade Szechwan. Just why he should have chosen Szechwan in particular is not precisely known. He was aware that this far western province was isolated, and that it would be difficult to employ it as a base for any dynastic ambitions. Furthermore, some of his officers tried to persuade him to advance east into the Chekiang-Kiangsu area, which was far more important both politically and economically than Szechwan.[7] But such a move would not have relieved him of the pressure of the opposing government forces, and apparently the belief that he could be the unchallenged master of Szechwan is the principal reason for his going there. At any rate, Szechwan was invaded and saw the culmination of Chang's rebellion. . . .

### The Establishment of a Government at Chengtu

It will be remembered that already while in Hupeh Chang had declared himself "King of the West," and had attempted to establish a

[3] *HLLK*, 16.11a-b, 17b, 18a; *PKC*, 7.4a-b, 16.9a-b; *MSPL*, 19.51a; *MS*, 309.30b, 31a; and *MSCSPM*, Chap. 57, pp. 51-52.

[4] During the Ming period modern Hupeh and Hunan were one province with the name *Hu-kuang*.

[5] All dates have been converted to the Western calendar.

[6] *HLLK*, 16.13a, 14b, 15a-b; *PKC*, 7.1b, 2a; *MCPL*, 19.55a; and *MSCSPM*, Chap. 77, p. 50.

[7] It is interesting to speculate what might have been the fate of Chang if he had moved into the Kiangsu-Chekiang area and established a center of power there. He would perhaps have been in a position to have dominated the Ming court after its flight to Nanking and used the pretender as a puppet. Interestingly enough, after his death one of his chief officers, Li Ting-kuo, did succeed in dominating for a time the last of the Ming pretenders. However, by this late date there was no chance for the Ming to recover power.

government. But it was in Chengtu that he made his most serious effort to found a dynasty. He gave his state the title of "Great Western Country" (*ta hsi kuo*), adopted Ta-shun as a *nien-hao* (reign title), renamed Chengtu "Western Capital," and occupied the palace of the deceased Prince of Shu.[8]

But more important than these rather fanciful imperial pretensions was his attempt to set up a government. This government was in complete accord with past precedents, and included such familiar offices as the Six Boards, Grand Secretariat, Ministry of the Left, and Ministry of the Right.[9] Of the nine persons who are known to have served as heads of these offices, four were holders of the *chin-shih*, and two held one of the lower degrees. Seven of the nine were natives of Szechwan, most of whom were either living in retirement after some kind of an interruption in their official careers or were awaiting a hoped-for appointment to office. The two most prominent members of the group were Yen Hsi-ming and Wu Chi-shan. Yen was a *chin-shih* and an ex-magistrate. He served concurrently as Minister of the Right and Grand Secretary. Wu was also a *chin-shih* and had been magistrate of Chengtu at the time of the city's fall. He served as President of the Board of Rites. Two members were what might be described as nongentry. They were Li Shih-ying, a Taoist priest who served as President of the Board of Punishments, and Wang Ying-lung, an arrow-maker who was made President of the Board of Works. But by far the most powerful member was a young man named Wang Chao-ling, who was from a prominent Anhwei family. He had been captured by Chang several years previously and had come to exercise great influence over him. He served concurrently as Minister of the Left and Grand Secretary.

Some of the early actions of the new government included the holding of official examinations, the minting of money, the distribution of ranks, and the establishment of a *pao-chia* system.[10] The coins were in typical Chinese style, round with a hole in the middle and bearing the charac-

---

[8] *MCNL*, 12.27b, 28a; *SKCL*, 10.20b, 21a; *MS*, 309.31b, 32a; and *KTS*, foll. 6b, 7a. Ta Shun was also the title which Li Tzu-ch'eng gave his dynasty. However, it is probably merely a coincidence that both Chang and Li chose this term which is equally appropriate for the name of a dynasty and a *nien-hao*.

[9] *KTS*, foll. 6b, 7a; *HS*, fol. 12a-b; *SC*, fol. 8b; *PKC*, 11.13b; *SKCL*, 10.20b, 21a; *MS*, 309.32a; and *HLLK*, 18.19b. The Six Boards were the Boards of Rites, Revenue, Civil Office, War, Punishments, and Works.

[10] *HLLK*, 18.22b; *SP*, 2.15b, 17a; *SC*, fol. 3a-b; *MCNL*, 12.30a; *HS*, fol. 12a; and *SKCL*, 10.21a. The *pao-chia* system was the association of families in groups of ten for such purposes as administration, self-defense, and social control.

ters *Ta-shun t'ung-pao*.[11] In conferring ranks, Chang seems to have wished to offer a conciliatory gesture and thereby win support for his administration. For example, a title was granted to the eldest son of the deceased Prince of Shu. Finally, the *pao-chia* system had a long history in China, and Chang was interested in it mainly as a means of social control, which had been one of its traditional purposes.

In addition to setting up a civil administration, Chang also expanded and reorganized his army.[12] Great numbers of Szechwanese were recruited, and definite divisions into camps were made. However, leadership was kept in the hands of a small group, all natives of Shensi, who had been associated with Chang since the beginning of his rebellion. Four of this select group, Li Ting-kuo, Ai Neng-ch'i, Sun K'o-wang, and Liu Wen-hsiu, were singled out for top command positions. They were given exalted titles, and according to a Jesuit source, were assigned definite responsibilities in a grandiose scheme for the conquest of all China as well as various outlying areas.[13]

In evaluating Chang's attempt to found a government, the Chinese sources, as one would expect, have almost nothing but evil to say for his efforts. It is interesting to note, however, that the Jesuits felt he at first gained considerable support. For example, one Jesuit source states:

> . . . He [i.e., Chang] began his rule with such liberality, justice, and magnificence by which he captivated all hearts that many mandarins, famous both in civic as in military affairs whom fear was keeping concealed, left their hideouts and flew to his side. And surely he was so equipped by nature with such virtues that, had not clemency been wanting and unbelievable wrath and more than beastly savagery and inhuman cruelty taken its place in his soul, he had seemed made king by nature.[14]

But whatever possibilities his civil administration might have had, his

[11] *Ta-shun t'ung-pao* means *coinage for general circulation of the Ta-shun period.* Chinese copper coins typically had inscribed on them the reign period during which they were minted combined with the term *t'ung-pao.* A reproduction of one of the coins issued by Chang's government is contained in *Ming-mo nung-min ch'i-i shih-liao* (*Historical Source Materials for the Late Ming Agrarian Uprisings*), Sün Yüeh, *et al.* (eds.), (Peking, 1952), p. 6.

[12] *HLLK,* 18.22b; *SKCL,* 10.20b; *PKC,* 11.13b; *MCNL,* 12.27a; *KTS,* fol. 7a; *SC,* fol. 2b; and *SP,* 2.15a-b.

[13] Thomas Ignatius Dunin Spot, "Collectanea Historiae Sinensis 1641 ad 1700" (microfilm of unpublished ms. in the Archives of the Society of Jesus in Rome; written in 1710), I, 112. Two Jesuit priests, Gabriel de Magalhaens and Louis Buglio, were engaged in missionary work in Szechwan at the time of Chang's invasion, and they subsequently came into close contact with him. Father de Magalhaens wrote an account of their experiences, which has now apparently been lost. However, Dunin Spot made use of it in the work cited above.

[14] Dunin Spot, *op. cit.,* Vol. I, p. 100.

main interest remained centered in his army, and his power continued to be based upon military domination. And as we shall see, later developments negated any initial success which his government had had.

### The Terror Policy

The traditional picture of Chang, based especially upon his activities in Szechwan, is that of a veritable monster who was guilty of the most senseless atrocities. In fact, the Chinese sources at times seem almost to vie with each other in recounting the most gruesome stories illustrating his brutality. For sheer imagination, a story in the *Shu pi* must be awarded the prize in this competition.[15] According to this tale, once, while he was suffering from an illness, Chang vowed that if he recovered he would offer two "heavenly candles" as a sacrifice. No one understood what he meant, but when he did recover, he ordered the small bound feet of many women to be cut off and placed in two piles. The feet of one of his favorite concubines were unusually tiny, and he had them severed and placed at the very top of each pile. Then oil was poured on and both piles ignited in fulfillment of his vow to offer two "heavenly candles."

But despite the obvious exaggeration in the sources, Chang did institute in Szechwan a ruthless terror policy. This policy was well under way by the middle of 1645, and increased in intensity, especially in 1646, when the decision was made to abandon Szechwan and move to Shensi. At first the gentry bore the brunt of the pogrom, and there is, for example, the famous incident when Chang enticed several thousand prominent Szechwanese to come to Chengtu by announcing the holding of an official examination.[16] Once assembled, he ordered them all killed. And later on the population in general suffered.

There are specific reasons why the terror policy was resorted to, and it was not merely a series of senseless slaughters. In the first place, Chang

[15] *SP,* 3.20b, 21a.

[16] *HLLK,* 18.19a; *PKC,* 11.13b; *MS,* 309.32a; *SKCL,* 10.26a-b; *SC,* foll. 6a, 7a-b; *MCNL,* 12.31b; and Martin Martini, *Bellum Tartaricum or the Conquest of the Great and Most Renowned Empire of China . . . ,* trans. from Latin (London, 1654), pp. 211-12. Martini's account of Chang's occupation of Szechwan, like that of Dunin Spot, is based on the now lost original of Father de Magalhaens. The description of the incident in Martini is so apt that it deserves quotation: ". . . he [i.e., Chang] called all the students of the country to be examined for their degrees, promising to give those honors to whomsoever should deserve them best; and the Chineses are so bewitched with the desire for these dignities that they did not conceive the perfidious strategem of the tyrant. There appeared therefore in the public hall deputed for that ceremony about 18,000 persons, all of which he commanded his souldiers to massacre most barbarously, saying these were the people who by their cavilling sophisms sollicited the people to rebellion."

considered that drastic measures were necessary to stamp out all opposition. We have noted that, following the capture of Chengtu, no substantial opposing forces remained. But resistance did continue, at times of a guerrilla nature and at times more serious.[17] Most of this resistance was organized by Ming officials who had managed to escape death or capture at the hands of Chang. These men were essentially war lords operating on their own, though they were theoretically subject to a special official who had been dispatched by the Ming Nanking administration to restore order, and who had his headquarters at Tsun-i in southeastern Szechwan. The most successful of these resistance leaders was Tseng Ying, who in the spring of 1645 managed to capture Chungking and defeat a determined effort made by one of Chang's lieutenants to retake the city. But neither Tseng nor any of the others ever emerged as a serious threat to Chang, and they usually limited their operations to the fringes of his main center of power. Still, the very fact that there existed any opposition at all exasperated Chang and made him willing to institute ruthless measures to suppress it. And as is so often true with terroristic policies, a limited amount of ruthlessness merely served to increase opposition and made necessary greater and greater ruthlessness.

Another reason for the terror program was conflicts within Chang's army. We have already noted that large numbers of Szechwanese were brought into the army, and there developed a conflict of interest between them and the older elements. Even these older elements were not above divisions among themselves, for they were after all of diverse origins. Some of them were remnants of formerly independent rebel bands, and others had been recruited throughout the wide areas of north China where Chang had operated. Of course, the continuing leadership of the original Shensi group provided a certain amount of stability, but this leadership was naturally resented. Thus, Chang thought it necessary to acquire discipline by applying the terror policy to the army itself, especially against the Szechwanese recruits.[18]

Finally, Chang's personal deficiencies as a leader, exaggerated by the unfortunate influence of Wang Chao-ling, constituted an important factor in the terror policy. From the evidence offered by the Jesuits, Chang seems to have been intelligent enough, but he did not have the wisdom and patience necessary for making the transition from raiding to organized administration. Still, he would undoubtedly have done a great deal better if it had not been for the advice of Wang Chao-ling, who unfortunately had none of the stature of Li Yen, the gentry adviser of

---

[17] *HLLK*, 18.23b; *SKCL*, 10.23a; *SP*, 3.2a-b; and *KTS*, fol. 10b.

[18] *PKC*, 12.9b; *SP*, 2.13a-b, 14a-b; and *SC*, foll. 9b, 10a.

Li Tzu-ch'eng.[19] We have already noted that Wang was a member of an Anhwei gentry family who in his youth had been captured by Chang. But the years which he had spent in the rebel group had apparently robbed him of his gentry orientation and made him an advocate of extremist policies. Chang seems to have subscribed originally to the position taken by such faithful lieutenants as Li Ting-kuo and Sun K'o-wang, who felt that support could best be gained by following a course of moderation.[20] But Wang succeeded finally in getting his own policy of ruthlessness adopted, and thus he must bear a considerable portion of the responsibility for the collapse of the Chengtu government. Interestingly enough, his advocacy of the terror policy finally cost him his life, for he was so hated by the other leaders that after Chang's death Ai Neng-ch'i shot him through the head with an arrow. . . .

Several reasons prompted Chang's determination to invade Shensi. In the first place, there was the complete failure of his Chengtu administration. Furthermore, he realized that if he was to have any chance of establishing a dynasty of his own, he must extricate himself from the isolation of Szechwan and move into a more strategic area in the north. Finally, the Chengtu plain undoubtedly had been fairly thoroughly plundered by 1646, and supplies for his army were no longer plentiful.

After abandoning Chengtu, he did not, however, move immediately toward the Shensi border. Instead, he proceeded almost due east and set up camp at Feng-huang-shan near Hsi-ch'ung in the Chia-ling River valley.[21] Apparently his plan was to gather supplies and move on to Shensi the following spring when weather conditions would be more favorable. He was perfectly aware, at least according to Jesuit accounts, that the Manchus had invaded Shensi and would be his major opponents.[22] However, he had no real appreciation for the military potential of the Manchus, and his army, still wracked with internal strife, was certainly no match for them.

[19] Li Yen was a member of a prominent Honan family who became widely noted for his humanitarianism. He served as one of Li Tzu-ch'eng's closest adviser and was primarily responsible for persuading him to adopt moderate policies in order to win popular support. See *MS*, 309.11a-b, 23b.

[20] *HLLK*, Appendix, fol. 7b; and *SC*, foll. 15b, 16a.

[21] *MCNL*, 12.33a; *HS*, fol. 19b; and *PKC*, 11.15b.

[22] Martini, p. 217; and Joseph Anne Marie de Moyriac de Mailla, *Histoire générale de la Chine* . . . (Paris, 1777-85), Vol. XI, p. 26. The Chinese sources, written during the Ch'ing period naturally gave little consideration to Chang as a rival of the Manchus. However, de Mailla quotes Chang as telling his troops before leaving Chengtu: "I already see these foreigners chased out of China." In like manner, Martini quotes him as saying: "I hope by your valor to obtain the empire of the world when I have expelled the Tartars. . . ."

But Chang was destined never to reach Shensi. Instead, he was surprised by a Manchu force at his Feng-huang-shan camp. This surprise was made possible by the defection of one of his officers, Liu Chinchung, who had been in charge of defending the Shensi-Szechwan border area.[23] Liu was a native of Szechwan and resented Chang's terroristic policy. Thus, when a Manchu force under Haoge reached southern Shensi late in 1646, Liu promptly surrendered and promised to lead the way to Chang's camp.

Haoge's group, apparently a crack unit numbering about 5000 men, moved rapidly southward under Liu's guidance. When it reached the Hsi-ch'ung area, scouts conveyed the news to Chang, who at first refused to believe the report. Finally, however, he was convinced, and as Martini expresses it, ". . . he being of a bold and courageous humor, burst out of his tent, and without either headpiece or breastplate, snatched up a lance, and went out with a few to view the enemy."[24] Chang and his small group met the Manchus across a narrow creek, and Liu Chinchung pointed out his former chieftain to a skilled Manchu archer, who shot and killed him.[25] Thus, early in January 1647 Chang suffered the fate which he had succeeded in escaping for almost twenty years. In a way, however, history had not seen the last of his influence, for a portion of his army fled south and joined the cause of the southern Ming. Thus, rebellion was now cast aside for the more important task of resisting a foreign invader. Li Ting-kuo, whom we have already noted as one of Chang's principal lieutenants, became a major figure in the struggle against the Manchus. He remained loyal to the bitter end and died in Burma after a vain attempt to rescue the last Ming pretender from his Burmese captors, who surrendered him to the Manchus.

### Conclusion

Chang's occupation of Szechwan was the climax of his rebellion both chronologically and developmentally, for it was there that he made his most serious effort to establish a government. This attempt ended in complete failure, and although for a time he made a pretense of ruling in traditional fashion with ministers, a court, official examinations, and a bureaucracy, his government remained a powerless trapping and his real authority was derived from armed might. He made all the wrong moves

[23] *HLLK*, appendix, fol. 7a-b; *PKC*, 12.9b; *HS*, foll. 19b, 20a-b; *KTS*, fol. 12a; and de Mailla, Vol. XI, p. 22.

[24] Martini, p. 222.

[25] *HLLK*, appendix, fol. 7b; *PKC*, 12.8a; *SKCL*, 10.29a; *MS*, 309.33a; *SC*, fol. 14a; *HS*, foll. 20b, 21a; Dunin Spot (see n. 13), Vol. I, p. 129; de Mailla, Vol. XI, p. 27; and *Tung hua lu* (Shanghai, 1887), Shun-chih 7, foll. 4b, 5a.

for one wishing to establish a regime on a firm basis. That is, he made no carefully planned and effectively executed appeal to the gentry; he chose as his principal adviser a man who was the antithesis of traditional gentry viewpoints; and, in exasperation, he sought to dispose of all opposition by resorting to sheer terror. Thus, his activities in Szechwan not only provide us with a history of the province from 1644 to 1646, but they also furnish an example of a peasant rebel attempting, and failing, to change from raiding to civil government.

## 24 / COMPARISON OF THE PROCESSES OF DECLINE IN THE EASTERN AND WESTERN PARTS OF THE ROMAN EMPIRE / A. H. M. JONES

... Neither economic factors, nor psychological factors* ... can be a complete explanation of the collapse of the empire. There is a very simple test, which Western scholars are prone to forget. It was only in the West that the imperial government broke down in the fifth century. Yet in the East Christianity was deeper rooted and more widespread, and monasticism was both more extensive and carried to greater extremes. The army in the East was fully as large and as expensive, and the bureaucracy as swollen and corrupt. Yet at the very time when the Western Empire was staggering to its fall, the Eastern was making a recovery. In the sixth century Justinian was able to reconquer substantial parts of the Western Empire—Africa, Italy with its adjacent islands, and even a part of Spain. Much of Italy was, it is true, almost at once lost to a fresh barbarian inroad, that of the Lombards, and at the beginning of the seventh century a simultaneous invasion by the Avars from the Danube and the Persians from the east almost brought the empire to its knees. Under Heraclius it made a marvellous recovery, only to face the new threat of the Arab invasions. To the Arabs it lost Syria, Egypt, and later Africa, but after initial setbacks it consolidated itself in Asia Minor and the Balkans, together with some surviving fragments of Justinian's reconquests—Sicily, Sardinia, and parts of Italy. Altogether the Eastern Empire showed a surprising vitality in comparison with the West.

These facts indicate that the empire did not, as some modern historians almost assume, collapse from internal causes. It succumbed to persistent attacks by invading barbarians. Strategically the Eastern Empire was, during the fourth and fifth centuries, far better placed than the

Reprinted with permission from A. H. M. Jones, "The Decline and Fall of the Roman Empire, *History*, **40**: 140 (October 1955), 220-26.

* See Ch. III.

Western. The main pressure came from the German tribes pushed westward by the Huns against the Danube and the Rhine, and later from the Huns themselves. The Eastern emperor ruled Thrace and Eastern Illyricum, and was thus responsible for the defense of the lower Danube. The Danube was frequently forced, and Thrace and Illyricum were so regularly ravaged that they became financially a liability rather than an asset. But the barbarian invaders could move no further eastward, for the Bosphorus and the Hellespont were always firmly guarded by the emperor who reigned at Constantinople. The barbarian invaders who crossed the Danube therefore always tended, when they had exhausted the resources of the Balkans, to move westward and add to the embarrassments of the West. On the eastern frontier, Persia could be a formidable adversary, but it was a civilized state with which treaties could be made: actually peace was kept over long periods between Rome and Persia. On the desert frontiers of Syria and Egypt there were only the Saracen tribes who were easily controlled by the judicious grant of subsidies until they were galvanized into united aggression by Islam. The greater part of the Eastern Empire—Asia Minor, Syria, and Egypt—was more or less immune from invasion, and provided the resources to maintain the imperial armies in the Balkans, which, though frequently invaded, were regularly recovered from the impregnable bridgehead of Constantinople.

In the West, the strategic situation was much less favorable. The empire had to protect two long fronts, the upper Danube and the Rhine, and the German tribes, moving on interior lines, could switch their attacks from one front to another. The tribes who broke through the Rhine defenses could ravage the whole of Gaul at will, and those who penetrated the Danube line had a choice of passes through which they could invade Italy itself. Spain behind the Pyrenees, and still more Africa, seemed secure, but simultaneous invasions of Italy and Gaul proved too much for the imperial armies. While the bulk of the army was heavily engaged in the defense of Italy against the Goths, the Vandals, Sueves, and Alans burst into Gaul, and thence penetrated the Pyrenees and found a lodgment in Spain, whence the Vandals moved on into Africa. The imperial government in Italy was thus encircled and deprived of its main sources of revenue and supplies, and was unable to maintain the struggle.

Not only were the areas governed by the Western emperor more exposed to attack than those under the rule of his Eastern colleague, they were [also] probably poorer in manpower and in revenue. For us today this is difficult to realize. The lands bordering the eastern Mediterranean, with the exception of Egypt, have as a result of centuries of misgovernment and the cumulative effects of denudation, receded absolutely in prosperity. It is certain that there is less cultivable land than under Roman rule, and that less of it is cultivated, and it is a reasonable guess that the population has shrunk considerably. By contrast the now prosperous lands of northern Europe—Britain, Gaul, and the Danubian provinces—were probably still underdeveloped under the Roman Empire. Much of the best soil seems to have been undrained marsh or uncleared forest. This statement is difficult to substantiate without more extensive archaeological surveys, but in Britain at any rate it was the light upland soils which were cultivated, and the rich river valleys were neglected. It is notable moreover that, under the empire, it was Africa which was regarded as the richest of the western provinces, and was in fact the granary of Rome. Africa has, it is true, receded in prosperity since Roman times, but its natural resources can never have compared with those of Gaul, if these had been fully exploited. Africa too was regarded as populous, which argues that the northern lands must have been very sparsely inhabited.

It would seem, then, that the emperors of the West, who were faced with the more difficult military task, had smaller manpower resources to draw upon for their armies than those of the East. This is probably one of the reasons why in the West barbarians were more freely recruited in the fourth century, and in the fifth the government—with fatal results— came to rely almost exclusively on hired federates. In the East, by contrast, during the fifth and sixth centuries the emperors maintained and built up a national army of Roman citizens and kept the element of barbarian mercenaries under control. The armies with which Belisarius and Narses won their victories were predominantly Roman, mainly raised by voluntary recruitment from the sturdy mountaineers of the Balkans and eastern Asia Minor, whence came the crack regiments of "Isaurians."

The Western emperors also seem to have commanded far less revenue than their Eastern colleagues, whether it was levied, as it mainly was in the fourth century, in kind, or was commuted into gold, as it mostly was during the fifth. The Eastern Empire was able not only to pay its army regularly and keep up its strength: it could afford to pay huge subsidies to Attila without undue strain, and, what was far more costly, to launch great seaborne expeditions for the recovery of the West. Leo's expedition against the Vandals is said to have exhausted the empire's reserves for a generation, but Anastasius nevertheless left a full treasury and a buoyant revenue. Justinian's wars undoubtedly placed a severe financial strain on the empire, but nevertheless it continued to be a going concern. In the West, on the other hand, the regular army was allowed to run down, and seems by the middle of the fifth century to

have melted away, while the federate troops which replaced it were re-
munerated with grants of land, under the system of *hospitalitas,* instead
of being paid in cash.

The greater financial resources of the Eastern Empire were probably
in part due, as suggested above, to the fact that the areas which it ruled
were more fully developed and richer. It must also be remembered that,
owing to the strategic considerations mentioned above, they suffered
less from the ravages of war. Asia Minor, Syria, and Egypt were virtually
sealed off from invasion. In the West, on the contrary, the revenue-pro-
ducing provinces were successively ravaged and then occupied by barbarians; the occupation of the rich provinces of Africa by the Vandals
was the final blow from which the Western Empire never recovered.

I would also suggest that the relatively favorable financial position of
the imperial government in the East was in part due to a difference in
the social structure of the eastern and western parts of the empire. This is
a point which, in the absence of statistics, must remain rather speculative,
but the evidence is, I think, strong enough to warrant stating it as a
working hypothesis. There seems to have been a greater concentration of
landed property in the hands of a few wealthy men in the West than in
the East. We have reliable evidence that the senatorial aristocracy of
Rome enjoyed fabulous incomes from their landed property: a senator
whose annual rents totalled 1500 pounds [of] gold and dues in kind to
the value of 500 pounds [of] gold was reckoned to be of medium wealth.
Two senators of Constantinople, one of whom had first ruined himself
by his extravagance and then brought ruin on his colleague by borrowing
from him and squandering 1000 pounds [of] gold, were both put on their
feet by a grant of 2000 pounds [of] gold from Anastasius. A typical Western senator had, that is to say, an annual income twice as great as the
capital wealth of a typical Eastern senator. At the other end of the scale
the peasant freeholder seems to have survived in far greater numbers in
the East than in the West. In the West at any rate he has left very little
trace in our records, and we hear almost exclusively of *fundi* and *massae*
in Italy, Sicily, Africa, Spain and Gaul. In the East, on the contrary, we
hear of villages of peasant proprietors still surviving in Syria in the mid-
fifth century, while Justinian legislated to protect the peasant freeholders
of Thrace and Illyricum from foreclosure by moneylenders. In Egypt
both the Codes and the papyri attest the existence of numerous villages
of freeholders down to the Arab conquest.

If my hypothesis is correct, less of the product of agriculture went into
rents in the East, and more was therefore available to the government
in taxation. In the West, great landlords absorbed more of the national
income in the form of rent, and as they were influential persons who

could get their estates assessed at a low rate, secure immunity from special or supplementary levies, or finally postpone payment till one of the recurrent general remissions of arrears, the government did not secure the full taxes from their lands. The concentration of land into great estates also had its effects on the recruitment of the army. Landlords were always most reluctant to give up their tenants as recruits; at a time of crisis in 399 we find the Roman senate successfully petitioning the emperor against a levy of recruits and being allowed to pay commutation in gold for the men assessed on their lands. In the latter part of the fifth century, tied tenants (*coloni adscripticii*) were debarred from military service in both halves of the empire. In the West, this concession must have cut off from the army its major source of manpower. In the East, there were ample resources of freeholders from whom Justinian could raise his armies, notably in Asia Minor and the Balkans.

The economic preponderance of the great landlords in the West was reflected in the government of the empire. From the end of Constantine's reign, members of the great senatorial families begin to occupy the praetorian prefecture, the supreme judicial and financial office, and by the fifth century they almost monopolize it. We may well believe, as Ammianus hints, that they protected their own interests and those of their relations, friends, and colleagues. In the East, the praetorian prefecture was usually held by men of relatively humble origins, imperial notaries in the fourth century, or later on, lawyers or, under Anastasius and Justinian, financial officials like Marinus the Syrian and John the Cappadocian. These men certainly lined their own pockets, but are admitted by their bitterest critics to have filled the treasury. They owed their advancement to the emperor, and had little motive for sparing the wealthy.

To explain this difference in the economic and social structure of the Western and Eastern parts of the empire, one must go back many centuries. The Roman senatorial aristocracy began building up their vast estates in the second century BC from the spoils of the Eastern wars and the exploitation of the provinces. Many of the old families died out in the course of time, but the order was filled by wealthy *equites,* often the descendants of men who, having made fortunes by tax collecting or money lending in the provinces, had invested them in land, and the fortunes of the extinct families generally remained within the order, passing through heiresses or by will or adoption to the newer families. The senatorial nobility thus accumulated through the generations the vast wealth of which we find it possessed in the later empire, and since it was to a large extent Italian by origin in the early centuries, and still in the second century AD predominantly Western, its estates lay mostly in the

Western provinces, and particularly in Italy: for senators were expected to reside in Rome and obliged to invest a proportion of their wealth in Italian land. In the East, wealth remained more evenly distributed. With the foundation of the new imperial capital of Constantinople and the establishment there of a second senate, a similar process of concentration began in the East, but Rome, after all, had five centuries start over Constantinople.

I have outlined what seem to me to be the principal causes of the empire's decline, and of its collapse in the West. It would be difficult, and probably profitless, to attempt to weigh their relative importance, for they interacted upon one another so as to form a single complex. The strategic vulnerability of the West not only exposed it to severe military pressure, but diminished the economic resources on which its defense was based, while its economic disequilibrium reduced its military manpower. The decline of public spirit led to the growth of the bureaucracy, and the weight of bureaucratic control crushed public spirit, while the heavy financial burden it entailed doubtless contributed to the general apathy of the population. Otherworldliness weakened the economic and military resources of the empire, and the resulting distress and defeats made men turn away from this world and set their hopes on another. The decline and fall of the Roman Empire was the result of a complex of interacting causes which the historian disentangles at his peril.

## 25 / FORMS OF POLITICAL CONFLICT IN THE BYZANTINE EMPIRE / C. DIEHL

### Forms of Political Anarchy

#### Popular Revolt

Revolutions were of different kinds. First, there were the revolutions originating among the people. We have already seen something of the plebeians of the capital; as in other great cities, they included numbers of vagabonds, adventurers, thieves, and beggars. They were credulous, excitable, impressionable, and noisy people, ever on the verge of panic or sedition; they loved bloodshed; the sight of pain fascinated them; they were foul-mouthed and uproarious, passionate and fierce. They claimed to be the heirs of the ancient Romans, and if they no longer cast their votes in the Forum, or elected tribunes and consuls, they reserved the right to demonstrate in the Hippodrome: to execrate or applaud, to howl or to cheer, until, indeed, the circus seemed "the final refuge of public

Reprinted with permission from C. Diehl, *Byzantium: Greatness and Decline* (New Brunswick, N.J.: Rutgers University Press, 1957), pp. 129-36.

liberties." They were armed, too. The famous factions known as the Blues and the Greens were not merely racing associations; they had a political and military organization which turned the people of Constantinople into a sort of urban militia, and enabled them to intervene in public affairs. This they did with an enthusiasm in which survived, perhaps, something of the democratic spirit of the ancient Greeks—to the grave danger of the state.

### The Nika Insurrection

The terrible revolt known as the Nika Insurrection, which in January 532 came near to overthrowing Justinian's throne, is a telling example of the people's power. It began with a violent scene at the circus, when the mob addressed the emperor directly, with howls, insults, and protests, in mingled wrath and derision. Uproar spread through the town; in one of the most beautiful quarters fires raged for a week, while furious men—and women, too—routed the emperor's troops, proclaimed a new sovereign in the Hippodrome, and made ready to storm the palace. A contemporary declared that "the empire seemed on the eve of its downfall." We know how Theodora's energy stiffened the courage of Justinian and his advisers, and how in the Hippodrome Belisarius crushed the rebels and strewed the arena with more than 30,000 corpses. This bloody execution subdued popular passion for some years, although often during the rest of the sixth century fights and plots disturbed the capital. But this frightful insurrection, which filled Byzantium with fire and ruin, gives abundant proof of what the many-headed monster could do.

### The Revolt of 1042

The rioting of April 19, 1042, is another example, rendered especially interesting through an eyewitness account by Psellus. Few pages in Byzantine history are more vivid. We know the cause of the rebellion. Emperor Michael V had just dispossessed the popular old Empress Zoë and shut her up in a convent; and in Psellus' account we can follow the whole course of the revolt. He describes in memorable terms the mounting roar in the city, the sudden cessation of all business, the groups muttering in the streets, and the crowds of both sexes and all ages, murmuring at first, then menacing, while "a dark veil of pain and wrath sank over the city, as in times of great national disaster." In the squares there were pamphlets and protests; elsewhere, vociferous outcry. The women especially were in a state of fierce excitement. Even the most retiring of them—those who until then had seldom left the *gynaeceum*—mingled unveiled with the mob "like furies, huddled in a howling mass and uttering hideous imprecations." Soon the rabble were organized and armed, each snatching up whatever came to hand: axes, swords, cudgels, stones. They broke open the prisons and then headed for the palace "as if moved by some unseen power." "They stampeded in their thousands, feeling their strength increased tenfold. Their eyes flashed fires of resentment and rage." The homes of the emperor's kinsmen were sacked and demolished. The palace itself was invaded and despoiled, precious objects in the treasury broken, tax registers torn up, and money stolen. The emperor fled.

Delirious joy and triumph followed; there was dancing in the streets and the singing of songs improvised for the occasion. Then came the final act of the drama. In the religious house of the *studium*, where they had sought refuge and now clung desperately to the altar, the emperor and his uncle were surrounded by the mob. "All those wild beasts threatened to tear them to pieces." Agonized and half-dead with terror, they begged and pleaded. They were torn from the sanctuary and dragged by the heels into the square amid yells, savage songs, and taunts, hoisted on to a mule and led to the executioner, who was waiting to put out their eyes. Contemporaries were profoundly shocked by the atrocities of that day, and by the mighty and mysterious unleashing of the mob soul, $\mu\acute{\epsilon}\gamma\alpha$ $\kappa\alpha\grave{\iota}$ $\delta\eta\mu\sigma\sigma\iota\acute{\omega}\tau\alpha\tau\sigma\nu$ $\mu\nu\sigma\tau\acute{\eta}\rho\sigma\nu$, as Psellus wrote. Their reflections on the transience of worldly power are expressed in terms reminiscent of Bossuet. And indeed, few events bear such striking witness to the hideous brutality of a Byzantine mob when goaded to frenzy.

### Church Revolutions. The Event of 963

The people did not always act alone, but sought support either from the church or from the army. In August 963 Nicephorus Phocas, the empire's most illustrious general, had just proclaimed himself emperor at Caesarea in Cappadocia. His troops were at the gates of the capital, where the excitement was intense. The chief minister, the all-powerful Bringas, was attempting to organize defense, and had outlawed the kinsmen and supporters of Nicephorus. Bardas, the father of the pretender, had had no time to escape; he sought refuge in St. Sophia, where the Patriarch Polyeuctes received him. The people, who took his part, rushed to the Great Church and threatened and reviled the soldiers of the regent, who were trying to drag the fugitive from the sanctuary by force. In vain did Bringas order the patriarch to deliver Bardas to him; in vain did the "abusive, haughty man" harangue the crowd, threatening to starve them by denying them bread unless they yielded; in vain did he compel Bardas to leave St. Sophia and return to his house. For when the people attending afternoon service—it was Sunday—found the fugitive no longer in the Great Church, they raised such an uproar against the patriarch and the clergy who had let him go that Polyeuctes had hastily to invite him back. And when Bardas hesitated, they took steps to protect him by mounting guard [a]round the palace all night. Soon the rebels armed themselves and attacked the government troops; and in this street fighting, women did their share, hurling missiles from above. A leader had been found: the *Paracoemomenus,* Basil, natural son of Emperor Romanus Lecapenus. Arming the men of his household —he had more than 3000 people at his command—he plunged boldly into the struggle. At his instigation, the people broke into the palaces of the chief minister and his friends, looting, sacking, and razing the buildings to the ground. Fighting continued in the city for three days; the infuriated mob arrested and imprisoned people of high rank on the smallest pretext. Plundering and destruction were frenzied. The arsenal was captured and the fleet handed over to Nicephorus; and while Bringas, deserted by everyone, fled in his turn to St. Sophia, his victim, Bardas, took possession of the imperial palace until such time as his victorious son should make his triumphal entry into Constantinople.

## The Revolution of 1057

An even more active part was played by another patriarch in the revolution that carried Isaac Comnenus to the throne in 1057. At first, Michael Cerularius left the disaffected generals to plot together in St. Sophia, and when they departed, he was aware of their intention to proclaim Isaac emperor. Informed men regarded him from that moment as master of the situation. And indeed, while the insurgents were pitching camp at the gates of Constantinople, it was he who took charge in the capital and prepared the revolt. On the morning of August 31, 1057, a crowd gathered outside the Great Church, loudly demanding the patriarch. Having allowed them to wait some little time, Cerularius appeared in full canonicals, and in the crowded church listened to what the insurgents had to say. But soon voices were heard acclaiming Comnenus, and the patriarch made no protest. On the contrary, he soon openly assumed leadership of the revolutionary movement, compelled the emperor to abdicate, set up a provisional government with himself at the head, and unleashed rebellion and bloodshed in Constantinople. Once master of the city, he handed it over to Isaac Comnenus. On this occasion it was the patriarch who made the emperor.

## Military Revolts

The army, however, was the mightiest force of all, and in any really serious situation it was to the soldier that Byzantium turned for succour. Military *pronunciamentos* raised many fine emperors to the throne:

Heraclius, who delivered the realm from the tyranny of Phocas; Leo the Isaurian, who put an end to the frightful anarchy at the beginning of the eighth century; Nicephorus Phocas, who in the tenth brought such glory to the empire; Alexius Comnenus, who saved it from disaster at the end of the eleventh. This does not include the pretenders, such as George Maniakes, Bardas Phocas, Bardas Skleros, and countless others, who felt sure enough of their soldiers to assume the imperial crown and the purple boots, and who, less fortunate, never attained their goal. It was in camp amid their devoted troops that ambitious malcontents, as well as those who in critical times strove to uphold the might of the crown, sought and found support. More than once, indeed, it was the soldiers who coerced their hesitant leaders. It was thus that Nicephorus Phocas was proclaimed emperor, in his camp at Caesarea in July 963. Sword in hand, the high officers surrounded their general's tent and amid acclamation greeted him as Autocrat of the Romans. Nicephorus protested and refused, spoke of family bereavements that had drained him of all ambition, and declared that he had but one duty, one desire: to carry on the war against the infidel. Heedless of this, they dragged him from his tent and raised him shoulder-high. He yielded—not too unwillingly. Girded with his sword and leaning on his lance, he stood on a mound and addressed his soldiers for the first time; those soldiers who, says the historian to whom we owe this account, "loved him marvellously (δαιμονίως) and were proud to receive his praise."

All who feared for their lives in Constantinople sought refuge in the camps. When in 1057 Michael VI—"The Old," as his adversaries called him—was unwise enough to displease the leading army commanders and to reply to their representations with smooth words and jests, the generals did not hesitate to plot against him, being sure that the whole army would follow them; and from their conspiracy resulted the proclamation of Isaac Comnenus. Again in 1081, when Alexius Comnenus learned the evil designs of Botaniates' ministers, he fled with his adherents to the troops of whose loyalty he was assured, and marched resolutely on Constantinople. Rarely did the capital resist the military forces of usurpers for long; and as we have seen, there was always a party within the walls ready to serve them.

### Palace Revolutions

We know how important a place the palace occupied in Byzantine life, and how strong was the empress's influence there. Within those walls and in the seclusion of the women's apartments, among women, eunuchs, and courtiers, many plots and counterplots were woven to secure the succession to the throne. The Sacred Palace of Byzantium is full of grim stories. There the devout Irene had her son Constantine VI blinded, in the very room in which he had been born. There in 820, in St. Stephen's Chapel, Leo V the Armenian was assassinated by murderers lurking among the choristers while, according to his custom, he was conducting the singing. There Basil the Macedonian and his friends slew Michael III; and there also, one December night, Theophano had her husband, Nicephorus Phocas, assassinated and from a window displayed to the soldiers of the guard the severed, dripping head of their master.

## 26 / ECONOMIC FACTORS IN THE DECLINE OF THE BYZANTINE EMPIRE / *PETER CHARANIS*

It is now five hundred years since the Byzantine Empire was brought to an end by the Ottoman Turks. Scholars today quite justly reject Gibbon's assumption that the Byzantine Empire was, throughout its entire existence, in a state of decline. They have come to rank it, instead, as one of the great empires in history.[1] And this for good reasons. It endured for over a thousand years. Down to about the middle of the eleventh century, it was the center of civilization in Christendom. It preserved the thought and literature of antiquity; it developed new forms of art; it held back the barbarians. It produced great statesmen, soldiers, and diplomats as well as reformers and renowned scholars. Its missionaries, aided by its diplomats and sometimes by its armies, spread the Gospel among the pagan tribes, especially the Slavs, which dwelt along its frontiers and beyond. As a Czech historian has put it, Byzantium "molded the undisciplined tribes of Serbs, Bulgars, Russians, Croats even, and made nations out of them; it gave to them its religion and institutions, taught

Reprinted with permission from Peter Charanis, "Economic Factors in the Decline of the Byzantine Empire," *Journal of Economic History*, 13, No. 4 (Fall 1953), 412-15, 423-24.

[1] Not only specialists but generally cultivated people have come to have a high regard for Byzantium. The Norwegian Fridtjof Nansen wrote in his book, *L'Arménie et le proche Orient* (Paris: Paul Geuthner, 1928), p. 31: St. Sophia "is and will remain one of the most remarkable works of architecture, and if the Byzantine culture had created nothing but that, it would be sufficient to classify it among the greatest." And the philosopher A. N. Whitehead wrote in his *Adventures of Ideas* (New York: The Macmillan Company, 1933), p. 104: "The distinction separating the Byzantines and the Mohammedans from the Romans is that the Romans were themselves deriving the civilization which they spread. In their hands it assumed a frozen form. Thought halted, and literature copied. The Byzantines and the Mohammedans were themselves the civilization. Thus their culture retained its intrinsic energies, sustained by physical and spiritual adventure. They traded with the Far East: they expanded westward: they codified law: they developed new forms of art: they elaborated theologies: they transformed mathematics: they developed medicine. Finally, the Near East as a center of civilization was destroyed by the Tartars and the Turks."

their princes how to govern, transmitted to them the very principles of civilization—writing and literature." [2] Byzantium was a great power and a great civilizing force.

Yet in a sense Gibbon was right, for the Byzantine Empire did not come to an end as the result of a single blow as, for instance, the battle of Nineveh of 612 BC is said to have brought to an end the mighty Assyrian Empire. The empire which Mohammed II destroyed on May 29, 1453, had been wasting away for over three hundred years, although part of this time, notably during the period of the Comneni, it was not an insignificant force. By the time of the fall of Constantinople, however, the Morea, one or two islands in the Aegean, and Constantinople were all that had been left of its once widely extensive territories. Constantinople itself, which in the tenth century had a population of perhaps one million people, had been reduced to probably not more than 75,000 inhabitants. [3] As a center of commerce it had long been eclipsed by Galata, the Genoese colony on the opposite side of the Golden Horn. The Byzantine emperors became puppets in the hands of the Italian commercial republics, notably Genoa and Venice, served the Ottoman sultans as vassals, or miserably toured the West begging for help in return for which they were ready to sacrifice the religious traditions of their people. What a far cry from the august position of their predecessors of the tenth century who challenged East and West and challenged them not without success! "I shall conquer your lands," wrote Nicephorus Phocas to the Caliph of Bagdad, and I shall go as far as Mecca. . . . I shall conquer all the Orient and the Occident and I shall spread everywhere the religion of the cross." [4] The same emperor declared to the ambassador of the German emperor, Otto I:

> Do you want a greater scandal than that [Otto] should call himself emperor and claim for himself provinces belonging to our empire? Both these things are intolerable; and if both are unsupportable, that especially is not to be borne, nay, not to be heard of that he calls himself emperor.[5]

What brought the empire from this pinnacle of power down to the

[2] F. Dvornik, *Les Slaves byzance et Rome au IX° siècle* (Paris: Librairie Ancienne Honoré Champion, 1926), Vol. II.

[3] Peter Charanis, "A Note on the Population and Cities of the Byzantine Empire in the Thirteenth Century," *The Joshua Starr Memorial Volume, Jewish Social Studies, Publication No. 5* (New York: Conference on Jewish Relations, Inc., 1953), pp. 137-39.

[4] G. Schlumberger, *Un Empereur byzantin au dixième siècle: Nicéphore Phocas* (Paris, 1890), pp. 429 ff.

[5] F. H. Wright (trans.), *The Works of Liudprand of Cremona* (New York: E. P. Dutton & Co., 1930), p. 249.

abject position in which we find it in the fourteenth and fifteenth centuries is one of the most interesting problems in history.

In the history of the Byzantine Empire, war and religion were the two principal factors that molded the society of the empire and determined its external position.[6] War was the normal state of things throughout its long existence. The external crisis, however, that particularly affected the evolution of its society was that of the seventh century.

The advances of the Saracens and the incursions of the Slavs and Bulgars reduced virtually the whole empire to a frontier province. To cope with this situation, the emperors of the seventh century reorganized the provincial administration of the empire, introducing what is known as the *theme* system, the essence of which was the subordination of civil to military authority exercised in each province by the commander of the army corps stationed there.[7] But with the establishment of the *theme* system is connected the establishment of another institution, the system of military estates. These military estates, small in size and granted to individuals in return for military service, became the opening wedge in the formation of a new class of free peasant proprietors. The soldiers themselves constituted the nucleus of this class, but others gradually were added, for while the eldest son of a soldier inherited his father's plot together with the obligation of military service, the rest of the family were free to reclaim and cultivate the land that was vacant.[8] The free peasants, cultivating their own land, paying the taxes, and, if necessary, serving in the army, came to constitute the dominant element in the agrarian society of Byzantium. They became a bulwark of the state, lent to it new vigor, and enabled it eventually to recover its position in the Orient. By the end of the tenth century, Byzantium had become the most powerful state throughout the Christian-Moslem world.

The situation changed in the eleventh century. During the second

[6] This statement, made by me in my study, "On the Social Structure of the Later Roman Empire," *Byzantion*, XVII (1944-45), 57, has been repeated by others. See, for instance, D. A. Zakythinos, "Les Institutions du Despotat de Morée, VI: Justice," *L'Hellénisme Contemporain*, Ser. 2, 4th year (1950), p. 206. A most amazing interpretation has been given to it recently by a Soviet scholar. He writes: "The American historian P. Charanis extracts from the Fascist ideological arsenal the ancient glorification of war, carols its sham creative role; it is a pseudoscientific theory calling only to concur in the ideological preparation of a new war." A. P. Kazhdan, *Agrarnye otnosheniia v Vizantii XIII-XIV VV* (Moscow: Akademia Nauk SSSR, 1952), pp. 17-18. The translation is by G. Alef.

[7] The latest work on the origin of the *theme* system with the essential bibliography is by A. Pertusi, *Constantino Porfirogenito de thematibus. Introduzione. Testo critico* (Vatican City: Biblioteca Apostolica Vaticana, 1952), pp. 103-11.

[8] For a discussion of this with the essential bibliography see Charanis, "On the Social Structure of the Later Roman Empire," *op. cit.*, pp. 42-49.

half of that century, the empire suffered a series of military reverses from which it never fully recovered. The most serious of these was the disastrous defeat at Manzikert (1071). The battle of Manzikert decided the fate of Asia Minor and conditioned the subsequent history of the Byzantine Empire. But Manzikert was only a battle, and battles had been lost before without the serious consequences that followed Manzikert. What explains the decline that set in after it and that would lead eventually to the disappearance of the empire were the conditions which came to prevail in the social and economic life of the empire in the eleventh century and later. Manzikert itself was the result of these conditions.

The dominant fact in the social and economic life of the empire in the eleventh century is the triumph of the landed military aristocracy and the decline of the soldiery-peasantry which had for centuries served as the bulwark of the state. . . .

It has been said that "Byzantium's weakness, which led to her fatal decline in the course of the eleventh century" was "her rigid, defensive attitude toward the outside world . . . embodied in the cultural and economic barriers she raised against all outsiders." [9] The economic barriers spoken of in this statement refer no doubt to the strict controls that Byzantium had exercised over commerce and industry. It is extremely doubtful if this indeed was Byzantium's weakness. The simple observation that the period during which these controls were most rigidly enforced is the period of the greatness of the empire suggests the opposite, and this suggestion is reinforced by the further observation that the period of decline coincides with the breakdown of these controls. The power of a state and as a consequence its ability to maintain its position in the world is commensurate with its financial resources, the principal source of which is taxation. In Byzantium this source, seriously compromised by the disappearance of the free peasantry and the increase in the wealth, privileges, and power of the aristocracy was reduced almost to the vanishing point by the commercial privileges granted to the Italian republics[10] and the consequent loss by Byzantium of control over its urban economy. This was Byzantium's weakness that brought about its decline and final fall.

[9] A. R. Lewis, *Naval Power and Trade in the Mediterranean, AD 500-1100* (Princeton, N.J.: Princeton University Press, 1951), p. 253.

[10] An idea of what happened to the revenues of Constantinople is given by the statement of the Byzantine historian Gregoras that, while the annual custom revenues of Constantinople had shrunk to about 30,000 nomismata, those of the Genoese colony of Galata went up to about 200,000 nomismata. This was about the middle of the fourteenth century. Nicephorus Gregoras, *Byzantina Historia*, II (Bonn, 1829-30), 842.

# CHRONOLOGICAL TABLES

## Ancient Egypt*

### I.** ca. 2700–ca. 2200 BC—The Old Kingdom

The period of Egypt's most centralized absolutism, in the person of the king sanctioned as god-king. But at the same time, a period of progressive decentralization and weakening of the king's authority, especially by priestly groups. The period of highest material and intellectual powers.

### II.** ca. 2200–ca. 2050 BC—The First Intermediate Period

The first period of chaos and disintegration of central rule.

### III.** ca. 2050–ca. 1800 BC—The Middle Kingdom

Egypt reunited by force of arms. The kings became again absolute rulers through the perpetuation of the traditional dogma of divine absolutism. The Middle Kingdom brought back to Egypt the benefits of peace, prosperity, and world dominion.

### IV.** ca. 1800–ca. 1550 BC—The Second Intermediate Period

The collapse of the Egyptian State as a result of a combination of inner developments and external exigencies, especially the invasions of the Hyksos.

### V.** ca. 1465–ca. 1165 BC—The Empire

In the first part of this period (until ca. 1325 BC) Egypt extended its frontiers and regained internal and external security. The dogma that the king alone was the state continued, but the complexity of administrative organization gave also rise to the development of a somewhat independent bureaucracy.

This was followed by a period of civil disturbance (Amarna heresy) and the Hittite invasions from outside. In this period, ca. 1325-1100 BC, there is a weakening of the central government.

* Based on John A. Wilson, *The Burden of Egypt*, Chicago, The University of Chicago Press, 1951.

** There exists no evidence about the exact dates of these periods.

## VI.* ca. 1150–663 BC—The Post-Empire Period

Period of stagnation and decline.

# The Roman Empire**

## I. 27 BC–AD 96—From the Establishment of the Principate to Julio Claudius and Flavians

A period of tremendous territorial expansion over all the lands around the Mediterranean Sea.

The changes within the political system marked a tendency toward the establishment of hereditary dynasties that, however, were never fully legitimized.

## II. 96–AD 180—The Enlightened Emperors

In this period the Roman Empire reached its maximum territorial extent, population, and material prosperity. This was due to the combination of internal peace and effective government. This epoch is looked upon as the Golden Age of the Roman Empire.

## III. 180–AD 395—The Military Autocracy until the Partition of the Empire

Disorder reigned within the Empire, as a result of continuous civil war between the different armies of the Empire and struggles among their leaders for the possession of the throne. This was also a critical period for the whole of ancient Western civilization because of the continuous influx of barbarian invaders.

## IV. 395–AD 476—From the Partition of the Empire until the Fall of the Western Empire

In this period there still existed the fiction of imperial unity, but there was a complete separation of different administrative authorities. The period is marked by the complete breakdown of Roman resistance to barbarian invasions, and the occupation of the western provinces and Italy by peoples of Germanic stock. In AD 476 Odovacar, the leader of the Germanic mercenaries, forced the emperor Romulus to abdicate and enthroned himself.

# The Byzantine Empire†

## I. 330–AD 610—From the Foundation of Constantinople to Heraclius I

The shaping of the Eastern Empire as a Christian Empire. In this period the Byzantine Empire still maintained apparent continuity with Rome (e.g., Latin remained the official language).

* There exists no evidence about the exact dates of these periods.
** Based on Arthur E. R. Boak, *A History of Rome to 565 A.D.*, New York, the Macmillan Company, 1921.

† Based on C. Diehl, *Byzantium: Greatness and Decline*, New Brunswick, New Jersey, Rutgers University Press, 1957.

## *II. 610–AD 717*—Period of Acute Crisis and Internal Crystallization

The period of invasions by the Persians, Arabs, and Slavs. At the end of this period the Byzantine Empire, though diminished in size, was strongly organized and relieved of the weight of the Western inheritance.

## *III. 717–AD 1025*—Period of Maximum Development

The period of peak Imperial power, economic prosperity, territorial expansion, and centralization of administration.

## *IV. 1025–AD 1453*—Period of Increasing Aristocratization Leading to the Decline and Fall of the Empire

A period of court intrigue, civil war and rebellion in the capital, and strengthening of the feudal powers in the provinces, combined with new invasions from the East—by the Turks—and conflict with the Normans in the West.

Generally a period of shrinkage and decline, with but a few years of temporary recovery.

## The Chinese Empire*

## *I. 221 BC–AD 222*—The Ch'in and Han Dynasties

The period of political as well as cultural unification, accompanied by the suppression of individual freedom. During the first century AD Confucianism was established. This is therefore the formative period of the Chinese Empire that lasted for two millennia.

## *II. 222–AD 589*—The "Six Dynasties" Period

At the end of the Han Dynasty there began a period of civil strife and internal division that lasted for almost four centuries.

This is a period, as in the Roman Empire, of invasions by peoples from Central Asia, causing the disintegration of the administration and threatening China's cultural unity.

At the end of this period Buddhism was introduced.

## *III. 589–AD 618*—The Sui Dynasty—Unification of the Second Empire

Period of political unification and of the beginning of prosperity.

## *IV. 618–AD 907*—The T'ang Dynasty

A period of political, economic, and cultural prosperity. In the seventh and eighth centuries China's frontiers were expanded; economic prosperity and cultural creativity sphere (in art as well as in philosophy) increased.

* Based on Kenneth S. Latourette, *The Chinese: Their History and Culture*, New York, The Macmillan Company, 1960.

## V. 907–AD 960—The Five Dynasties

The period of collapse of political unity that lasted for half a century. Nevertheless, this was a period of great cultural activity.

## VI. 960–AD 1279—The Sung Dynasty

A period of continuous, strong rule, characterized by very great achievements, especially in the cultural sphere, by which many of the forms of orthodox Chinese intellectual life were moulded.

In this period, however, the Chinese never succeeded in conquering the tribes that threatened its northern borders. Between the years 1127 and 1279 the Empire was split—the Southern Sung Dynasty reigning in the south of China, and the Chin Dynasty in the north. There were frequent wars between them, which led to a heavy taxation.

The establishment of the Southern Sung Dynasty was followed by an immigration from north to south. Characterized by political weakness, the period was nevertheless marked by cultural flourishing—in literature, art, and especially philosophy (the Neo-Confucian school)—and by the extension of education.

## VII. 1279–AD 1368—The Yüan Dynasty—the Rule of the Mongols

With the Mongol conquest China became a part of the huge Mongol Empire, which, however, soon broke down and was divided into several parts. The Mongols in China became mostly absorbed as the ruling dynasty of the Chinese Empire.

This was a period of cultural stagnation.

## VIII. 1368–AD 1644—The Ming Dynasty

The last native Chinese dynasty. The period was marked by territorial expansion and economic prosperity, whereas its cultural achievements were smaller in comparison with the T'ang and Sung periods.

The Ming Dynasty ruled over all the area that is known as China proper, and for shorter and longer periods also ruled Korea and Japan, and lands as far south as Ceylon recognized its sovereignty.

The leading cultural achievements were in the applied arts (building, etc.). In the philosophical sphere there was a loyalty to accepted ideals.

## IX. 1644–AD 1912—The Ch'ing Dynasty (Manchu)

The long rule of the Manchus can be divided into two periods:

(a) 1644-1838—Period of prosperity and stability.
(b) 1838-1912—Period of conflict with the European forces—the period of decline.

During the first period China achieved its greatest territorial expansion. At the Empire's height the Manchus ruled over China proper, Manchuria, Mongolia, Sinkiang, and Tibet and received tribute from many other countries— from Korea in the north to Burma in the south. This was also a period of economic prosperity. Internal order had never been better maintained over so long a period, and the population multiplied. First contact with Europe was established.

This was a period of cultural stability and relative lack of innovation. The Manchus adhered to the past conventions and tended to suppress cultural heterodoxy.

From 1838 until the fall of the Ch'ing Dynasty in 1912, the greatest cultural revolution the Chinese ever knew took place. Under the impact of the West, the traditional political, intellectual, economic, social, and religious institutions underwent great change, and the first processes of modernization took place.

Due to the Western impact and inner disorder, the old Empire disintegrated and the Manchus were overthrown in the Revolution of 1912.

# SELECTED BIBLIOGRAPHY

## I. General

Eisenstadt, S. N. "Internal Contradictions in Bureaucratic Polities," *Comparative Studies in Society and History,* 1: 1 (1958), 58-75.

———. *The Political Systems of Empires.* New York, 1963.

———. "Processes of Change and Institutionalization of the Political Systems of Centralized Empires," in G. K. Zollschan and W. Hirsch (eds.), *Explorations in Social Change.* Boston, 1964. Pp. 432-51.

———. "Political Orientations of Bureaucracies in Centralized Empires," in his *Essays in Comparative Institutions.* New York, 1965. Pp. 216-50.

Ibn Khaldun. *The Muqaddimah.* London, 1958. Vol. I, Chap. 3, § 12, 23; Vol. II, Chap. 3, § 41, 45.

Mosca, Gaetano. *The Ruling Class.* New York, 1939. Chap. 3, § 6; Chap. 8, § 1-4.

Weber, Max. *The Theory of Social and Economic Organization.* New York, 1947. Part III.

———. "Bureaucracy," in H. H. Gerth and C. W. Mills (eds.), *From Max Weber: Essays in Sociology.* London, 1947. Pp. 196-264.

Wittfogel, K. A. *Oriental Despotism.* New Haven, 1957.

## II. Historical and Sociological

### Ancient Egypt

Wilson, John A. *The Burden of Egypt.* Chicago, 1951.

### The Roman Empire

Baynes, N. H. "The Decline of the Roman Power in Western Europe: Some Modern Explanations," *Journal of Roman Studies,* 33 (1943), 29-35.

Boak, A. E. R. "The Role of Policy in the Fall of the Roman Empire," *Michigan Alumnus Quarterly Review,* 56 (1950), 291-94.

Henderson, B. W. *Civil War and Rebellion in the Roman Empire.* London, 1908.

Jones, A. H. M. "The Decline and Fall of the Roman Empire," *History*, 40: 140 (Oct. 1955), 209-26.

Rostovtzeff, M. I. *Social and Economic History of the Roman Empire*, 2nd ed. Oxford, 1957.

Westermann, W. L. "The Economic Basis of the Decline of Ancient Culture," *The American Historical Review*, 20 (July 1915), 723-43.

——. *The Slave System in Greek and Roman Antiquity.* Philadelphia, 1955.

### China

Eberhard, W. *A History of China.* London, 1948.

Fairbank, J. K. (ed.). *Chinese Thought and Institutions.* Chicago, 1957.

Pulleyblank, E. G. *The Background of the Rebellion of An Lu-shan.* London, 1955.

Weber, Max. "The Chinese Literati," in H. H. Gerth and C. W. Mills (eds.), *From Max Weber: Essays in Sociology*, London, 1947. Pp. 416-44.

Wright, A. F. (ed). *Studies in Chinese Thought.* Chicago, 1953.

### The Byzantine Empire

Boak, A. E. R., and J. Dunlap. *Two Studies in Later Roman and Byzantine Administration.* New York, 1924.

Charanis, P. "Internal Strife at Byzantium in the Fourteenth Century," *Byzantion*, 15 (1940-41), 208-30.

——. "On the Social Structure of the Later Roman Empire," *Byzantion*, 17 (1944-45), 39-57.

Dvornik, F. "The Circus Parties in Byzantium: Their Evolution and Their Suppression," *Byzantina-Metabyzantina*, I (1946), 119-33.

Jenkins, R. Y. H. *The Byzantine Empire on the Eve of the Crusades.* London, 1953.

Ostrogorsky, G. *History of the Byzantine State.* Oxford, 1956.

### The Islamic Empires

#### General

Lewis, B. *The Arabs in History.* London, 1950.

Cahen, Claude. "The Body Politic," in Gustave E. von Grünebaum (ed.), *Unity and Variety in Muslim Civilization.* Chicago, 1955. Pp. 132-63.

——. "L'Histoire économique et sociale de l'Orient Musulman médiéval," *Studia Islamica*, III (1955), 93-116.

——. *"Les Facteurs économiques et sociaux dans l'ankylose culturelle de l'Islam,"* in R. Brunsvick and Gustave E. von Grünebaum (eds.), *Classicisme et déclin culturel dans l'histoire de l'Islam.* Paris, 1958. Pp. 159-217.

——. *Leçons d'histoire Musulmane.* Cours de la Sorbonne (mimeo.). Paris, 1958. Vols. I-III.

Saunders, J. J. "The Problem of Islamic Decadence," *Journal of World History,* 3 (1963), 701-720.

### The Abbassids

Muir, W. *The Caliphate: Its Rise, Decline, and Fall.* Edinburgh, 1924.

### The Ottoman Empire

Fisher, S. N. "Civil Strife in the Ottoman Empire, 1481-1503," *Journal of Modern History,* 8 (1941), 449-66.

Gibb, H. A. R., and H. Bowen. *Islamic Society and the West.* London, 1950.

Lewis, B. "Some Reflections on the Decline of the Ottoman Empire," *Studia Islamica,* 9 (1958), 111-27.

Stavrianos, L. S. *The Balkans Since 1453.* New York, 1958. Chap. 8.

Stoianovich, Traian. "Factors in the Decline of Ottoman Society in the Balkans," *Slavic Review,* 21 (Dec. 1962), 623-32.

### Absolutist Europe

Beloff, M. *The Age of Absolutism.* London, 1954.

Goodwin, A. (ed.) *The European Nobility in the Eighteenth Century.* London, 1953.

Hartung, F. *Enlightened Despotism.* London, 1957.

Swart, K. W. *Sale of Offices in the Seventeenth Century.* The Hague, 1949.

# DATE DUE

| NOV 17 '70 | | | |
|---|---|---|---|
| | | | |
| | | | |
| | | | |
| | | | |
| | | | |
| | | | |
| | | | |
| | | | |
| | | | |
| | | | |
| | | | |
| | | | |
| | | | |
| | | | |
| | | | |
| | | | |
| | | | |
| GAYLORD | | | PRINTED IN U.S.A. |